By the same author

Halliwell's Hundred
Halliwell's Filmgoer's Companion (eighth edition 1984)
Halliwell's Film Guide (fourth edition 1983)
Halliwell's Television Companion (with Philip Purser)
  (second edition 1982)
Mountain of Dreams: the Golden Years of Paramount
The Clapperboard Book of the Cinema (with Graham
  Murray)
The Ghost of Sherlock Holmes: Seventeen Supernatural
  Stories

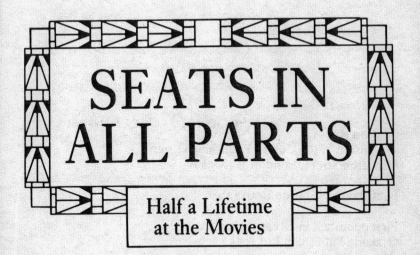

SEATS IN ALL PARTS

Half a Lifetime at the Movies

LESLIE HALLIWELL

GRAFTON BOOKS

A Division of the Collins Publishing Group

LONDON GLASGOW
TORONTO SYDNEY AUCKLAND

Grafton Books
A Division of the Collins Publishing Group
8 Grafton Street, London W1X 3LA

Published by Grafton Books 1986

First published in Great Britain by
Granada Publishing Ltd 1985

Copyright © Leslie Halliwell 1985

ISBN 0-586-06923-2

Printed and bound in Great Britain by
Collins, Glasgow

Set in Times

I think
MY MOTHER
would have liked to read
this book

Contents

8 CONTENTS

Preface

There have been Halliwells in Bolton for many hundreds of years: it is the one town where I don't have to spell my name a dozen times a day. You see it on the destination board of the bus which takes you to a rather grubby industrial district on the edge of the moors: a place full of pubs, and chip shops, and six-storey mills which no longer fulfil their original function of processing cotton. There is still a Halliwell Road, a Halliwell Lodge, a Halliwell House. Those prepared to do a little scrambling may even find traces of the original holy well. But accept no imitations. Helliwell is an imposter from Yorkshire, Hallowell comes from Cumberland, and Hallewell is thoroughly confused.

If there were any rich Halliwells, I didn't know them. Not in the early 1930s. The other Halliwells we mixed with were mill folk like us, though the boys and girls my age may have been sitting for grammar school scholarships. Their parents had just put the clogs-and-shawl atmosphere behind them, and wanted something better for the next generation than the constant oily smell of cottonseed. One of the saving graces of these extremely hard times was the Lancashire sense of humour. Another was the enthusiasm for various forms of public entertainment: not only for Handel's *Messiah* and the Amateur Operatic but for the church concert and the *palais de danse* and the music hall and above all the cinema. The cinema was the most conveniently and constantly available, and it took people furthest out of themselves, into a wondrous and beautiful world which became their Shangri-La, though they never expected to find it in reality. In order to experience that world they would willingly queue for hours; besides, it was cheaper than lighting the fire.

In preparing these reminiscences I have been grateful to all who shared those far-off years with me. The book is above all a tribute to my indefatigably crusading mother, though there may also be a little social history in it. Additional thanks are due to my meticulous editors, Anne Charvet and John Bright-Holmes; and to three photo libraries, those of the *Bolton Evening News* (Gordon Readyhough), the Rank Organisation and the Cambridgeshire Collection.

LH, Summer 1984

Preface to the paperback edition

I was overwhelmed by the hundreds of letters I received following the publication of the hardback edition of this book, mostly from people whose memories are similar to mine, and who continue to enjoy the films of the thirties and forties above all others when they are revived on television. I hope I replied to all correspondents, but in any case I would like to take this opportunity to underline my appreciation of their enthusiasm.

In this paperback I have merely clarified a few points and corrected half a dozen errors of primary interest to Boltonians.

LH, January 1986

ONE

Shadows Before

The Queen's Cinema maintained a curious dignity, especially when viewed from the opposite corner of the junction which it dominated. Whenever I passed by there in recent years, on my occasional visits to the town in which I grew up, I used to imagine, despite the iron trellis which now closed off the foyer, that I could still hear the metallic whirring of its ancient projectors, or catch a whiff of the heady scent which permeated the hall in its heyday. It was an aroma compounded of soft plush and worn carpet and Devon violets and sweat. It was that scent, perhaps, which first made me a film fan; for it was to the Queen's in Bolton that I ventured on my first remembered visit to any cinema, one wet and windy afternoon in 1933, when I was four.

The fivepenny entrance was at the screen end, and what confronted me as we took our first steps into the unexpected darkness of the front stalls was a vista of row after row of upturned faces, transfixed by some monstrous luminescence high on the wall to my right. My mother handed our tickets to a smart young lady in a pillbox hat, but it was not until we had followed her flashing torch halfway up the nearest aisle that I glanced over my shoulder and saw the miracle for myself. The screen was astonishing. It astonished by its size, by its simplicity, and by its gentle brilliance. It was a window through which I could gaze into an incredibly glamorous, magical, monochrome world. And it really did look silver, just as the film magazines said.

Open-mouthed, I took a few backward steps, tripped over a piece of torn carpet, and sat down heavily on my infant rear. Somebody chuckled in the darkness; Mum grabbed my wrist and drew me down into an end seat which squeaked as I settled into it. But the man in front of me was so tall that all I could see was the back of his bald head; and after a minute of whispered consultation Mum decided that we should make a journey to the far side of the cinema, which was much less crowded. By now I had accustomed myself to the hushed atmosphere; it was rather like being in church, but more exciting. While holding my mother's hand firmly, I kept my eyes on the screen the whole way, watching the giant faces transform themselves as we reached the front row into ludicrously emaciated caricatures, then correct themselves to normal proportions as I trotted, backwards again, up the far gangway. By the time I was satisfactorily positioned behind a female tot even smaller than myself, I was already an addict.

Family tradition, unsupported by proof, holds that this was my second visit to the Queen's. On the first occasion, it appears, I had to be carried out screaming: I was overcome by the noise, and the crowds, and the darkness, and allowed myself insufficient time to get used to them before letting out my instinctive protest. It would be pleasant to know which was the movie that provoked this outburst, but the fact was neither recorded nor remembered by my embarrassed family. Now, at the time of this second experiment, the stars seemed more propitious. The cinema management, Mum thought, *must* have forgiven her, even though a framed notice reading

CHILDREN IN ARMS
DEFINITELY
NOT ADMITTED

had been hung prominently in both foyers. And so, after dinner one weekday (midday dinner, for this was darkest Lancashire) she dressed me in my natty new britches and my floppy cap, and we went to a matinée. All the way on the deafeningly noisy tram, from the top of Parkfield Road to the bottom of Trinity Street, she lectured me firmly on how I was to behave in the pictures, urging me that if I should be frightened or otherwise upset I was to inform her in the smallest of whispers, so that we could take our leave without disturbing other people. She need not have worried. As she announced to the family at tea time, I was as good as gold.

The attraction that afternoon was Sylvia Sidney in a non-singing version of *Madame Butterfly*, with Cary Grant as Pinkerton and Charlie Ruggles for light relief. It was hardly a suitable introduction to film art; and it might have put an impressionable infant off for life. Luckily, however, I was far too busy absorbing the wonder of pictures that walked and talked to be critical of the pace or the plot, which I barely understood. I vaguely remember the hara-kiri finale, and Mr Grant in a white uniform, but my recollection is much clearer of the trailer for the following week's attraction. *Orders is Orders* it was, a British army comedy which I never managed to see despite my later fondness for its imported American star James Gleason, the epitome of all hard-boiled, soft-centred, wisecracking Brooklyn Irishmen. What made the trailer so memorable (and Mum failed to explain to my satisfaction why it was *called* a trailer) was its use of flashy white lettering and dazzling optical trickery. I can see now the ladder of star names as they appeared one by one, and it annoyed me that evening that none of my family could tell me how it was done. I remember too that during the interval, pink-tinted slides were flashed on to the screen announcing a forthcoming Al Jolson film, which must have been a re-issue of *Mammy*. I pleaded to see this because Mr Jolson, in blackface, was the living image of my beloved golliwog.

After two hours and a quarter over the celluloid rainbow, Mum and I emerged at four-thirty into the drab, harsh world of Bolton, or Bolton-le-Moors as the General Post Office insisted on calling it. It was a gloomy but suitably melodramatic place for a film fan to grow up in, and after that momentous introduction to the art I expected the familiar cobbled side streets to provide adventures at least as exciting as those which I came to witness so regularly on the screen. Even *Madame Butterfly* must have sharpened my awareness of the world around me, for I remember with absolute clarity a tiny incident on our journey home. The wind had died down, but we still had to dodge the puddles as we hurried along Bradshawgate and bought a large loaf at Catterall's. We turned up Great Moor Street to board the Great Lever tram, which waited impassively in the gloaming, at its terminus opposite Gregory and Porrit's lighting emporium. Just inside on the left was a long wooden-slatted seat which we habitually occupied; and when the conductor leaped on to the vehicle and clanged the bell rope, he turned out to be the same one who had escorted us into town just before two o'clock, so Mum naturally explained with some pride that I had been to the pictures and had behaved like a little angel. The conductor chucked me under the chin and punched our tickets. Moments later the vehicle stopped at a traffic light, and there clambered aboard the scruffiest, smelliest, wheeziest old man I had ever seen. He flopped down opposite us, and Mum nudged me to edge along so that we should not be directly in the line of fire from his spectacular exhalings. The conductor returned from his brief tour of the lower saloon. 'Fares, please, Dad,' he said cheerfully. The old geezer (as Mum described him later) coughed horribly and long, and made an elaborate pretence of searching his tattered pockets, without result. At last he turned his head up plaintively and said in a voice which was no more than a croak: 'Ah'm only gooin' to t' station.' The conductor paused, rubbed the end of his nose violently, half-looked at Mum over his shoulder, then touched the old man lightly on the lapel and hurried upstairs. I stared rudely at the old man until he had the grace to look sheepish; but he did get off at the next stop, only to disappear rapidly into the public bar of the Railway Hotel. All that evening I was jealous of him for riding free when Mum had had to pay.

It would be fitting, no doubt, if that visit to the pictures were my very earliest memory. But there lingers in my mind another series of images, a confusion of my third and fourth birthdays. The third is clear to the extent that I woke up in Mum and Dad's big bed to find its patchwork counterpane littered with exciting parcels, and beyond them a view through the sash window to the steaming mill pond from which it was said that Dad had once rescued a drowning man. In the distance were a score or so of the mill chimneys, tall, dark and satanic, which littered the Bolton landscape. My mind mixes up the presents: a wooden tricycle, a beaker with Little Jack Horner on it, a toy gun that shot sparks. Which birthday do these belong to? It was certainly on my fourth that I received that most influential of all gifts, *Film Fun Annual*, a cornucopia of crudely illustrated adventures: Joe E. Brown, magically dressing himself with the aid of assorted springs and hooks; Lupino Lane, fleeing from an assortment of African animals;

Wheeler and Woolsey in a haunted house.

Members of my family have always proved willing to fill me in on the early bad habits which I conveniently forgot to remember: hiding under the table from the doctor, refusing to go to bed until everyone else did likewise, stealing all the jam I could lay my hands on. On the other hand, they were proud that I could read by the time I was three: newspapers, too, none of your baby books. I certainly can't recall *learning* to read. What I do have is a cosy impression of endless happy evenings stretched out on the fireside rug, demonstrating my prowess by reading out selections from the *Bolton Evening News*. It was a well-printed paper boasting a circulation of 70,000, just under half the town's population at that time. I broke my reading teeth on its advertising pages, and especially on the cinema advertisements which used biggish type and were often well spaced out. Not surprisingly, I could say Laurel and Hardy before David and Goliath, though I knew little enough then about either pair.

Some of the publicity slogans, laboriously spelled out on those rich Dickensian evenings climaxed by a mug of steaming cocoa, still jingle in my mind. There was a campaign for *Strange Interval* (the English title for Eugene O'Neill's *Strange Interlude*) which announced it as 'the film in which you hear the characters THINK'. An advertisement which totally perplexed me read:

RAIN!
is predicted by
JOAN CRAWFORD
at the
THEATRE ROYAL

When *Fra Diavolo* turned up, I pronounced the words to

my own satisfaction but was absolutely unable to find out their meaning. (What were grown-ups for if not to explain things?) *Gabriel over the White House* was billed as 'a wonderful justification of the film industry as well as a great evening's entertainment'. *Rasputin the Mad Monk* sounded like a great thrill, since it boasted 'the three Barrymores, together on screen for the first time'. What exactly *were* Barrymores? And the whole family was impressed by the warning given in bold type for *The Good Companions*: 'NB. This picture takes *nearly two hours* to screen.'

For months – it seemed like years – I made a nuisance of myself, urging my mother that if I was old enough to read about 'the pictures' – and I had now graduated to my sisters' twopenny film magazines – then surely I was old enough to see a few. The fact was that I had not the faintest idea what 'pictures' were like, and for week after week Mum put me off with 'not after your behaviour last time'; to which I responded, more or less, that since I could not remember my behaviour last time I should not be held responsible for it. Mum managed, however, to protect me from the great mystery until after my fourth birthday, shrewdly diverting my interest to our small stock of six-penny gramophone records (mostly Parlophone with a few Woolworth's thrown in) and to the great polished cabinet which she would wind up at the side before standing me on a chair so that I could watch the needle make contact with the shiny black revolving disc. My favourite was Jack Hulbert singing 'The Flies Crawled Up the Window' but I could be almost equally tempted by 'Sandy Powell at the Zoo'; this involved a great many animal noises and a catch phrase 'See You in the Monkey House', which I still use to the bewilderment of my friends. Then there were 'Tiptoe Through the Tulips' and 'Play to Me, Gypsy', and Tommy Handley singing about 'Maggie's Cold':

Was it by the fire with Jeremiah
That Maggie caught a cold last night? Oh, no!
Was it by the wall with Archibald
That Maggie caught a cold last night? Oh, no!
Did she go, did she go,
Down where the water lilies grow . . .?

That was very daring for 1933, and a real family favourite which grew scratched in our service. So was Gracie Fields singing 'Walter, Walter, Lead Me to the Altar' and 'The Biggest Aspidistra in the World'; and so also were The Two Leslies (Leslie Holmes and Leslie Sarony) whose first names naturally endeared them to me, especially when they warbled 'Shut the Gate':

Good Morning, Mrs So-and-So, d'you want any meat today?
I've got some lovely pickled pork, I'm very glad to say.
She said, me husband's in the house, I've got one pig already,
So shut the gate! –Bother the gate! Gee up, Neddy!

These were riches indeed.

But my time finally came; and, once initiated into the delights of filmgoing, I quickly became a regular. The Queen's, apart from being convenient for the Great Lever tram, was at that time Bolton's plushiest and most respectable picture palace, and it was here that I received most of my first year's tuition. Whether she actually liked the film on offer or not, Mum enjoyed being 'taken out of herself', and must have sadly regretted the lack of opportunity while I was still too young to be trusted. The snug little cinema below the station bridge was a friendly place, and Mum had such a winning way with people – her eyes could tell a hard luck story while her lips were still closed – that she usually managed to get me in for nothing till I was about six and a new hawk-eyed manager took over. For an extra penny we could have sat in the back stalls or even the rarefied circle, but we seldom ventured into the former because the barrier interfered with my view of the screen, or into the latter because it was draughty and the steps were a trial for Mum's perpetually swollen ankles. When we did splash out one day and ascended the silent curving staircase with its rubber nosings, we found we were the only upstairs customers, and sat in great splendour in the exact centre of the front row, watching *Gold Diggers of 1933*. At first I could not understand how from this level we could be watching the same screen as the people in the stalls, but it came to me suddenly in a flash of inspiration, like grasping the basic principles of algebra. I tried to prove my theory by leaning over the circle rail to point out our usual seats below, and was promptly seized and suppressed by a vigilant usherette.

Two cinematic experiences stand out from that first year at the Queen's. One is *Zoo in Budapest*, an exotic Holly-wood romance which climaxed with Loretta Young being carried in the arms of Gene Raymond through a steamy lake. The other is Cecil B. de Mille's *The Sign of the Cross*, many scenes of which haunted me for years. I had little sympathy for the persecuted Christians, even when they were being rather realistically devoured in the arena by hungry lions to make a Roman holiday, but I rather cared for Claudette Colbert as the wicked Poppea, bathing in a hundred gallons of asses' milk (which according to the magazines kept curdling in the studio lights); and of course Charles Laughton as Nero ('delicious debauchery') was utterly irresistible, and I did imitations of him for my aunts on the following Sunday. I was most interested to note that the Christians in the film introduced themselves to each other by drawing crosses in the dust with their sticks, and determined to adopt similar methods; but Bolton did not seem to have the right kind of dust, and a friend commented that there was very little point in belonging to a secret society if one drew attention to oneself by making silly signs in public.

The Queen's in the early 1930s must have had prior claim to all films from the Warner Brothers. We seemed to experience dozens of their brash and lively Broadway-set musicals, with those dazzling Busby Berkeley numbers shot from overhead so that the lines of chorus girls turned into gyrating kaleidoscopic patterns. There was *42nd Street* and *Footlight Parade* and *Dames* and *Flirtation Walk* and *Fashions of 1934* and several in the *Gold Diggers* series, mostly featuring demure Ruby Keeler and debonair Dick Powell and wisecracking Joan Blondell and hard-boiled Glenda Farrell, with comic support provided by a selection from Zasu Pitts, Guy Kibbee, Hugh Herbert, Ned Sparks, Alice Brady and Frank McHugh. 'I can't stand those noisy musicals,' said Auntie Flo once as we walked home from church, 'they put years on me.' My mother protested that even musicals could remind one of serious matters, instancing the unemployment number in *Gold Diggers of 1933*, and Al Jolson among the hoboes of Central Park in *Hallelujah I'm a Bum*, and even Shirley Temple in *Stand Up and Cheer* leading the nation's poor in a patriotic finale of which President Roosevelt must have thoroughly approved, for he was quoted in *Film Weekly* as saying that 'it is a splendid thing during this Depression that for just fifteen cents an American can go to a movie and look at the smiling face of a baby and forget his troubles'. Auntie Flo had absolutely no answer to that, and I remember she was (I think uniquely) among our party when in 1936 the whole family, on the crest of the wave of enthusiasm for the dazzling footwork of Fred Astaire and Ginger Rogers, queued at the Queen's for *Top Hat* and sat most of it through twice. My imitations henceforth included the

wounded but threatening tones of Eric Blore as the
eccentric manservant Bates, and the high-pitched dithering
of Edward Everett Horton, one of the most accomplished
and professional figures in the history of Hollywood comedy. Half a lifetime later, in 1969, just months before he
died, I met him over lunch at the Savoy, and on his way out,
at my special request, he gave us a final sample of his
unique double-take, a practised combination of pout and
head-shake.

Mum and I had our favourite seats at the Queen's, just in
front of the velvet-covered mid-stalls barrier. At the head
of the forward aisle were two seats which gave an uninter-
rupted view of the screen, and to secure them was bliss
indeed. I remember we had them for *Lives of a Bengal
Lancer*, which was quite an achievement since the whole
town turned out to see this oddly-titled Indian adventure,
in which the splendidly saturnine Douglass Dumbrille may
have been the very first screen villain to say: 'We have ways
of making men talk.' We were lucky to get in at all for *It
Happened One Night*, which was one of the rare films to
command the attention of my father and two sisters as well
as the serious filmgoers of the family, for news of its
multiple Academy Awards had percolated even into our
remote neck of the woods. Actually Dad backed out when
we got into town and went to the Nag's Head instead; but
he was waiting outside the Queen's when the film ended, so
we counted that as a gesture at least, and told him all about
it as we walked home, with a pause while we held our noses
for the passage through Walker's Tannery. From that
evening on, Clark Gable and Claudette Colbert were
officially welcomed into our band of familiars; and if the
bedroom scenes did evoke anxious glances from Mum, I
think she must have satisfied herself that any innuendo
sailed straight over my head.

Packed houses were also the order of the day for *Sing as We Go*, which was billed as 'Bolton's own film'. This civic proprietorship stemmed from the fact that scenes had been shot in local cotton mills, including the finale when Gracie Fields leads her unemployed workmates triumphantly back to the looms in the rousing final chorus of a song which makes no sense but still brings a catch to my throat:

> Sing as we go, and let the world go by,
> Singing a song to march along the highway . . .
> Say goodbye to sorrow;
> There's always tomorrow
> To think of today . . .
> Sing as we go, although the skies are grey,
> Beggar or king, you've got to sing a gay tune;
> A song and a smile make your life worth while,
> So sing (tra la la la la la la la la la la) as we go along.

If the film had been set in Timbuctoo, Boltonians would still have flocked to hear the performer we most loved. Born a few miles away in Rochdale, Gracie was one of us; and as J. B. Priestley's boisterous script unfolded, you could almost smell the tripe and onions. A great deal of the film was shot in Blackpool, which was only eighty minutes away by daily charabanc, two-and-ninepence return, and there were plenty of knowing chuckles at the boarding house sequences; we had all suffered during Wakes Week from landladies like that. This time Dad really did come along, as he had watched the local filming during one of his unemployed afternoons: as a cotton spinner in the mid-thirties he was at home more often than at work. He wanted to know whether he could be spotted in the crowd scenes; but he could not.*

After the first months of 1937, the Queen's booking policy began to suffer from increased competition. A brand new cinema, the Lido (some Boltonians still call it Lydo), was visible from its stalls entrance, and only five minutes away a genuine colossus, the Odeon, was rising above the notorious slums of Ashburner Street, near the wholesale market. The Queen's put up a very poor struggle; for lack of evidence to the contrary we assumed that its management was now content with second best, or even third, which meant a staple diet of Johnny Mack Brown westerns and second-feature whodunits (not even Charlie Chan, but Mr Wong).

One of the last big fishes it caught, however, was Alfred Hitchcock's *The Lady Vanishes*. That was in 1939, and by then the Queen's was so well advanced on the slippery slope that we decided the film must be poor, despite its title. We almost didn't go. However, I passed by the cinema during the week, for my town centre routes always contrived to cover as many cinemas as possible, so that I could study form in the shape of stills and posters for coming attractions; and I was attracted from across the width of Bradshawgate by the huge red pictorial poster which covered almost the whole of one wall at ground level. In the centre was a train, steaming out at me, and this was surrounded by cameo heads of an array of familiar faces in attitudes of fear. Surely this had to be worth fivepence? I

*Forty-five years later, for a television programme, I searched Bolton high and low for the mill gates through which the singing star leads her mates back to work. Finally given directions, I found it down a long dead-end which I had never previously explored. The mill seemed to have become a chemical works, and on the gates was a little old man who looked like Albert Tatlock from *Coronation Street*. I asked him whether these were really the gates from *Sing as We Go*. 'Aye,' he said, 'they were, that. I were 'ere. I were a little piecer in them days.'

was vaguely attracted too by the name of Hitchcock, which
I associated with a delightful comedy-thriller we had seen
on a wet afternoon during a Blackpool holiday some three
or four years earlier. It had marvellously atmospheric
scenes in a music-hall, on a train, and on the Scottish
moors, and it was called *The Thirty-nine Steps*. Mum's
other reason for not wanting to see *The Lady Vanishes* was
that she had not cared for Margaret Lockwood in *Lorna
Doone*; but I talked her into it, and on Wednesday evening
we caught the tram in a state of pleasurable anticipation,
having been assured by other people that we would enjoy
ourselves. On the Saturday we went again, very early to
avoid the queue, for this was the kind of entertainment that
came along less than once a twelvemonth. The name Froy
written in steam on a carriage window; the nun with high
heels; the Test Match demonstrated with lump sugar; the
conjuror's cabinet; the drugged drinks; the mummified
patient; the danger, the excitement, the immense relief of
the happy ending. All the ingenious details of that harrow-
ing but often hilarious train journey were indelibly printed
on my mind from its very first acquaintance with them,
even though the plot is based on a nonsense. After all, if
one had vital secrets to transmit across Europe, surely even
in the thirties one would have picked up a phone instead of
translating them into a whistled tune and committing it to
the memory of an elderly governess who had to make a
slow and dangerous journey by train and boat?

I have no idea why, like a duck to water, I took so easily
and instantly to the cinema, except perhaps that my
mother, having herself been deprived of secondary schooling, urged me to absorb every educative influence in sight.
Besides, I was the sort of small boy who loathes rough
games; and being the youngest in the family (by thirteen
years) I could hardly fail to concern myself chiefly with

adult interests, since I had no contemporaries. So the cheap westerns, the serials, and the 'U' certificate Saturday matinées, with their noisy orange-eating crowds of smelly kids, were not for me.* From the beginning, it was 'A' films I chiefly wanted to see. Mum used to explain that 'A' only meant there was a murder in it; but even brief observation revealed the fallibility of this theory. The category also covered sophisticated comedies and urban dramas in which life was depicted as my sisters' magazines would have liked it to be, replete with champagne cocktails and Alpine holidays and dinner jackets and grand pianos. (We had an upright at home, for my elder sister's benefit, but she lost interest and I never learned to do more with it, before it succumbed to the damp of wartime winters, than pick out *Swanee River* with one finger.) Real life was fascinating, but untidy and sometimes sad; the kind of life shown on the silver screen had dramatic progression, and its loose ends of plot were always tied up. (Well, *nearly* always.) It was highly moral, and it taught me such things as how to behave at table, how to speak to a lady, and what was involved in various kinds of adult activity. For instance, to be a reporter you had to wear your hat in the house, and know more about crime detection than the police. It gave me an idea of what happened in history, admittedly a hazy one since Disraeli and Voltaire and Richelieu and Rothschild all seemed to look like George Arliss. It gave me a taste for the rhythms of popular music and the styles of American wisecracking. It introduced me to hundreds of people who

---

*The censor's categories were enforceable by law. 'U' (universal) meant that even unaccompanied children might be admitted; 'A' (adult) that their ticket must be bought, and they themselves accompanied, by a parent or guardian. 'H', which did not become 'X' until 1951, was a complete prohibition of the entertainment to anyone below the age of sixteen.

were handsomer or wittier or more clearly defined than anybody of my real-life acquaintance. It gave me things to dream about.

If filmgoing was also a lonely kind of hobby, that suited me too, for even at the age of five or six I was an inward-looking child. I was adored by old ladies, and considered by aunts and uncles to be full of fun and mischief, for I willingly entertained them with riddles and jokes I had picked up from my comics. But I wanted even then to think for myself. I liked long silent walks, in such countryside as was to hand. The treeless high moors gave me a taste for the world's barren places, where you can see the real shape of things. My father, of whom I saw little during the week, liked a walk too, the fresh air making a change from his long days in the mill, and on many Saturday afternoons I trotted beside him the three or four miles through the Red Sands to Little Hulton or Walkden; here we sat and chatted in the backyards of his cronies, most of whom seemed to keep hens. On occasional Saturday mornings I would walk to the home of my infants' class teacher, the diminutive but ever busy Miss Fyles, and take vegetarian lunch with her and her 'invalid' sister (who outlived her by thirty years).

Before I was five Mum, who had always longed to be a teacher herself but had been condemned by circumstance to work in the mill from the age of eleven until her marriage, made me a junior member of the Great Lever Branch Library, an imposing brick building at the end of the row below us, with a hushed reading room in which old men slept peacefully from lunch until closing time. Its iron shelves, arranged in a fan shape, held few enough books on the cinema, yet it was here that I first encountered Paul Rotha's *Movie Parade*, which revealed to me the surprising fact that some films were made in languages other than English, and that talking films were an invention quite new in the year of my birth. At home, I was fascinated by our new acquisition, the Murphy wireless set ('It's a console', my mother would tell her friends, adopting salesman's jargon). It seemed to alternate each evening between Henry Hall and his Dance Orchestra, the current comedy hit 'You Can't Do That There 'Ere', and Frances Day singing about being lost with her dog in a deep, deep fog in London. Though a friendly and amusing convenience it never seriously rivalled the cinema in my affections.

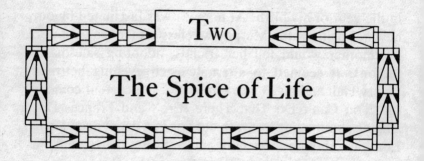

Two

The Spice of Life

For a film fanatic, Bolton was almost like Mecca. At one time there lay within my easy reach no fewer than forty-seven cinemas of varying size, quality and character. None was more than five miles from Bolton's town hall, and twenty-eight were within the boundaries of the borough. Many of them remained mysteries until I reached the years of sufficient discretion to seek them out for myself, but I quickly found ways of cajoling my relations into taking me to the halls nearest their homes, which were seldom the most salubrious since we were a distinctly working-class group. Wide, straight main roads shot out of Bolton like spokes from a wheel, and in the time of which I speak, the most striking and well-lit buildings (apart from the mills in winter) were likely to be picture houses; bare, smelly and well-worn halls bearing such grandiose names as the Carlton, the Majestic, the Palace, the Empire, the Plaza, the Ritz and the Regal. For the time being, I could judge most of them only by the literacy of their advertising.

Further afield, the industrial wasteland of south Lancashire was studded with comparable solar systems. Preston was eighteen miles away, Blackburn twelve, Burnley fifteen, Oldham thirteen, Warrington seventeen, Wigan eleven. I consulted their newspapers when I could, but we seldom made the journey unless we particularly

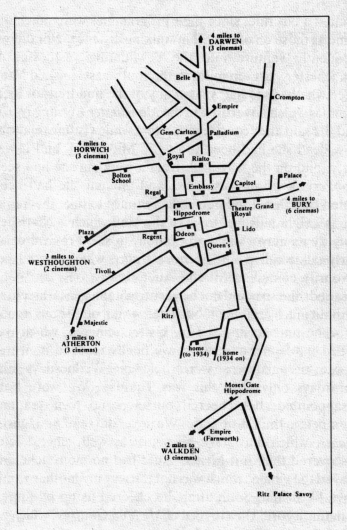

Bolton Cinemas of the 1930s
(*not to scale*)

A map cannot convey the excitement of reading their brightly-coloured posters, which because they changed so frequently were the cleanest items in our damp and sooty town

wanted a bus ride, since their programmes were much the same as those on offer within walking distance. Nor did we frequently venture into the bewildering vastnesses of Manchester, just ten miles to the south-east. I asked Mum once whether she had visited any of the hundreds of local cinemas which advertised in the *Manchester Evening News*, and she said after consideration that while visiting relations now dead she had been to one in Middleton, and it was dirty; and on the way back from a wedding she had seen *Rookery Nook* in Rusholme, and thought she had been bitten by a flea. I did persuade her once to take the bus as far as Leigh, a dismal town of the kind which is cherished only by its mayor and corporation, to see a revival of an early talkie called *The Monster Walks*, which starred her favourite comedian Mischa Auer. It was only an 'A', I pleaded, and so could not be very frightening. She assented without much argument, but when we got off the bus it took us some time to find the back street cinema, which was called the Sems; and, when we finally reached it, it was closed, as matinées were held on Wednesdays and Saturdays only, and this was Tuesday. We were both disappointed, but cheered ourselves up over tea and crumpets in the Co-op Café. We never did see *The Monster Walks*, which may have been just as well, since I later discovered that in it Mischa Auer had no moustache and played the villain, which was not the way my mother would have liked him. Soon after, he cheered us up by impersonating a gorilla in a revival of *My Man Godfrey*, which we had missed on its first release.

With the passing of years I patronized all the Bolton cinemas except one, and the omission still troubles me. It was the Gem, in Shepherd Cross Street, and by a series of misadventures I never even passed its front door. It always took, in the *Evening News*, an advertisement space larger than befitted its station in life, and the top line invariably had the word **CINEMA** in bold capitals in the middle, with **GEM** in each corner. So of course it was constantly referred to as the Gem Cinema Gem. It can't have been a real fleapit, as it was close to snooty Church Road, but we never established the truth because we were quite satisfied with two cinemas more convenient of access, the Tivoli and the Crompton, which were part of the same circuit and showed precisely the same programmes, though on different days to permit the bicycling of prints.

The reason we withdrew our patronage from the Queen's was not so much the declining quality of its attractions as the increasingly obvious defects in its presentation. Mum had long suspected that, since the change of manager, the place had been inadequately cleaned; something was once muttered about his 'bringing his own women in', which I was clearly not intended to interpret. Certainly the frequent journeyings of the usherette with the brass spray, which deposited great droplets of cheap scent on the heads of everyone in its range, may have been a rather obvious effort to cover up a multitude of sins. So far as I was concerned, the occasional reek of carbolic soap was even more offensive. Then there were the projection breakdowns, ever increasing in frequency. Once the light failed about twenty minutes from the end of the main feature. For the best part of half an hour we all waited fairly politely, after which the lights dimmed abruptly and on came the News, without a word of apology or explanation from anybody. We had to sit the whole programme round in order to catch up with the bit we missed: we had not become so bold as to feel capable of asking for our money back.

Whenever the performance did run into a technical hitch, we could deduce from the length of time before the lights went up that nobody ever stood by the projectors and watched the show. We knew this in any case before we paid to come in, because the Queen's snuggled into a hill and as we hurried down it after buying our bag of Liquorice Allsorts at the station kiosk we often encountered the projectionist standing at his door with an illicit cigarette, just below the notice which ordered NO SMOKING in massive red letters. On one occasion I even spotted him hurrying across the road to the chip shop, the door wide open to reveal whirring machinery absolutely deserted. After half a minute of no sound, or no picture, or both, or the film whizzing wildly through the gate with sprocket holes hopelessly disengaged, the usherettes would start to flash their torches at the projection port-holes, and eventually this might, or might not, have some result. As the management did not seem to care about these short-comings, and the manager himself was seldom seen by patrons other than those of the Railway Hotel, we gradually transferred our principal allegiance to the Hippodrome, for it was decently run, cheerful and comfort-able. Moreover, its programme policy was an infallible magnet for those who liked a good laugh, and there were few who did not among the grime and unemployment of industrial Lancashire during the run-up to World War II.

The Hippodrome stood opposite the General Post Office, at the western end of Deansgate, as far away from the Queen's as it could be while still remaining in the town centre. Despite a certain austerity of design there was something irresistibly jolly about it, for it was built in Edwardian times as a music-hall, and across its façade the old name was still visible in superbly crafted stone letters: EMPIRE & HIPPODROME 1909. Inside, the rather cramped stalls were enhanced by a splendid gilded pro-scenium, complete with tragic and comic masks at top centre; these became rather more appropriate in later years when the Hippodrome was taken over by a repertory company. The broadly curving dress circle was spacious and airy, with no upper balcony to make it claustrophobic; while under its steep slope there was tucked away a tiny but welcoming café, which seldom served anything more ambitious than pots of tea and toasted tea cakes, but did so with friendly efficiency.

Crowded along the walls of the narrow corridors and staircases were more than sixty glazed frames (I counted them) containing signed photographs of popular stars of the time. Other frames held sets of cigarette cards such as 'Stars of Stage and Screen' and 'Actors in Natural and Character Studies'. A few larger composite frames, clearly designed to hold an assortment of stills, now announced coming attractions in a variety of lettering styles, impeccably executed by the house artist whom we sometimes saw at work during a matinée. (The Hippodrome never went in for stills, perhaps because of some dispute over the hire fee, and we never missed them because the stars were always too well known to require this kind of photographic representation: the portraits were come-on enough.) The whole building reeked of mothballs, but we thought that a clean smell; there was no perfume save that which rose from the artificial grass which covered the boarded-over orchestra pit, when it absorbed the heat from the footlights.

As the Hippodrome took over our support, so the usual timing of our visits tended to change, for the Hippodrome ran no weekday matinées except during the school holidays, preferring to concentrate its energies on two supposedly separate evening shows. By now of course I was at school anyway, and even when I could manage the afternoon, the Hippodrome's two pm start for its separate matinée made it a bit of a rush for Mum after she had prepared and 'sided' dinner for my two sisters, who dashed home for it from their work at the Co-op Drapers and Whitaker's Department Store. It was much more relaxing in the evening. The first house began at six pm; the second at 8.15; but nobody was ever turned out between them, so that determined seekers of value for money could easily sit through both programmes. We usually arrived just in time for the first run of the feature, for it was impossible to get there as early as six o'clock. Our routine on Hippodrome nights was for Mum to have Dad's tea ready when he came in from the mill at a quarter to six, to chat with him through it but to catch the ten past six bus into town, leaving the half-washed dishes in the sink and the master of the house somnolent in front of the fire with the *Evening News* on his lap. 'Off to th' Hippo?' he would ask, nodding to himself as we closed the door.

The Hippodrome was so very British in its ambience that I can remember only two or three American films that played there, apart from supporting two-reelers starring the likes of Buster West, Thelma Todd and Patsy Kelly, or the Three Stooges. A less comic series of two-reel shorts starred Floyd Gibbons, a tough, eye-shaded, real-life crime reporter. He appeared in an item called *Attic of Terror*, at the start of which I was prepared to hide under my seat, but Mum said the title was probably the only frightening thing about it, and as usual she was right. No, what kept the Hippodrome popular and prospering was its nourishing diet of British low comedy in the music-hall tradition. It even played a record of that catchy variety theme tune, 'The Spice of Life', before the main feature. Tom Walls and Ralph Lynn in the Aldwych farces, Will Hay, Leslie Fuller, Flanagan and Allen, Cicely Courtneidge, Jack Hulbert, Gracie Fields, Leslie Henson, Max Miller, Dug-

gie Wakefield, Gordon Harker . . . they were all regular
favourites, and whoever the star of the week happened to
be, his next attraction could usually be glimpsed among the
innumerable 'Coming Shortly' slides which were flashed
rapidly on to the screen during the commendably brief ice-
cream interval. (We tended not to bother with cinema ice
cream in those days. The tubs contained hard, dull, tasteless stuff, and the Snofrute bars, being nothing but frozen
juice with bits of fruit left in, tended to melt very suddenly
and run through the open-ended carton right down one's
sleeve. They tasted delicious, and were fine for the open air
when bought from one of the familiar Wall's tricycle men,
but the Hippodrome soon abandoned them, since they
resulted in pools of sticky mess on the carpet.)

The Hippodrome's array of interval slides was an
entertainment in itself. Trailers, like stills, had clearly been
banned as too expensive, but the staff artist had worked
overtime on the slides. Each one was crammed with drawings, photographs, ornate lettering and other decorative
detail, with the film title in dashing rococo style as its
centrepiece; the whole was suffused in some startling
colour considered appropriate to the theme. *Alf's Button
Afloat* is still a green film to me, *Boys Will Be Boys* yellow
and brown, *Pot Luck* crimson; as each appeared, the
auditorium would fill with oohs and aahs of anticipation.
Squibs for some reason was advertised in a chilly black and
white, and a chilly film it remains in my memory. It was a
1937 talkie remake of George Pearson's silent comedy
about a cockney flower girl winning the Calcutta Sweep; it
starred the now matronly Betty Balfour in a forlorn comeback, along with Gordon Harker and Stanley Holloway to
give it zest. We had been looking forward to it for weeks,
but when the time came Dad was out of work, it was winter,
and the house had run out of coal because of a strike. Dad

went off to the Spinners' Union for company; Mum and I
headed for the pictures mainly to keep warm, but we both
had colds and sniffled through the show. The cockney
humour failed dismally to make a North Country audience
laugh, the settings were (quite suitably) drab, and Mum
said Miss Balfour should have stayed in silent pictures, as
her voice was torture to listen to. In order to save the tram
fare we walked there and back. A penn'oth of chips in
Newport Street cheered us a little, but when we got home
there was a row on some long-forgotten subject, and I went
to bed crying.

On the whole, however, the Hippodrome brings back
only the happiest of memories. There was something very
satisfying about seeing music-hall comedy in an old music-
hall. We sat always in the fourpenny stalls, which meant
entry through a little side street pay box. The cashier was a
maiden lady of uncertain age; she had tightly marcelled
hair, and repeatedly told us (and presumably everybody
else) how terrified she was of a recurrence of the night she
was attacked by 'footpads' while the commissionaire was
inside. I liked to pay for my own ticket, using pennies
handed to me by Mum as we walked briskly through the
back streets from Victoria Square; but when an 'A' film
was the attraction, the law said she must get the tickets for
both of us and hand them to the doleful old doorkeeper, the
one with the drooping moustaches and the dirty white
gloves. He would then lift the dust-filled red velour curtain
which allowed us to enter the inner sanctum by the doorway to the left of the screen. Invariably we arrived towards
the end of the shorts, but sometimes there was a cartoon
just before the news, and of course I always insisted on
seeing that through twice. The shorts in fact were very
often the best part of the programme. Since main features
then seldom ran more than 75 minutes, there was room in a

two-hour programme not only for a two-reel comedy and a cartoon but often for a couple of 'interests' as well, selected from such series as *Stranger than Fiction*, *Speaking of Animals*, *Sportslight* (with Grantland Rice), *Screen Snapshots* and *Unusual Occupations*. Then there was the news. World events at my age were a bit of a bore and I often went for a stroll to the Gents as they unfurled, but I did like Gaumont British News for its cheerful signature tune and its fancy title sequence where a gallery of rapidly changing news items centred on a bell-ringing town crier whom I used to insist was the comedian Sidney Howard in disguise. (Perhaps it was.)

The best vantage-point for a small boy was obviously the middle of the front row, and Mum sometimes agreed to sit there; although it can't have done her eyes any good, and people making their way to the toilets used to tread on her feet, which were tender at the best of times. There was no rowdyism, however: the front stalls at the Hippodrome were occupied chiefly by respectable middle-aged couples or family parties, and any hooligan elements would have been quickly and firmly dealt with by the patrons themselves if the commissionaire had chosen to be otherwise engaged. Wherever we sat, it was always a thrilling moment when the lights dimmed and the censor's certificate for the main feature flashed on to the dividing, floodlit red curtain, to be laboriously and audibly deciphered by an eager audience.

The stars whose adventures we watched on the Hippodrome's milky-textured screen seemed always more real, more vital, than those observed elsewhere. This may have been partly because it was such an intimately shaped hall, but mainly I suspect because low vaudeville comics most easily found a level on which to meet audiences whose roots were in cotton spinning and who had lived, generation after generation, in the long shadow of the mills. In Lancashire they worked hard, and they liked to laugh hard, sometimes at subjects which southerners might have thought in poor taste, like drunkenness, underwear, and funerals. Beefy Leslie Fuller might have been my uncle, George Formby a comical cousin and Gracie Fields a young spinster aunt. It required no effort of imagination for us to be interested in their doings; they were only a slight exaggeration of our everyday life.

In 1934 my mother had urged us out of our gaunt old terraced house in Parkfield Road into a brand new Bradford Road semi, only half a mile away but set on a hill above the common level: from its front gate the mill chimneys, apart from one just below us in Carter Street, could be seen only as distant symbols. The house cost all of £450, freehold, and was secured with the help of the Oddfellows and a mortgage from a local building society; I think my parents scraped together £50 to put down, by withdrawing all they had from the Co-op Bank. Dad, with his lunch in a red handkerchief, still walked every day, when there was cotton to spin, through Doe Hey to the Textile Mill, where he ran a fearsome 'set of wheels' on the sixth floor; but at least he now had a handsome house to come home to, even though he never paid much attention to it. He always said he had been comfortable where he was, and the move was for the benefit of the women of the family (and, he hinted with a glance, for me). Certainly my only remaining grandparent, my mother's mother, was delighted with our improved circumstances, and was waiting for us at the new house when we arrived on the van; she gave me a brand new 1934 halfpenny as a souvenir, and I kept it for years. I soon got used to the new house, but I began to understand as time went by that each and every one of our relations, who all still lived in terraced cottages without indoor

sanitation, thought the Halliwells were getting too big for
their boots. Bradford Road or not, we could tell them that
life was still a constant battle against the acid soot which fell
in showers from the industrial chimneys not only of Bolton
but, when the wind was blowing from the south, of
Farnworth too. Curtains and window bottoms were full of
it, and front steps had to be 'dolly-stoned' every day as a
sign that the occupants were as 'prick-meat' as circumstances would permit. In 1934, in the terraced rows of
Eustace Street, Woodgate Street and Melville Street just
below us, the older women still wore grey shawls; the earth
closets at the bottom of the yard were emptied by sinister-
sounding 'nightmen'; and the clatter of clogs on the pave-
ments was heard all day long; but the aura of respectability
was unmistakable.

And so we were aiming at the soft under-belly of the
middle class, my mother being determined that, since my
sisters had been robbed of a secondary education by illness
and bad timing, I should preserve the family honour by
winning a scholarship, whether she could afford it or not.
Auntie Flo once said it was the pictures that were turning
Mum's head, that by watching these grand folk drinking
their champagne she was getting ideas above her station.
This was not true; I don't think we ever connected the films
we most enjoyed with the world in which we had to live.
Certainly if the films of the Aldwych farces had any real-life
parallels, it was not in any life that we could recognize. Ben
Travers had created his own never-never land of comic
fantasy: it was alleged to lie in the affluent South of
England, but we strongly suspected that it could not have
been found there either. What did exist, and what mattered, was the brilliant timing and incredible mobility of
expression on the face of that perfect silly ass Ralph Lynn;
the bluff racetrack humour of Tom Walls, always with a

roving eye for a trim ankle; and the traumatic tribulations of that littlest of little men, Robertson Hare, whose 'Oh, calamity!' was at first hearing added to my gallery of impersonations. Tribute must also be paid to the regular supporting company of damsels in distress, incompetent maidservants, lordly butlers, nosey landladies, *nouveau riche* matrons, suspicious wives, saucy mistresses, ancient noblemen and roaring Blimps. I treasure the memory of Mr Lynn in *A Cuckoo in the Nest*, staying at a country inn with a lady not his wife and having his shaky signature in the guest register scrutinized by the landlady. 'You don't write very clear,' she remarks accusingly. 'Er, no,' he says, 'I've just had some very thick soup.'*

The film of *Rookery Nook*, despite its primitive technique and lack of directorial style (Tom Walls was said merely to line up his actors and tell them to get on with it), probably showed the Aldwych company at its best, and some of its fine googly lines still linger: 'Earlier than that I cannot be'; 'The other rooms is elsewhere'; 'If he's her stepfather, it's a very slippery step'; 'You swine of a Twine'. I especially treasure the early scene when Mr Lynn, having arrived in advance of his wife at their rented holiday home, pops out to get his bags from the car and returns to find sitting on the hall table a pretty young lady in pyjamas, the legs of which (he shortly discovers) are soaking wet from running through the fields away from her Teutonic stepfather Putz, who went nuts because she ate wurst. Mr Lynn stops dead in his tracks at the door. His monocle drops from his eye; his jaw sags; his long-fingered hands dangle limply from his wrists. He returns to the door to make sure he is in the right house. He comes back,

*In his autobiography Ben Travers says that this line was contributed not by him, but by the active-minded Ralph Lynn. Mr Travers thought at first that it was a bit over the top.

makes a helpless gesture, tries to cough. She is unaware of him. He puts up a hand, doesn't know what to do with it, scratches his head. He passes a finger round his collar, moves timidly closer, drums his fingers on the corner of the table. It is so gentle a noise that even a stethoscope would not pick it up. When she finally realizes his presence and tells her halting story, it is Mr Lynn who looks embarrassed, with the convenient aid of a loofah which he passes from one hand to another round his neck, behind his back and between his legs. This is great farce acting, and vintage Lynn; but all the Aldwych films, creaky as art, are full of choice moments. It may be objected that fruity farces which involve girls in cami-knickers and gentlemen without their trousers were hardly suitable entertainment for an impressionable lad of six or seven. Nonsense. I laughed at the comedic skills of all concerned, never quite understanding what the characters were really up to.

After Aldwych, Will Hay certainly came next in our affections. His films were fast, funny, wry and a little pathetic, the work of a great modern droll. It was not so much the badinage of the famous schoolmaster act ('How Hi is a Chinaman') that made us love him; we would eventually have wearied of the cheeky boys and the excruciating puns. Luckily he found writers to take him outside the classroom and establish him as a clever caricature of a human being. Whatever the disguise – fire chief, prison governor, stationmaster, colonial official, policeman, correspondence course organizer – Hay was always the likeable seedy incompetent attempting to carry off by bluster a task well beyond his powers. His failings were well known to his assistants, who taunted him unmercifully, but when danger threatened they always pitched in on his side to rout the villains. The casting of Graham Moffatt, like the fat boy from Pickwick, as the younger of these foils, was

clever enough; but Moore Marriott as toothless old Harbottle, constantly berated by the others but full of ancient
wheezes, was an inspiration. *Oh! Mr Porter*, rising to
heights of lunatic invention in a pub, a windmill and a
moving train, is undoubtedly their most perfect film, but
Ask a Policeman, in many respects a carbon copy, has a
priceless sequence when Harbottle persuades his old father
(also played by Moore Marriott) who must be at least a
hundred and ten, to remember a traditional rhyme which
proves to be the key to the plot:

> When the tide runs high in the smugglers' cove,
> And the headless horseman rides ab*ove*,
> He rides along with a wild hallo,
> And that's the time when the smugglers row out in
>   their little boats to the schooner and bring back the
>   barrels of brandy and rum and put them in the cave
>   below.

Hay made films with different support, and Mum and I
were especially fond of one of his first, *Those Were the
Days*, in which he played a more or less straight role. An
adaptation of Pinero's *The Magistrate*, it had the best re-
creation I know of a Victorian music-hall, and so seemed
especially suited to the Hippodrome.

I was keen enough on the debonair Jack Buchanan,
though Mum always said he looked a sissy. We were
divided too about George Robey, whom she had admired
for years on the halls, though to me, instinctively I suppose,
he seemed not to have weathered the changeover to film
technique. Gordon Harker, of the cockney twang and the
jutting lower lip, was always reliable, especially in a well-
plotted crime thriller. George Formby was unengaging in
his first films, *Off the Dole* and *Boots! Boots!*, but
they were virtually amateur efforts; decent scripts and
production soon turned him into a real star, and you could

have heard a pin drop whenever he bashfully reached for
his ukelele and sang a saucy song:

> The blushing bride, she looks divine,
> The bridegroom, he is doing fine,
> I'd rather have his job than mine,
>   When I'm cleaning windows.

Yes, I added that too to my fireside impersonation
routine; no wonder I got some funny looks from Auntie
Edith.

Cicely Courtneidge with her husband Jack Hulbert (and
sometimes his brother Claude) seemed always eager to
please, and they brought with them a whiff of London
cabaret. The brothers had a fine time in *Bulldog Jack*, with
its final thrilling race through underground train tunnels,
and Cicely was particularly splendid in *Under Your Hat*
when disguised as an ex-Indian Army matron telling young
schoolgirls in song that the future was theirs:

> When I was in Delhi,
> I lay on my (hm, hm)
>   In a flat-bottomed canoe.
> They all thought me barmy,
> But I know the army!
>   The nation depends on you. . .

We did not care for Flanagan and Allen until they became
part of the Crazy Gang in *OK for Sound*, in which they
shared honours with the famous baritone Peter Dawson,
who offered his rendering of *The Road to Mandalay*. Mum
thought this one of the most wonderful performances she
had ever heard, and could not understand why I was
impatient for the slapstick to start again. The Gang went on
to make two classics: *Alf's Button Afloat*, the only film I
know in which hero and heroine are eaten by a bear, in

Kent, and *The Frozen Limits*, in which Moore Marriott leads a multiple nightshirted sleep-walking scene so hilarious that I still send myself to sleep chuckling about it.

For a small boy even the more mediocre comedies usually seemed to have redeeming features, but the serious British output, what little there was of it, could be cheerless indeed, as anyone will know who has ever sat through *Drake of England* or *Royal Cavalcade*. My sisters adored Anna Neagle in all her guises: historical in *Nell Gwyn*, fustian in *Peg of Old Drury*, romantic in *The Three Maxims*, sentimental in *Limelight*. I tolerated them without much enthusiasm. Until *The Lady Vanishes* we did not follow Alfred Hitchcock's name or even then understand a director's function, but I remember thinking *Secret Agent* a rambling mess and *Sabotage* rather unpleasant after some striking early scenes. *The Thirty-nine Steps* was quite another matter. A revival of its tongue-in-cheek adventures, laced with humour and chilling suspense, warmed us up on a December night when the Hippodrome's heating system broke down. The enthusiasm and excitement of 800 people seemed to heat every part of us except our toes, and it was in high spirits that we headed for home, humming Mr Memory's tantalizing theme tune and trying to work out what exactly were the thirty-nine steps anyway? Not that it mattered to one's enjoyment of the film: they were just a Hitchcock McGuffin, a bald device to link the suspense sequences. Hitchcock's *The Man Who Knew Too Much* was also a Hippodrome movie, being from Gaumont British. Equally skilful, and similar in mood, it seemed rather less likeable because the life of a kidnapped child was at stake, and one could hardly laugh and cheer as one would have wished, even at the scenes in the dentist's surgery and in the East End chapel which was a cover for the anarchists. Peter Lorre, who played the kidnapper, became the current man we loved to hate, and the street sets had a deliciously sleazy atmosphere which I tried in subsequent weeks to recreate after dark by walking with half-closed eyes through Bolton's lamplit alleys.

When I was nine, the Gaumont British version of *King Solomon's Mines* seemed to me a masterwork. Even though neither Mum nor I normally went in for *Boy's Own Paper* stuff, we had both enjoyed the Rider Haggard book when I borrowed it from the library, and the film version seemed eminently satisfactory, although we were disappointed that Roland Young as Captain Good had so little to do. Cedric Hardwicke might have been born to play Quartermain, and you could scarcely imagine a finer Umbopa than Paul Robeson. An elderly actress called Sydney Fairbrother was also very vivid as the evil old African witch Gagool. We must have been extremely late that night, for her big final scene in the mountain caves was just beginning as we crept to our seats, and jolly frightening she was too.

The only American film I specifically remember seeing at the Hippodrome is *Mystery of the Wax Museum*, a shocker in the literal sense. Based on the ingenious though unconvincing idea of a crippled wax sculptor who carries on his trade by giving real corpses a wax coating (a process he has applied to his own horribly injured face), it played as an amalgam of Gothic horror with a standard Warner Brothers crime reporter yarn. In this case the reporter was a lady, or shall we say a woman, since at one point she instructs her editor, when he gets home, to throw his mother a bone. She then blows him a raspberry, to which he responds: 'A cow does that, and gives milk besides.' Such ripe badinage (which disappeared from Hollywood films after 1934, when the Legion of Decency came to have its way with all scripts) contrasted piquantly with the scenes in the horror chamber, with its daunting sets by Anton Grot. The whole curiosity was dipped in two-colour Technicolor, which added a bizarre tinge by making everything orange or turquoise. For this remarkable attraction, the Hippodrome had uniquely gone to the expense of a trailer, all winking eyes in the dark museum, with scrawny hands ready to clutch at the frightened heroine (Fay Wray, who after *King Kong* became known to the trade as the greatest screamer in the business). She of course had stupidly got herself locked in after closing time. Mum tried to distract me when the trailer was on, and said I should not think of going in case it gave me nightmares. But I persisted, and she had to admit that she liked Lionel Atwill, an English actor in Hollywood who was playing the smooth-tongued criminal lunatic Ivan Igor. Glenda Farrell, as the reporter, was also a favourite of ours, and besides, the film boasted nothing more admonitory than an 'A' certificate, since 'H' had not yet been invented. And so we turned up as usual, but had to queue for an hour, and were admitted just as the unmasked and horrific Igor is foiled in his plan of turning Miss Wray into the Marie Antoinette his burned hands can no longer create, and falls into his own vat of boiling wax. I shrank back into my seat, half afraid of getting splashed.*

I must have had a few bad dreams after all, for Mum refused point blank to take me to the Hippodrome's next horror film, *Werewolf of London*. The advertising slide for that was bathed in *two* colours – red and green – and there was an evil leering face in each corner. I pleaded that it

*In the early fifties it was discovered that the negative of *Mystery of the Wax Museum* had deteriorated and that all known prints were lost. In my then capacity as programme buyer for ITV, it delighted me to be able to direct the copyright owners to an interesting if faded print from which new copies could be made; these from time to time still turn up on British television; while the involved script has more recently been the subject of a scholarly thesis at the University of Wisconsin.

could not be very horrifying since dear old Warner Oland, so gentle and endearing as Charlie Chan, was in it. Mum's response was to point a firm finger at the *Evening News* advertisement, which read:

THIS FILM HAS TERRIFYING SCENES
AND PARENTS ARE ADVISED
NOT
TO BRING THEIR CHILDREN TO SEE IT

So for once the Hippodrome lost two customers, and it took me thirty years to catch up with *Werewolf of London*. It did not then seem worth the wait.

When fate turned our Hippo into the wartime haven of the Lawrence-Williamson Repertory Company, which stayed for more than twenty years, it became of great educational importance to me, serving as my means of introduction to many famous if faded theatrical hits. Nevertheless I remember it most clearly as the home of movies that made me laugh, and I have never forgotten the thrill when its house lights dimmed and its red footlights illuminated the parting curtain as some familiar trademark appeared, most frequently the dignified Gainsborough lady bowing to us from her gilded cameo as she introduced yet another ribald comedy. Gainsborough once had a special inspiration. For a comedy called, I think, *In the Soup,* the part of the bowing lady was played by Ralph Lynn himself, in drag, to our unanimous hilarity and delight.

THREE

Portrait of the Author as a Young Fan

Bolton seemed to me, at that time, a pretty good place to grow up in; but the only comparisons I could make arose from occasional visits to relations in Chorley, Wigan, Blackburn and Bury. (I put seaside resorts outside my range; only the really privileged could expect to live there.) Geographically, Bolton is quite fortunately placed. It lies in a natural basin, and from even its smokiest district you could look up to see the bracing, barren Lancashire moorland to the north. It had wide clean streets, traditional shops, an enormous Town Hall with steps enough to delight a Roman emperor, two splendid covered markets and plenty of local activity, including the Little Theatre, the Operatic Society, and *Messiah* every Christmas in the Victoria Hall. Even so, southerners today are seldom much impressed, and would have liked it still less in the thirties before slums were cleared to make way for a million-pound neo-Victorian civic centre, still unfinished in the eighties despite being officially opened by Lord Derby in May 1937. Nowadays there's a smokeless zone, and the useless old mills, redundant since the decline in the British cotton trade, have been turned into mail order stores. The tall chimneys no longer stab the sky like menacing triffids; but in the middle thirties, the raw, damp, sooty air was all-pervading. In summer, like a sponge, it soaked up the polluted smoke from more than fifty thousand hearths (for coal fires were almost the only cooking facility) into a continuous cloud that hung over the town like a pall. From the moors one could see it stretched out, a great grey blanket, over the familiar streets, discouraging any adventurous sunbeams from penetration of the deep cup. In winter the smog was at its most lethal, attacking one's head and chest and nasal passages, following one craftily into homes which were usually draughty and heated only at the centre, causing women to huddle as close to the ashy grate as they could without risking chilblains, and men to hurry after work to sample the clean refreshing taste of mild or bitter beer at the local. These Northern industrial towns shared a common joke, much favoured by music-hall comedians, about a traveller who woke up in a train and asked what was the tunnel from which the train had just emerged. He was told that it was Bolton; or Sheffield; or Rotherham; or Halifax; or any one of forty towns in which the tale might be told.

Living in the comparatively clean but undeniably dull suburb of Great Lever (the exact boundaries of which were hard to define) we suffered an extra handicap in the shape of our route into the town centre just over a mile away. The bus from Townleys Hospital, next to the workhouse, stopped every five minutes outside our door. Two hundred yards down the hill it stopped again, virtually on the industrial level, with one mill to the right and to the left the huge pond or 'lodge' of another. Across this stretch of water the wind cut like a knife from Richelieu Street (pronounced 'Richy-loo'). No boats were ever seen on it, and its banks were edged with overgrown rhododendrons whose slightly tacky leaves were black with grime and filthy to touch. Round the corner, past yet another mill and a couple of dingy factories, one climbed steeply to pass under the footbridge linking the two sections of Walker's Tannery, alleged to produce the best leather in England but a vision of hell to the passer-by who glanced through any of its low windows and witnessed the processes applied to the fresh skins. It also exuded a noisome smell which clung so defiantly to clothing that one's friends knew instantly the route one had taken. Once through this inferno, the direct avenue into town lay past the slaughterhouse, which frequently provided horrors of its own. The only way of avoiding it was to turn right over the pedestrian bridge which crossed the multitude of railway lines branching away enticingly to such dreary places as Radcliffe, Moses Gate and Pendleton. A left turn on the other side took one past the railway sidings to the corner on which the Queen's Cinema stood beckoning.

Similarly noisy, bustling, dirty and dramatic were most of the inner districts of this efficient but unromantic community, and it seemed to me sometimes that apart from its excellent shopping facilities, the town centre served no purpose except to hold them together. This was especially true in the evenings, when the pubs and the cinemas were the only public venues open; I doubt whether Bolton had a restaurant serving evening meals until well into the fifties, since the normal eating day finished with high tea; but fish and chip shops stood on a hundred or more corners and offered succulent supper fare best eaten straight out of the newspaper in the cold night air. The uncomfortable trams with their blinding headlights would clang towards you like bats out of hell when you crossed Victoria Square, threatening at each corner to leave their rails as they jolted past one gaslit building after another. It was no backdrop for an aesthete, but Hitchcock, had he ever ventured so far north, might have thought it a highly suitable setting for a thriller.

One of Bolton's virtues was its strongly developed sense of community. For so vast and sprawling a place its relationships were astonishingly village-like: not a single resident, I sometimes thought, could be unrelated or unknown to my family. A trip with my mother to the town centre shops or the UCP Café (UCP = United Cattle Products, i.e. tripe and brawn) always involved long sessions of standing in doorways or on corners, chatting to garrulous friends of both sexes; and when the *Evening News* arrived, its Births, Deaths and Marriages column always provoked enough comment to keep conversation going at least through tea.

'Ah see Bill Openshaw's gone, then.'

'Nay, 'as 'e?'

'Aye. Ah can remember 'im in my class at St Mark's. They thought 'e 'ad consumption then, you know.'

'Always looked poorly.'

'Aye, but 'e always got over it. Then 'is mother went with double pneumonia, poor feller.'

''E wasn't a bad lad at all, old Bill. Ah say old because 'e always looked old. Same age as me, really. It makes you think. It does that. Aye.'

'Let's see, was it Bertha Kenyon 'e married? Or Doreen Greenhalgh?'

Despite my mother's ambitions, my favourite urban walks still ran through the cobbled working-class thoroughfares which were never far away in any direction and are now immortalized in *Coronation Street*. I traversed them especially at weekends when I made the obligatory visits to relations. My father's mother died before I was born, and his father soon after, but they had several children. Walter was sufficiently ambitious to become a mill manager, and died of stress and a hardened artery in 1935. Henry I never knew: pneumonia claimed him before the century or the cinema were much advanced. Alice kept a tripe shop in Morris Green Lane, and died suddenly before ever making my acquaintance. Polly (really Mary Ann, but she cried if you said it) was a simple soul, happiest by her back fireside, or cooking while her husband Jesse mended shoes on the hearthrug. Bertha, unsentimental and determined, absented herself from the family for years, then in middle life became an unqualified mental nurse and later ran a rambling boarding house in the Jewish district of Manchester. Not much encouragement there for a budding film fan.

My mother's side of the family was quite different. Believing firmly in bettering themselves, all the Haslams liked to be instructed as well as entertained, to know all that was going on and to take part in it; they frankly regarded the Halliwells as an idle lot and insufficiently houseproud. Above all they liked a good laugh. They were always laughing: at home, on church outings, at church suppers, in the mills. My mother, born in 1885 (two years after Dad), was the eldest of four, three girls and a younger boy. Her father had died in his forties, the prevailing legend being that, like Prince Albert, he had got his feet wet; though another school of thought had it that with his weak lungs he was never the same after helping to carry Canon Doman's coffin the three miles from St Mark's to its interment at Deane Church. Her mother, however, lived until 1937, a frail but indomitable old lady with a fearsome eight-foot-long hearing tube. For many years a mill worker, as a widow she had become a conscientious washerwoman, but I knew her simply as the perfect Grandma who every Thursday walked two miles to have tea with us, and then set off on the two miles back. I cried bitterly when we lost her, and kissed her forehead as she lay in her coffin. She had apparently enjoyed the occasional silent film, but being stone deaf was only infuriated by the talkies. Mum and I once got her as far as the Theatre Royal to see Sidney Howard in *Night of the Garter*. She laughed not at all, and on the way home in the tram said it was a 'soft' picture (i.e. childish, silly). But later, when she was having a cup of tea by the roaring fire, she chuckled and admitted that one or two scenes had made her smile to herself, while Mr Howard had reminded her of a long-dead St Mark's curate who had been unable to get anything right.

My mother's young brother Tom, gassed in World War I, had a painful and very limited life for the next thirty years, being skeletal and bedridden for the last ten of them; but he saw a joke even in that. His was the kind of Lancashire wit that laughs at any adversity, even at Albert being eaten by the lion. He went only to see comedy films, especially those of Leslie Fuller, and I suspected that a great many of his jokes came from them. His sisters Edith and Florrie, both stay-at-homes until just before Grandma died, were patchy cinema-goers, regarding no film as more important than an hour's gossip, and seldom able to recall on the following day either the title or the stars. When Florrie was forty she unexpectedly married an amiable if slightly eccentric widowed bank clerk, Tom Twigley; and after Grandma's funeral Edith simply moved in with them to become the perfect auntie, making the cakes and doing the washing-up. When in later years they qualified for the old-age pension and the cheap cinema admission, they went twice a week for a while in the spirit of not missing a bargain. But sitting in the dark was not for them, so they transferred their allegiance to the repertory company and occupied the same circle seats every Wednesday for many years.

I visited all these aunts and uncles regularly, passing as

many cinemas as I could on the way, and entertaining them by regaling the plots of the films I had recently seen. I also called on an old friend of Grandma's who had attended so many funerals that she was known as Mother Mourning Coaches; three spinster sisters who really were called Faith, Hope and Charity; and a whimsical old gent called Llewellyn Jones who taught me to swim at the High Street Baths. I was that kind of boy. I almost walked my shoes off, up Settle Street and through the ginnel, through Bobby Heywood's Park to Daubhill, up Lever Edge Lane to Four Lane Ends, always with the sweet sickly smell of the mills in my nostrils. My curiosity was insatiable. I explored the murky towpath of the River Croale, the decaying streets under the High Level, the Dickensian muddle of the district called Haulgh (pronounced Hoff) below the Parish Church. These streets saw very little wheeled traffic, but they teemed with life, especially in the evenings when the men, exhausted by work, sat smoking on their doorsteps with a jug of draught ale at their side, chatting to each other in voices loud enough to be heard across the street.

Everybody in Bolton knew everybody else's business. If somebody died, it was the woman next door who consoled the bereaved and laid out the corpse. So nobody tried to hide anything except the courting couples, who might try a quiet twilight stroll through Farnworth Park, or by the Darcy Lever canal if the midges were not too troublesome. It was an intensely local life for most people, very moral, very lively within limits, very church-oriented. The daily life of cotton-spinning families was improving only slowly on the lot of their Victorian predecessors. They worked long, arduous hours, Saturday mornings too, and holidays with pay were only an incredible promise which none of them expected to see fulfilled in their working lifetime. Few had ever in their lives travelled south of Manchester, or further than Blackpool or the Isle of Man, and there were still many who had never crossed the boundaries of Bolton, and did not care to. Their hard lives were kept cheerful by various comings-together of friends and relations, principally at weddings and funerals, at either of which families would be likely to see the same faces telling the same stories in the same private room with the squeaky chairs and the hat-racks at the back of the Co-op Restaurant.

Although my mother and father maintained impeccable spelling and handwriting, both had left school for the mills at the age of eleven, and for several years Mum had an hour's walk in all weathers before work began at 6.30 am. Dad beat his own father's record by working nearly seventy years in the mills, staying at his 'wheels', in a reduced capacity, till he was approaching his eightieth birthday. There was no need for him to go on working, but it passed the time, and he liked the company. People knew him to be unambitious, but he was always respected, fond in his spare time of Conservative Clubs and Spinners' Unions and Oddfellows' Halls: or any palatial setting where beer could be thoughtfully sipped by benevolent men in threadbare suits. He never really approved of unions unless they were quiescent. We were always Conservative, our family, less from political conviction than because we liked to vote for someone we could look up to rather than a member of our own class who had no means of leading us to a better life. Labour followers in fact were considered low. Nor was Dad a capacious drinker. He could linger for hours over a pint if the company was good; but his metabolism was such that even small amounts of alcohol made his cheeks flame with purple-red patches, and Mum grew furious if he was seen in public with what she called his erysipelas face. He tried sometimes to please her, but he was not a homebody, and the lure of the great hotels with their gilded ceilings and marble columns, their cast-iron chandeliers and mahogany doors, was too great. In such surroundings one could feel oneself to be a person of importance.

Dad had nothing against the cinema, but it simply did not enter into his scheme of things. He occasionally agreed to take me for a Saturday laugh at one of the broader comics, but he failed to understand how people could regularly bother to concentrate on shadows when for as little money an evening's real entertainment might be had in a comfortable bar with one's cronies. He did, however, like Uncle Tom Twigley, enjoy a weekly visit to the Grand Theatre, Bolton's gilded music-hall in Churchgate, perhaps because it had a bar at the back of the stalls. I was always delighted to accompany him. The Grand was usually filled to overflowing at both evening performances, and its rich theatrical atmosphere was invigorating. I was bored by ballad singers like Cavan O'Connor and Monte Rey, but the rest was pure magic, especially the comedians and novelty acts. Max Miller, against his inevitable painted backdrop of a modernistic street corner with flat roofs and metal windows (the Grand seemed to possess no other), always enjoyed a bit of barracking from the bar patrons, who popped in and out of the auditorium to shout a few words of encouragement or derision. It would have been a tawdry world if we hadn't all enjoyed it so thoroughly, if the artists hadn't given the impression of doing their stuff for more than a pay packet. Perhaps backstage was a melancholy place, but if it was they never let it show. Meanwhile a parade of great names passed before our astonished eyes: George Robey ('I stopped, I looked, I listened'); Frank Randle ('I'll bet tha's a hot un'); Gillie Potter ('Good evening, England'); Old Mother Riley ('Where've you been, who've you been with, what've you been doing, and why?'); Hatton and

Manners, Murray and Mooney, Nat Mills and Bobbie, Florrie Forde, G. H. Elliott, Clapham and Dwyer, Stainless Stephen, Norman Long, Terry Wilson, Albert Whelan, Norman Evans, the Ganjou Brothers and Juanita, Florence Desmond, Hetty King, Jimmy James, Teddy Brown, and Wilson Keppel and Betty in their famous sand dance, 'Cleopatra's Nightmare'. All these and many more played the Grand at least once a year, and if they brought back the same act we never minded. At the festive season there were brisk, efficient, twice-nightly pantomimes with traditional stories and even more traditional routines ('I can prove to you that you're not here'); while every six months or so there was a circus, and we all wondered how they fitted the wild animals into that cramped backstage. (They didn't: there was a convenient warehouse down the alley.)

Despite my mother's willing support, I think it was my sisters who first aroused my insatiable curiosity about the movies, because it was necessary for their own social standing that they should be *au fait* with the latest public and private exploits of John Gilbert, Clark Gable, Ricardo Cortez and William Powell. I remember lying on the hearthrug, the home-made black one with a blue diamond in the middle, listening to them chatter about these mysterious people as they put the finishing touches to their faces in the cracked mirror over the kitchen sink. They liked best the genteel romantic pictures in which the shop girl who could take care of herself (usually Jean Arthur or Claudette Colbert) eventually married a millionaire and lived happily ever after to the accompaniment of popping champagne corks. Tinkly musicals, melodramas with a message, and adventure stories with strong silent heroes were also greatly to their taste; and in the middle thirties they could find something to their taste every week. If they shared an idol, it must have been the elegant and debonair Ronald Colman. I remember most clearly now the occasions when they stepped out of character. Edith, for instance, went to see *Dirigible* because it was advertised as having 'positively NO war scenes'; and Lilian went rather timorously to *Dracula's Daughter* because a lucky number had won her free admission. They joined forces to see John Barrymore in *The Mad Genius* because they were bemused by the weirdest of publicity campaigns:

A STORY OF THE STRANGEST PASSION
ONE MAN EVER HAD FOR ANOTHER! IT STANDS,
A MONUMENT TO ITSELF, FOR ALL TIME!

Lilian once had an argument with her boyfriend as to whether that evening they should go to see Barbara Stanwyck, who was young and sultry, or Marie Dressler, who was over sixty and no oil painting. Much to my surprise Marie Dressler won, possibly because that marvellous, shapeless, vivid old character actress had a marked resemblance to my mother. The advertising always made the most of her homely qualities:

WITH PRIDE AND PLEASURE
WE PRESENT
OUR MARIE-
GOD BLESS HER!!!

When she died in 1934 it was like losing a member of the family.

The girls were also lured to something advertised as

THE LADY REFUSES!
Why?

And great fuss was made of the revival at the Embassy,

after Clark Gable had become the King of Hollywood, of one of his early movies called *Night Nurse*. Edith came back indignant at having had to queue for a film in which Mr Gable played only a minor menace and had no more than a dozen lines apart from some shots of his feet crossing the floor. She came close to demanding her money back.

Still, it was with my mother that I saw my first few hundred films. Our frequent outings strengthened the natural bonds and made us pals, diminishing almost to nothing the years between us. A heavily built, often ailing woman, forty-four when I was born and (like most mill town women) looking older, she got such fun out of her filmgoing that it was a pleasure to be with her. She never entirely forgot a film she had seen, though names would sometimes elude her and we often spent an enjoyable ten minutes trying to ferret out a title from the clues she was able to offer. 'You know, it was where he was a doctor, the hero I mean, it might have been Franchot Tone, but I don't think it was. She feels she's not good enough for him so she persuades him to go with the other girl, and then there's that fire where he saves the baby . . .or was that *Men in White*? No, I think it was the other one, the one with that nice fellow, the one that looks like George Raft but isn't. And Frank Morgan was in it, I'm sure of that.'

Like millions of other people then, Mum relied on her pictures to lend sparkle to a life which was otherwise fairly humdrum. By the time I was of movie-going age my sisters were grown up and full of their own interests, though dutiful to the extent of spending most of Sunday (between Eucharist and Evensong) on their knees polishing the skirting boards. As for Dad, the first flush of joy in his relationship with Mum had long faded, and they preferred to seek separate interests since they could not agree on communal ones. She objected to his pipe and his beer, while he felt that her presence constrained him to a dull, respectable circle in which he could not shine, especially since tea might be the only beverage on offer. In fact Mum did enjoy a jug of draught oatmeal stout, but at home by her fireside, brought by me from the off-licence and warmed in the winter by the insertion of a poker red hot from the fire. As we did not encourage a large circle of visiting friends, partly because we could not afford to keep the parlour heated all the year round, she found evenings at home a dullish end to the long hard days, even after the advent of radio. Mysterious headaches of increasing intensity prevented her from concentrating solely on the spoken word when it came out of a box in the corner. So she looked for excuses to take her 'out of herself', and she found them through me, and through our joint fascination with the movies.

Slowly the shape of the family became distorted, Mum's primary interest being focused on me and my progress at school. At St Simon's I was the darling of all the teachers, being always top of the class and going twice a week to the library in search of the extra reading matter recommended by Miss Fyles, Miss Maurice and Miss Southern. There was a feeling that the headmistress, Miss Crompton, tried to hold me back because I was too bright and might sap my own mental strength, but the staff ganged up on her. In this way I graduated from *Little Black Peter* to *Alice in Wonderland*, from *David Copperfield* to *Treasure Island*, and like Oliver Twist I was always in search of more. In considering this remarkable thirst for knowledge Mum conceived the idea, with the connivance of the teaching staff, that I should sit as soon as possible for a scholarship to Bolton School, the splendid red sandstone pile in the Chorley New Road, endowed by Lord Leverhulme and established since the sixteenth century. She conceded that such a result was unlikely and that I might have to put up with the Church Institute or the Municipal; but it would be one or the other. A secondary education of some sort I was going to get, by hook or by crook. Eventually, by an accident of my birthday, I sat for what is now the eleven plus when I had just turned nine, and learned a few months later that I had come third out of five in the county who had been awarded major Lancashire scholarships to public schools. It was an achievement that scared all of us, and in some way changed our lives.

Meanwhile my father had become a rather shadowy figure, seldom seen between tea and bedtime. After being fed, and left alone by the fireside for twenty minutes, he would creep upstairs to scrape a shave, and emerge smelling of carbolic in his best collar and tie. Muffler, bowler hat and overcoat were donned in the hall, the pipe was lit in the back kitchen, and he was away for the evening. When he did return at about 10.45 it was with equal stealth, so that he could pop his collar into the dresser drawer and be away to bed before Mum could start an argument. He left the running of the house entirely to her; when his wage packet arrived on Fridays, he was happy to hand over to her the entire responsibility of spending it, keeping back only an agreed amount of pocket money. Under this system he thought it reasonable for him to ignore the manila envelopes which accumulated at the back of the mahogany dresser, though he was quick to spot and open the kind of letter which might invite him as a conference delegate to a weekend at Southport or Llandudno. However, we did all come together for such events as the Bolton New Year Fair where my special treat, apart from sessions on the Waltzer, was to enter one of the large tents which served mugs of black peas and vinegar.

In 1937, firmly propelled by my mother into meaningful

activity, my father won enough votes at the Co-op election to get on to the Education Committee, and stayed there for fourteen years. This suited her very well for, apart from the honour, it meant that she knew where he was at least on the twice-weekly committee evenings. The Co-op then had a local influence almost unimaginable, and most of its 56,000 members relied heavily on the 'divi' which they collected each quarter after laboriously filling as many gummed sheets as possible with their little yellow shopping receipts. The General Committee's proceedings were of more interest to Boltonians than those of the Palace of Westminster. The educational sub-group was an eccentric body of eight good men and true, devoted to the improvement of our educational, social and cultural life. The means to this end included winter classes about the history of Co-operation, going back to Robert Owen and the Rochdale Pioneers; weekly meetings of men's and women's guilds; and free use of the splendid marble and mahogany Bridge Street centre, which included two large halls for dances and concerts, a restaurant and café with private rooms, and a heavily ornate library filled with the rather unsettling busts of Victorian gentlemen who always seemed to be looking straight at me. All these functions, in the high season, required considerable attention from committeemen, so that from the time of his election we saw less of Dad than ever unless, as often happened, we went along to the Saturday activities and watched him proudly doing his turn as master of ceremonies.

I liked the concerts best, when the baritone and tenor combined to sing 'The Two Gendarmes' ('We run them in, we run them in'), or when the middle-aged contralto, Emmy Walmsley, tried to look demure and played with her georgette handkerchief as John Baron crooned at her: 'Tell me, pretty maiden, are there any more at home like you?'

And there was always potato pie at the interval, trundled in huge steaming vats from the restaurant's kitchen to the long trestle tables in the corridor, and served with the help of enormous ladles. The events of the year were the 'trips', cheap holiday packages offered in Wakes Week at the end of June, with committeemen acting as couriers. (They also had a few free days at Easter on the pretext of trying out the hotels.) We were due to go to Lugano – it would have been Dad's turn in 1940 – but the war stopped us. In the previous summer, though, the whole family (at reduced rates) helped him shepherd 400 people to, from and around the Isle of Man. Everyone agreed that he did a grand job, handing out rosettes, chatting up the bandleader, and forever checking numbers. Memory says that I spent most of the week intoxicated by the luxuries of the Alexandra Hotel, cheekily persuading bulky matrons to join me in dancing and singing to 'Boomps a Daisy' and 'Under the Spreading Chestnut Tree'; but I also managed to squeeze in a couple of films.

The people of whom I speak could seem caricaturish to modern onlookers. Their dress was different, usually displaying a cheap formality: striped suits for the men, and for the women swoopingly styled coats to follow their heavily corseted figures. The predominant colour was black. Everybody wore a hat. The older women tended to large hips, and their aggressive busts did not prevent a general shapelessness. Only constant sweat kept the men trimmer, but they lacked vitality, as well they might after long days in the steaming mills. As with the figures on Blackpool's saucy postcards, the act of marriage seemed to take these people instantly from innocent youth to clumsy middle age: the comic concepts of browbeating wife arose naturally from the appearance of most of the women. My own family was particularly heavily built, and we all had loud clear voices: nothing was ever misunderstood.

The houses were pretty cheerless, with only one room really used. It was used for everything, like a perpetual performance of *You Can't Take It with You*. But it was warm, and there was always enough money for good cheap things to eat. Especially cakes: malt wheatbread and vanilla slices and Russian sponge. Pies were marvellous too. I was often sent at midday to get them steaming hot from the little bakery at the top of Ena Street: tuppence for meat, three ha'pence for meat and potato, a penny for apple. Outside, the roadways were mostly cobbled, with great round stones like cottage loaves: you could break your ankle on them. Street lamps at night gave only a faint gaslit glow, so that one hurried on from each to the next in case bogeymen were on the prowl. (If one asked for some female who wasn't there, the favourite jokey response was She's run off with a black man, and the reply to anything complicated was Our cat's run up your entry: both were chilling images redolent of mystery and danger.) Awesome too were the magnificent and ubiquitous wrought-iron fences, ten times as solid as the stuff one sees today. Most gardens boasted a stretch, and they ran all round the parks, holding in the rhododendrons. During the war Lord Beaverbrook ordered them ripped out to make armaments, and the town was never the same; some of the scars in the stonework are still visible.

FOUR

Three Growls from the Lion

Until the Odeon was built in 1937, the grandest cinema we had in Bolton was the Capitol. Any night, if we arrived a minute after a quarter past six, we probably had to queue for the best part of two hours, until the 'first house' ended. If we knew we had to wait, we would hurry three or four doors further along Churchgate to an establishment called Ye Olde Pastie Shoppe. It had Dickensian bow front windows, and its freshly made meat-and-potato turnovers were certainly the finest in our experience and very possibly the best in England. Armed with prime examples of this steaming hot sustenance, we would hurry up the marble steps and through a heavy glass-and-chrome double door into the long sloping yard down which the sixpennies queued. (Never less than sixpence at the Capitol, and no half price.) Just beyond the door there was a little window in the wall, behind which an obscure person handed out tickets in return for money. Progress, superintended by an impressively bedecked commissionaire, was then along the cinema wall to a low roofed area, where queue barriers permitted an orderly zigzag of two to three hundred people to await admission by the little green door below the screen. We seldom minded the wait. The pasties tasted better in the open air, and there were usually people on whom I could try out riddles. ('How many hairs in a cat's tail?' – 'None, they're all outside.') Because there were so many people it was always warm, and we had the barriers to lean on. Besides, when the wind was in the right direction or we were able to place an ear next to the cinema wall we could hear quite a bit of dialogue from the feature then showing.

Just occasionally, when I was surrounded by tall or smelly people and began to feel claustrophobic, I might grow tired of standing still. (How my mother, with her bad feet, put up with it I've no idea.) At such times, my place safely kept, I would saunter off to inspect the delights of Churchgate. This, though barely a hundred yards long, was Bolton's Theatre Street. It was dominated at one end by the forbidding, soot-encrusted parish church above its steep and sudden slope; at the other by a tall cross commemorating the execution of the Earl of Derby after the Civil War, when Bolton (quite incredibly) was a Roundhead fortress. Between these sombre relics was a wonderland of bright lights and social activity. Next to the Pastie Shoppe was Sabini's Ice Cream Parlour, its product generally acknowledged as superior to that of Messrs Tognarelli and Manfredi, who operated from other parts of the town. Also open in the evenings were two sugar confectioners (Gent's and Walsh's, as I recall), their rainbow windows filled with unwrapped boiled sweets, very hard on the palate but irresistible all the same. There were three busy public houses, one vulgar, one ancient and one baronial. Closed, but with windows of moderate interest, were a UCP tripe shop, a shoemaker (in whose cellar my Uncle Jesse worked), an emporium of musical instruments, a gown shop which seldom had more than two garments in the window, and Toyland, which appeared to subsist on the sale of Hornby trains and Meccano sets. Then there was the arcaded Theatre Royal, in those days a cinema; a temperance bar which sold 'Vimto' from a barrel; and the Grand Theatre of Varieties. Wandering hopefully past the stage door of the latter, I once said hello to a surprised Sandy Powell as he was taking a breather. 'Hello thisself,' he replied.

Now and then I would become so engrossed by the crowds as to stay too long, only realizing my error when the Capitol's first house multitudes poured out suddenly into the roadway, and I had to struggle back to Mum against the tide. She would be cross if we had lost our place after waiting so long, in which case, when we got inside, some bounder might have bagged the front row centre seats which at the Capitol were set well back and which we felt were ours by right, despite the draughts which sometimes swept at us from the mysterious stage wings.

Austere, featureless and unwelcoming, the Capitol always seemed to us a bit toffee-nosed, but that may have been because it invariably collared the big Metro-Gold-wyn-Mayer pictures. That elegant lion, framed in an absurdly inappropriate motto about art being for art's sake, was to me like one of the family, and of course I imitated him too, but it was the important films that drew us there. Some of them may have been over my head, but I recognized their quality, and it was at the Capitol that I could best persuade myself, when conscience stirred, of the cinema's effectiveness as an educational instrument. For instance, I told myself, one learned a good deal about Chinese geography from long, slow, boring films like *The Good Earth*, as well as enjoying the locust swarm and the sight of Paul Muni with slant eyes. More to my basic taste was *Mutiny on the Bounty* (1935 version), which boasted several favourite actors of ours in fancy dress, yet contrived to be based on historical fact. Charles Laughton, from whose every appearance, after his belching Henry VIII, we expected a great deal, transcended history by making Captain Bligh a double-dyed villain, whether ordering thirty lashes at random or investigating the loss of cheeses he had stolen himself. The words 'cast adrift in an open boat' were imitated everywhere, and not only by me, even though they do not occur in this precise form in the film.

Equal in stature with these epics were the Garbo films, each more sumptuous than the last. Enjoyment is not a word I would have precisely connected with them, but I always sensed that I was in the presence of a goddess. The image that lingers most vividly is that last long-held close-up in *Queen Christina* when, having lost both throne and lover, she stands in the bow of the boat as it takes her away to a fate unknown. Many years later I learned that the director's trick was to persuade her to empty her mind of all thoughts, so that each member of the audience could interpret the Sphinx-like expression to his or her own satisfaction. Garbo films of course were filled with incidental benefits. Their production values were staggering, and their mainly British casts read like a Hollywood edition of Debrett: May Whitty, Aubrey Smith, Herbert Marshall, Henry Daniell, Reginald Owen, Reginald Denny, Henry Stephenson. The Barrymore brothers appeared with her too, and they seemed almost important enough to be English. We liked *Marie Walewska* for Charles Boyer's impersonation of Napoleon in skin-tight white pants, *Anna Karenina* for the icy unpleasantness of Basil Rathbone as Karenin, *Camille* for the much-heralded new star Robert Taylor, promoted as everybody's ideal boy-next-door. But it was the indestructible, almost hermaphroditic loveliness of the unsmiling Swede that crowds clamoured to see. No star before or since has been placed on quite so high a pedestal by a public so eager to live up to her.

In 1937 I read in *Screenland* magazine that someone

called Irving Thalberg had died. It seemed that MGM's
policy of bringing great literary masterpieces to the screen
had been entirely his, so I was duly sorry. They had all
played the Capitol: one of my earliest visits there must have
been to see Garbo in *Grand Hotel*, in which she seemed ill
at ease, though she did say in it her most celebrated line, 'I
vant to be alone'. She was simply too big to be a ballet
dancer; but the five top stars and the sure-footed production brought about my first experience of being overwhelmed by a Capitol queue: it stretched the whole length
of Churchgate and turned the corner down the slope of
Bank Street. We queued too for the Wallace Beery version
of *Treasure Island*, which must have been the Christmas
attraction for 1934, and I have never forgotten my terror at
the sinister appearance of Blind Pew with his black spot. I
also think back longingly to 1934 for *The Barretts of
Wimpole Street*. Laughton's climactic confrontation with
the eloping Norma Shearer still seems one of the tensest
moments in all melodrama, and of course the entire
audience went home happy when he was prevented from
taking revenge on her dog. Certainly my private film
collection, if I had one, would include the last half hour of
San Francisco, with its devastating earthquake sequence;
after this it seemed impossible that so many extras could
have survived to lead the hill-top hymn-singing, but they
provided a rousing finish. Forty years later I took a boat trip
round San Francisco harbour. As we docked, the title song
from this film was being played, and I half-expected to see
Clark Gable and Jeanette MacDonald and Spencer Tracy
marching arm-in-arm along the quay to greet us.

Perhaps the most superlative of the MGM supers was
David Copperfield: even my aunts queued for it. When the
studio went in for Dickens, it did not do so half-heartedly.
Two hours was the normal length of the complete pro-

gramme, and when we heard that the film itself ran a few minutes longer than this we were saddened at first, for that meant no Mickey Mouse; but in the event we forgave all concerned. The papers had made a lot of fuss about W.C.Fields playing Mr Micawber, but despite his twangy accent he was such fun that we accepted him without reservation; besides, he was English by descent. Basil Rathbone as Murdstone seemed the very incarnation of evil, and the notion that in private life he might be a modest and retiring sort of chap simply did not occur to us. Roland Young as Uriah Heep brought more fireside impressions from me: 'I'm your very 'umble servant, Mr Copperfield.' But all the interpretations were impeccable: Lennox Pawle as Mr Dick, Jessie Ralph as Peggotty, Herbert Mundin as Barkis, and of course the splendid Edna May Oliver with her vinegar face, shooing the donkeys from her front lawn. MGM's subsequent Dickens film, *A Tale of Two Cities*, was even more splendid to look at, but we all liked it less, partly because of the doleful ending but mainly because Ronald Colman appeared without his moustache.

It seemed that we had scarcely got over the shock of losing the star of *Tugboat Annie*, Marie Dressler, when a pall was cast over the town – and probably most of the world – by the incredible death at the age of twenty-six of that wisecracking blonde Jean Harlow, who had always seemed so able to take care of herself. Rumours abounded, but it was made clear in the end that she had died of a rare case of uraemia, and had failed to take advice because she had been brought up a Christian Scientist. Whatever the truth, she left a film unfinished. It was called *Saratoga*, and our genuine grief was tempered by considerations of how it might be completed without her. A local platinum blonde, Wendy Butler, with whom I later acted in some amateur productions, was allegedly one of hundreds of girls considered as possible stand-ins in a worldwide campaign, but no shots of her, not even from the rear, found their way into the picture. When it played a year later we were dismayed to find the doubling so obvious as to seem in poor taste; but then *Saratoga* itself was so plodding as to have been better left unfinished.

MGM in those days made frequent claims to have under contract 'more stars than there are in heaven', and the studio relied heavily on famous faces to make super-productions out of witless pot-boiler stories. Wallace Beery was a particular victim of this, and ended his career in 'B' features; he always gave good value, though Mum for some reason thought he was probably a dirty old man. Frank Morgan was seldom billed above the title, but we always favoured films which included him in the cast, for even at the very end of his life he was one of the screen's most delightful ditherers, with a marvellous uncertainty in his voice which may have been due to his partiality for the demon rum; in his last few films, so the story went, he had to be invisibly propped up while delivering his lines. The Barrymores also retained their prestige in adversity. However, our appreciation of John's villainy in *Maytime* was diminished by our knowledge from the gossip columns that he could not remember his speeches and had to use an idiot board. Lionel developed trouble with an arthritic hip, complicated by a fall; having already played Shirley Temple's crusty grandpa, he became crustier still when confined to a wheelchair, but made a fine comeback as the acid-tongued Dr Gillespie in the *Dr Kildare* medical series. Spencer Tracy had a drink problem too, but you'd never know it from the smiling, reliable image he presented on the screen; we were only sorry that he never seemed to get the girl. Norma Shearer, Joan Crawford, Robert Montgomery, Melvyn Douglas, Fredric March . . . none of them ever seemed to let us down, and nor did their lighting cameramen. Films like *The Bride Wore Red*, *Piccadilly Jim*, *Petticoat Fever*, *Yellow Jack*, *Forsaking All Others*, *No More Ladies* and *Mannequin* may be remembered now only as titles in a reference book, but to us in the thirties they were fine Saturday night entertainments with the ability to provide talking-points for our entire acquaintance. *Manhattan Melodrama*, for instance, never hit the history books except as the movie which John Dillinger, America's Public Enemy Number One, was watching just before the FBI gunned him down; but it set Bolton alight for a week because it teamed Clark Gable and William Powell and Myrna Loy. (All I really remember of it, from my very first year as a film fan, is a shot of Gable looking up at Brooklyn Bridge from the night ferry.) The Powell and Loy movie which made more of a hit than anybody expected was *The Thin Man*, and it always has to be explained that despite the sequels, the actual thin man was a character killed off in the first reel. (Powell himself was rather portly by this time.) The sophisticated marriage it presented had an asperity new to us, and as well as a cracking who-done-it plot it also had a delightful dog called Asta, so who could ask for anything more?

Expensive and elaborate as MGM's musicals always were, they seemed to occur only as unimportant breaks between the meatier stuff. Jeanette MacDonald and Nelson Eddy were the reigning monarchs of this realm and, even though anonymous critics had cruelly dubbed them The Iron Butterfly and The Singing Capon, a queue of Boltonians would form at the mere mention of their names. Since my sisters were fans of light opera and musical comedy, it was inevitable that I should find myself sitting through *Naughty Marietta* and *The Girl from the Golden West* and *Rose Marie* and *New Moon*, and equally inevitable that I should consider them a little on the dull side, especially in comparison with the Warner musicals which always scorned period finery to concentrate on chorus girls and gangsters. Nor was I much more taken by the occasional extravaganzas starring Eleanor Powell, except for the last few minutes when she tip-tapped her way into the spectacular finale. But musicals at least demanded comic relief, and it was through attending these basically boring spectacles that I became acquainted with such skilful caricaturists as Felix Bressart, Sig Ruman, Ray Bolger, Leo Carrillo, Raymond Walburn and Herman Bing; while if the villain was Douglass Dumbrille, as so often proved to be the case, well, that was all right too, for we loved him dearly despite his suave anti-social behaviour.

It seemed so odd when an MGM film escaped the Capitol's net and had to be sought elsewhere that we felt vaguely uncomfortable throughout the performance, especially since we suspected that the unusual booking must indicate some unpopularity in the film's track record. Even Leo the Lion, we thought, looked homesick when he roared us into *The Women* at the Queen's. This all-star, all-female dust-up, advertised as '135 women with men on their minds', seemed a bit skittish for MGM, but we enjoyed the performances, especially Joan Crawford in a bathtub and Rosalind Russell screaming for blood. The other notable Queen's capture was *Night Must Fall*, in which Robert Montgomery was the oldest pageboy in the business and Rosalind Russell a most unlikely member of the home counties jerseys-and-pearls set. The film did good box office because word had got round about the hatbox with the head in it; we half-expected to see the contents!

The Capitol, however, had to fulfil its British quota, and in doing so it usually turned up something fairly mouth-watering in the way of a thriller. *At the Villa Rose* was a good one, and modest items like *Première* and *Murder Will Out* seemed to please at the time, though memory now confuses Ralph Richardson in *The Return of Bulldog Drummond* with John Lodge in *Bulldog Drummond at Bay*. The Capitol also flew the flag for Richard Tauber in *Land Without Music*, and for Hitchcock's last British film *Jamaica Inn*. Everyone said this was disappointing although Mum and I thoroughly enjoyed the unadulterated ham of Charles Laughton's performance as the mad and wicked Sir Humphrey Pengallan. But in order to know that the Capitol's ship was truly on course you had to see that lion, if not heralding the film of the evening then at least ushering in the trailer for next week's attraction.

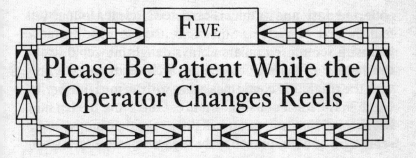

FIVE

Please Be Patient While the Operator Changes Reels

Directly opposite the Capitol stood the Theatre Royal, which had a long, low glass-roofed canopy with solidly sculptured iron uprights. I always thought the style better suited to the Victorian gentilities of Southport than to the depression-influenced realities of Bolton, but it did add a little elegance to Churchgate. Apart from the brief spell of glory to come during World War II, when it became a haven for number one theatrical tours driven from Manchester by the blitz, it was a jinxed house. Built in the twenties as a luxury legitimate theatre, it had one of the finest and broadest stages in the North of England, and all the trappings to go with it. But when talking pictures caused a temporary theatrical recession, the management of The Theatre (as all Boltonians called it, with accent on the 'a') jumped on to the movie bandwagon and stayed there determinedly, despite their all too obvious lack of policy, booking strength, or know-how. Barnum and Bailey were not among The Theatre's patron saints. It was wrong, not only spiritually but physically, for the shadowy world which it had entered. Its long stately corridors with vast mahogany cloakrooms were clearly intended for the passage and care of opera hats and mink coats: the cloth caps and mufflers of its regular clientele seemed out of place. It had two regal, curtained stage boxes which only collected dust; and its thickly carpeted circle tea lounge was half the size of Victoria Square. It had a marble entrance hall with sculptured pillars always delightfully cold to the touch, and a yawning proscenium arch decorated not only with the tragic and comic masks but with an intriguing relief frieze in the form of a Greek maze. Only from the outside, because of that untidy and slightly sagging canopy, did it seem a bit of a jumble: once through the casemented swing doors (and you could choose from eight of them) you were in one of the most beautiful theatres of my experience, always warm and cheerful because the predominant colour of its décor was red and the very richness of its fittings gave the building a pleasantly opulent smell.

Yet all these virtues went for next to nothing, for as a working cinema it was pitiful. The first film I saw there, with my sisters on this occasion, was *Morning Glory* with Katharine Hepburn. They complained bitterly that such an outstanding attraction should be shown at The Theatre, which everybody knew to subsist on other people's throwouts. Why, they might easily not have bothered to go. Certainly anything printed with sprocket holes had much to contend with from The Theatre's projectionists, a team of people whom, in imagination, I frequently tossed into the local reservoir, a pit of boiling oil, or the flames of Hell. Breakdowns were so frequent that I felt sure the management must schedule them at the rate of, say, ten minutes an hour in order to keep up with their advertised times. Then these same fools would adopt the infuriating habit of flooding the credit titles, and sometimes half the first reel, with bilious pink or green light, not only rendering the entertainment invisible but half-blinding one in the process. In later years they varied this with a Brennergraph effect which added kaleidoscopically-changing patterns to a screen already suffused with unwanted colour, even when they were presenting a film which had essential action behind the titles (such as *Ladies in Retirement*, which was well under way before I could make out what was going on). Once, when I was wearing my neatest suit, I plucked up sufficient courage to speak to the manager about these outrages, but all he had to say was that he was sure his chaps knew what they were doing. We did not share his faith, especially since we knew that the climax of each film was also likely to be ruined. As soon as the last word of dialogue had been spoken, the projectionists would let fly again, even if half a reel of essential silent action was still to come.

The Theatre's cheap and tatty category board was an outrage to the gilded entrance-hall in which it stood, a pathetic thing on a wooden easel, looking as though it had been picked up for a shilling at a church jumble sale. Its celluloid letters were supposed to clip into slots above and below semi-circular rods, but the process had always defeated the person whose duty it was, and they stuck out at all angles, one or two usually being visible on the tesselated floor. The titles were frequently misspelled, and instead of the attractions being arranged in order of performance, The Theatre insisted on giving the feature first, and the rest in diminishing order of their supposed importance, thus making it almost impossible to calculate the length of the programme without much complicated arithmetic and a dash of intuition. It was as though the owners wanted to prove films a flop so that opera and pantomime and *The Quaker Girl* might have a home to come back to.

Despite these inconveniences I enjoyed a great many films in The Theatre, whenever possible from my favourite seat. The front stalls were divided by one aisle, the rear stalls by two. This meant that in the front row of the rear stalls there was one centre seat where a small boy might stretch his legs and have nothing at all between himself and the screen but a gently sloping aisle and (on occasion) a brightly smiling ice cream girl. I never paid more than the front stalls price, but the usherettes knew me for a regular and usually looked the other way, except on Saturday nights.

I did have to sit elsewhere, however, for *Lost Horizon*, a Columbia film which The Theatre had presumably acquired because it had played so many of the second features which were Columbia's normal output. On that occasion Mum and I were lucky to get in at all, for the place was packed and had queues stretching both ways, much to the astonishment of the elderly and apathetic commissionaire. Even the rarely used gallery had been opened and rapidly filled; but we took the two singles which were being offered as we approached, and soon got together inside. I felt pleased for The Theatre's sake that it had a hit on its hands, though the projectionists could not resist one short breakdown, right in the middle of the climactic escape.

I expected *Lost Horizon* to be good, and it was. For many weeks it had been the chief topic of the fan magazines, special attention having been given to the fabulous expensiveness of the sets, the accuracy of the props, and the difficulties of filming a snowstorm in a Los Angeles ice house. (I couldn't think what an ice house might be, and for years imagined the inhabitants of Los Angeles to be Eskimos.) In due course all the Halliwells got to see it, and we agreed it to be the most thoughtful and satisfying film of the year. This may have been partly because half-employed people in a Lancashire mill town had more need than most of a Shangri-La to turn to. Not that we really believed in the existence of a land in Tibet where the climate was perfect and all was for the best in the best of all possible worlds; but we applauded the concept, and had serious discussions as to how each of the kidnapped air passengers should ideally have behaved. We did not presume to compare ourselves with Ronald Colman, but the lesser mortals seemed within reach, especially Edward Everett Horton as the fussy palaeontologist (a character which, I discovered to my chagrin, did not even appear in the novel which I promptly borrowed from the library). Meanwhile the range of my fireside impersonations was extended to include Sam Jaffe as the whispering 220-year-old High Lama.

It would be August of 1938 when we were asked at school to write a 'composition' about how we had spent the Bank Holiday. I started off in fine style about our family excursion over the moors via Scotchman's Stump and Walker Fold, and included a touching account of the way in which cows were reunited with their calves when they came in from the fields for milking. I concluded with our visit to The Theatre to see Will Hay in *Old Bones of the River*, and unfortunately retailed an unsuitable joke from the opening reel. Black chief Umbopa is asking white chief Sanders for permission to take another wife. 'But Umbopa,' says the surprised official, 'you have seven wives already'. 'Yes, master,' comes the reply; 'but the nights are so long!' Miss Southern blushed from head to toe when she read it, and I couldn't think why.

As the thirties progressed, Warners seemed to transfer its centre of operations from the Queen's to The Theatre. Gangster thrillers and giddy musicals alike did steady business, being used as forms of escapism, although both were subject to the law of diminishing returns. Familiarity, however, did not breed contempt for Jimmy Cagney, who varied hoodlum ethics with nimble tap dancing, or for Edward G. Robinson, who personified law and disorder with equal aplomb. A fellow called Bogart made frequent appearances in minor roles, but my mother did not care for his fleshy lips. Bette Davis guaranteed a full house after *Bordertown* and *Dangerous*, neither of which I bothered to see; when I did catch up with her in *The Petrified Forest*, she and the film seemed equally dull. Paul Muni, a man who clearly spelled Actor with a capital A, was a genius in our eyes, behind whatever whiskery disguise he chose to hide; in *The Life of Emile Zola*, however, solid educational entertainment that it was, we thought Joseph Schildkraut outclassed him despite his unpronounceable name. But it was not until the Saturday evening on which we chose, for want of anything better, to catch the last house at The Theatre of a mild medical romance called *The Green Light* that we caught up with Errol Flynn, whose billing in *Captain Blood* ('Six feet four of strapping English manhood!') had quite put us off; clearly his future films would be events we should not miss.

Warner movies were mostly made on the cheap, and used melodramatic shadows instead of expensive sets, but they were friendly productions which seldom failed to provide a satisfying evening, even the double-featured 'B' films in which the stars were on the lesser level of Joan Blondell, Aline MacMahon, Alice Brady, Glenda Farrell, Frank McHugh, Dick Powell, Ralph Morgan, Donald Woods and Warren William. We knew all these people intimately, the more so from Warners' useful habit of identifying them with a moving image at the beginning of each film. We considered this a device which other studios might profitably have copied.

RKO Radio films, being among the also-rans of Hollywood, also appeared quite frequently, and those floodlight-crazy projectionists always chose to bathe the pip-pipping radio station trademark in a chilling green. RKO films were mostly bad, but every six months or so these were counterbalanced by something really big, usually acquired for distribution from independent producers such as Goldwyn or Disney. Thus The Theatre was able to establish a claim to the wonder movie of 1938, *Snow White and the Seven Dwarfs*, though it had to be taken on concurrency with the newly finished Odeon. We chose to see it at The Theatre because we thought there would be a better chance of getting in; even so we had to queue for hours. It was not only the charm and brilliance of the animation that drew the crowds, nor the novelty of a feature-length cartoon, but mainly the fuss about the 'A' certificate, on which the British Board of Film Censors had insisted because of mildly frightening scenes with the witch, who at one point was seen kicking a skeleton out of her way. Most local watch committees had reduced the 'A' to a 'U' after a tiny cut but Bolton had demurred, so Churchgate was swarming with children clamouring to be taken in, as blatant a flouting of the law as I have ever witnessed. Mum thought it was a lot of fuss about nothing: 'Why, they'll be putting an "A" on Mickey Mouse next,' she said scornfully. I never heard of infant members of the audience having nightmares; on the contrary, for the next month the entire town seemed to be singing 'Whistle While You Work'.

SIX

Full Supporting Programme

Whenever two feature films shared a programme, it was a tip-off that neither was thought by its makers to be particularly good. Occasionally we held a contrary opinion, but on the whole we preferred one copper-bottomed star attraction plus forty minutes or so of shorts. If torn between two cinemas we would study the category boards and elect the one with the more promising supporting programme. The words 'comedy' or 'cartoon' were encouraging, but we liked the description to be more specific: Popeye or Woody Woodpecker, Andy Clyde or Leon Errol.

For the most part these shorts were American. If cinemas then had to uphold a British quota, they must have kept it for the weeks when nobody went. The majority of British shorts were excruciating, the *Secrets of Life* series with its stop-frame nature photography being an honourable exception. Very occasionally the GPO Film Unit would come along with an eye-popping item like *Night Mail*, an account of a train journey from King's Cross to Edinburgh. In Mum's words it was almost as good as a real film, even if it didn't have a story. Of course we did not then understand the word 'documentary'; non-fiction films were usually labelled 'interest', which is something they seldom did. The more professional American type, very slick and superficial, was usually over in nine minutes, and the most welcome of these were MGM's *Passing Parade* and *Pete Smith Specialties*, the equivalent of a light-hearted feature article in a tabloid newspaper; at least they kept us watching as they imparted nuggets of information about anything from gold prospecting to the prophecies of Nostradamus. On a much more ambitious level, *The March of Time* came in with a flourish of critical acclaim, but at twenty minutes it seemed dry and overlong to us, telling us things we did not want to know about countries of which we had scarcely heard. What we did enjoy about it, for we then knew that the endurance test was over, was the spontaneous chorus which rose from stalls and circle alike to echo the commentator's last portentous 'Time Marches On'.

Crime Does Not Pay was more to our liking. This consisted of two-reel crime dramas, allegedly taken from life and usually introduced by the governor or police chief of some American state, showing how retribution overtakes the evildoer. Coming from MGM, the two-reelers had good stars and directors, and were used as a training ground for young hopefuls: Robert Taylor appeared in one, and Fred Zinnemann directed several. The plain fact of the newsreels, however, was not for me at that stage, and the so-called magazines were little better; *Pathé Pictorial*, for instance, consisted of snippets about model railways and kite flying and architectural eccentricities, topped off with an extremely flat studio presentation of some moderately well-known music-hall act. The dullest filler of all, however, was *Signs of the Times*, a primitive advertising magazine consisting of brief items about home life or the countryside. Those which were not plugs for some invaluable household product ended with an apt quotation or moral tag in crude gothic lettering.

Cartoons were always popular, and the presence of Mickey Mouse on a bill meant almost as much as that of

Greta Garbo, but only slowly was black-and-white simplicity giving way to the sophistication of colour. Colour
however seemed to diminish Popeye the Sailorman, rob-
bing him of his former zip; but at least it showed us the
colour of his energy-giving spinach, then a vegetable
seldom found on Lancashire plates. 'I yam what I yam what
I yam', we all recited happily at school, but repetition soon
staled the rather limited bag of tricks, and Tom and Jerry
were beginning to absorb our affections. The accident-
prone cat, by the way, was black to begin with, and the
decade was nearly over before he settled into his familiar
shade of elegant grey.

Walt Disney, of course, was the star in the cartoon
firmament, having given us not only Mickey but also
Minnie and Donald Duck and Goofy (an animal of indeter-
minate pedigree) and Pluto; and, more briefly, Horace
Horsecollar and Clara Cluck. Disney cartoons provided a
vivid introduction to Technicolor: *Flowers and Trees* was
the first one, and although it did not try to be funny we
applauded it enthusiastically. Colour could not have
improved on the macabre *Skeleton Dance*, set to the music
of Saint-Saëns; here in a cemetery skeletons rattled and
gyrated and performed crude ballet movements, and left us
in *frissons* of pleasurable fear. On the whole, however,
though the 'Silly Symphonies' won awards, we preferred
the cartoons with the regular comic characters, and when in
the mid-thirties Mickey and Donald and Goofy and Pluto
appeared together, in such brilliantly-conceived adventures as *Lonesome Ghosts* and *Boat Builders* and *Clock
Cleaners*, our admiration and delight were unrestrained.

As much as anything else, and sometimes more, both my
mother and I enjoyed the slapstick comedies. Most of our
favourites in this department knew their limitations, and
were seldom seen in anything longer than a two-reeler. The

original Three Stooges – Larry, Moe and the close-cropped Curly – were at their freshest and best in the mid-thirties, with sharp editing and genuinely funny situations to relieve their rather unsympathetic orchestrations of eye-poking and head-bashing. We had considerable affection too for that great professional Charlie Chase, who usually played the Milquetoast husband accidentally floundering in deep waters; for Hugh 'Woo Woo' Herbert, a shapeless bundle of nervous energy; for El Brendel with his fractured Swedish English; for Buster West with his scissor-legged leaps and his curious way of walking across a chair; and for Andy Clyde, a willing and whiskery general practitioner often found in unequal combat with ghosts.

In the case of two of these knockabout comics an Academy Award for long and faithful service would not have been inappropriate. Edgar Kennedy, he of the stiff-fingered, face-hugging 'slow burn', and for whom the *Chopsticks* signature tune perfectly echoed his frustration, personified all blustering, accident-prone husbands helplessly at odds with wife, brother-in-law, mother-in-law, boss, policeman, and any inanimate object which might happen to get in the way of a peaceful suburban life. Edgar, bald-pated and temperamental, was particularly at a loss when confronted by mechanical or electrical gadgets, and if not demolishing the family car was likely to be blowing a hole in the family roof. He may have been a bully, but the world sure owed him a living, and none of us ever failed to sympathize when he sat amid his self-created havoc and attempted to massage his beefy face by pushing his tensed fingers into it.

Leon Errol was a burlesque and Ziegfeld comic of vast experience. He was seldom the innocent, being typically cast as the errant husband on the tiles who cannot resist the lure of a sultry blonde. Essentially, his two-reelers were potted French farces, but he brought such perfect skill and timing to his presentation of a fumbling drunk in frantic trouble that we thought of him as a reprehensible but basically lovable friend of the family. Mum often said he was the one star she would like to meet in real life and find out whether he was as entertaining as his acting suggested, and she was delighted when, towards the end of his career, in the *Mexican Spitfire* series, he found a real showcase for his talents in which he could play not only Uncle Matt, always behind the eight-ball, but also the drunken, yoke-shouldered English aristocrat Lord Epping. Sometimes he was also Uncle Matt *pretending* to be Lord Epping, which took some sorting out.

For the sake of fifteen minutes of one of these performers we would frequently sit through a boring feature. But two stars in particular rose above the rest in our affections. Perhaps they were particularly attuned to the people of our mill-ringed streets, most of whom, like this matched pair of screen characters, ambled through life full of good fellowship and blissful ignorance. One of them indeed was born in Ulverston, only forty miles away as the crow might fly; but as Stan and Ollie they were ubiquitous, the world's favourite foolish uncles. As a rule they turned up first at the Capitol, after which other cinemas squabbled among themselves for the second run, and the third, and the thirteenth. Since in this way each of their shorts supported a variety of attractions, and since my mother and I were remarkably catholic in our tastes, we sometimes saw their adventures seven and eight times over, laughing louder and longer on each occasion.

Once when a new short of theirs was on the bill, the Capitol's publicity man hit upon a particularly happy turn of phrase. 'In addition,' the advertisement read, 'we have pleasure in presenting our dear old friends, MR LAUREL

AND MR HARDY'. That was all. Not even a title: it was not necessary. Whatever they were up to, we wanted to be part of it, for they were friends indeed, and we all imitated them and loved them. Oddly enough my father had a distinct look of Stan, especially about the rather blank pale blue eyes; and when on a Sunday morning he and his portly brother-in-law Jesse put on their best dark suits and bowler hats to walk down from Auntie Polly's for a modest half-pint at the Green's Arms, the resemblance was so unmistakable that I was far from the only one to whistle the Cuckoo Song as they passed.

Once you knew and loved the characteristics of Laurel and Hardy, there was no great element of surprise about their comedy routines. Their very predictability was what made us roll about in helpless laughter. Everybody except these gentle innocents knew precisely what the outcome of any given situation must be, because it would proceed naturally from the kind of people Stan and Ollie were: children in the clothes of men. Ollie's selfish pride, for instance, in preceding Stan through a doorway, would be promptly followed by a painful fall as he collided with something. (They had a score of ways to enter or leave a room, all of them hilarious.) Stan's insatiable curiosity and wonder would land the pair of them in one fine mess after another. Whenever, as henpecked married men, they might decide to let respectability go hang and enjoy an illicit night on the tiles, their devices would be so obvious that cataclysmic retribution must speedily follow. If, as occasionally happened, Stan did something miraculously clever, such as clicking his thumb into flame and lighting his pipe from it, Ollie would diligently practise the feat until he did himself an injury. These simple basic themes always came up fresh because infinite variations were worked on them, and because the jokes were always full of human truth.

Typical of their interplay was the tit-for-tat routine which they brought to perfection. Sometimes, as in *Two Tars* or *Big Business*, a whole film was devoted to it. The basic routine was an exchange of physical violence, usually involving a third party, beginning with a light unintentional injury but with each reaction growing in fury and inventiveness until the whole scene took on the appearance of a national disaster area. Essential features of the routine were the 'slow burns' which punctuated it: each injured party, instead of exacting immediate revenge on his attacker, would quietly simmer while thinking up his next onslaught, an onslaught which his victim would make no attempt to avoid, watching instead with interest as the scissors or the eggs or the gluepot were procured and wielded. A brilliant example of this appears in what otherwise might be considered among the team's poorest films, *The Bullfighters*, made near the end of their film careers in 1945. The boys are patiently waiting for somebody in a hotel lobby dominated by a fountain with a circular seat around it. A stranger sits here reading a newspaper, and Ollie, with all his usual self-importance, places himself next to the man, with a little nod; he then proceeds to watch the world go by. Stan, sitting a little way from Ollie, is quickly bored; his fidgeting hand, which Ollie cannot see, comes into contact with a little tap, which he naturally turns. Promptly, a stream of water shoots out of the fountain and hits Ollie on the back of the neck. By the time Ollie has leaped two feet into the air and looked round for the perpetrator, Stan (who is totally unaware of the result of his action) is innocently twiddling his thumbs; but just at that moment the man with the newspaper chances to look up and give Ollie a neighbourly smile. Ollie eyes him uncertainly, looks at the camera for help which does not come, and finally decides to let the matter pass. But a few moments later, the whole pattern is repeated. This time Ollie's fury knows no bounds, but being a Southern gentleman he contents himself with a restrained reproof. He dips two fingers into the water, shakes them almost dry, taps the newspaper-reader's elbow, and with a little smile and a shake of the head flicks the drops of water into his face. The man is astounded, but is not to be got at in this way. Laying aside his newspaper, and doing a few double takes, he dips all his fingers into the fountain and flicks them at Ollie without draining off a drop. Ollie emotes violently in close-up, then grabs a handful of water and flings it. The man retaliates with two hands full. Olly reaches for his bowler . . . Very soon the whole foyer is flooded, the two protagonists are wringing wet, and Stan, the undetected cause of it all, is still twiddling his fingers and expressing surprise at the madness around him.

Once enjoyed, Stan and Ollie can never be forgotten, for in them is some part of all of us. Besides, they make an irresistible image, unified by their bowler hats and their strange dignity. Stan, unless provoked, is placid and willing and dumb, his long pale face animated from time to time by a curious set of almost involuntary expressions and gestures. There is the beaming self-satisfied smile from ear to ear; the head-scratching, accompanied by eyebrows raised in incomprehension; the myopic peer down the tilted nose for closer inspection of anything difficult to understand; the rare determined walk with swinging hips and flailing arms; the infantile tears. Ollie on the other hand has a large and expansive physical presence (which makes his agility on the run all the more remarkable) and is always sure of himself, a little too much so at times. His trade marks include his fascinated awe of women and his nervous banter in their presence ('A lot of weather we've been having lately'); his instinctive protection of the weaker Stan even when, as so often, the latter is in the wrong; and his incurable optimism that their joint fortunes will soon change for the better. Till the good times come he will remain philosophical about their many setbacks, relying on his ever-misunderstood courtesy, allowing us the privilege of seeing his tie twiddle and his camera look, or hearing his long-sustained yell as disaster strikes off-screen.

The secret appeal of Stan and Ollie may well be that in their external behaviour they have reverted to an age of irresponsibility, and most of us would dearly like to follow suit. But many of their features are recognizable in adults, too, adults of our literary as well as our real acquaintance. Is there really less to savour in the adventures of this immortal pair than in those of Don Quixote or Mr Pickwick? In their heyday they were so successful in the public's eye that the critics tended to sneer at them as mere buffoons. It irked my mother as much as it irked me that they might never get the recognition they deserved. Our fears were proved needless, but, alas, the recognition came after both Stan and Ollie had died.

When my mother thought of the cinema, I know it was Laurel and Hardy she thought of first, filling the screen with their benevolent presence. Even now, as for the last fifty years, when I lie wakeful at night, instead of counting sheep I run through in my mind some of the most hilarious Laurel and Hardy routines, and I soon doze blissfully away, thinking of Stan visiting Ollie in hospital with a gift of hard-boiled eggs and nuts, or the pair of them hiding their oddly-named dog Laughing Gravy from an irate landlord, or singing 'Honolulu Baby' to a small guitar. For they could sing, and dance too, and their rendering of 'The Trail of the Lonesome Pine' rather incredibly became Top of the Pops forty years after they first performed it. Children still imitate it. As for me, just let me hear their 'cuckoo' signature tune and I'm happy. I whistle it loudly every evening when I near my front door, as a signal to my wife to put the kettle on.

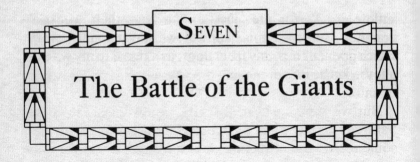

SEVEN

The Battle of the Giants

Late in 1936, men began to clear a slum site in Ashburner Street, on the town centre side of the wholesale market and close to the less used of Bolton's two railway stations. It would have had to go before long, as its ramshackle and smelly old mill cottages provided too great a contrast to the new million-pound civic centre, all neo-Victorian vastness and inconvenience, which had been built two hundred yards away. But there was high excitement when gossip reported, and the *Evening News* confirmed, that the site was booked for a flagship cinema in Oscar Deutsch's rapidly spreading chain of sleek modernistic Odeons, an amenity with nearly three thousand seats, a car park, and a balcony café. Well, it took them twenty years to pave the car park, and the café was long notorious for serving the toughest buttered crumpets for miles around, but the rest of the dream came true, and for many months the unvarying hobby of Bolton's unemployed was to watch it rise from the surrounding squalor, brick by brick and tile by tile. Progress was sure but infuriatingly slow: so slow in fact that a rival project, conceived and announced several months later, contrived to open first. This was the Lido in Bradshawgate, as unprepossessing and unVenetian a building as could be imagined despite its gondola-filled proscenium frieze. Financed by a small Salford-based circuit, it was little more than a cheap shell. The foyer was bare and cramped, and the centre stalls exits were by crash doors which opened from the auditorium straight out into the side alleys, sometimes drenching the adjacent customers in rain or snow.

But we were unaware of such inconveniences on the Saturday in 1937 when we queued for the gala opening. For some reason the attraction chosen for that one night only was a revival of Jessie Matthews in *Evergreen*, very welcome but quite uneventful, since we had previously seen it at the Hippodrome. The place nevertheless was mobbed, and we found ourselves in a low point of the front stalls from which it was difficult for me to see more than the top half of the screen over the heads of the people in front. I was comforted, however, by a handful of sample packets of a confectionery, then new, called Maltesers: the usherettes were practically throwing them at everyone who came in, and I grabbed as many as I could from the tray on the way to my seat.

We went again on Monday to see the Lido's first première, which was *Song of Freedom*, starring Paul Robeson. It was enjoyable enough while the star held sway, and I responded to his voice as to no one else's since Al Jolson, who seemed unaccountably to have retired from the screen; but by now we had discovered two of the Lido's failings. The first was its long, long intervals for ice cream sales, drastically curtailing the supporting programme we expected; the second was an even longer non-attraction called *Younger's Shoppers' Gazette*, a compilation of crude advertising filmlets (I once counted twenty-eight on the one reel). This was certainly not value for money, especially since the Lido was also the proud possessor of a Christie organ, and the interlude for this could stretch the gap between solid celluloid items to as much as thirty-five minutes. Though it had the advantage of a phantom piano attachment, the Lido organ did not rise from the orchestra pit as we expected, nor did it change colour as it came. From some of the side seats you could see it waiting in the wings throughout the performance, and since the main curtain hung slightly short, front stalls patrons could count the feet of the men who pushed it onstage at the appropriate moment. This musical marvel was operated by one Reginald Liversidge, an eager-to-please young man with a gleaming smile and a fine head of skin; his natty tailcoat and graceful manners probably endeared him to the matrons, but not to me. So far as I was concerned, his slide-accompanied concerts of 'Tchaikovskiana' were just one more nail in the coffin of a disappointing venue in which I had expected to spend many delightful evenings.

And so I was not impelled, in the years before the 1939 war, to visit the Lido very often. Its schedulers did not have the booking power of the established cinemas, and certainly not of the new Odeon which was to menace them all. It was too often content to take the cheapest programme available, and I was happiest when it settled for a re-issue. One such attraction was the 1931 Fredric March version of *Dr Jekyll and Mr Hyde*, which my mother wanted to see again, having been impressed by it when I was still in swaddling clothes. It was my first experience, in our well-behaved town, of an audience cat-calling and rough-housing during a performance. Mum said comfortingly that they only did it to prove they were not scared by Jekyll's transformations into Hyde; I was, but tried not to show it, my fear being tempered by a burning desire to wear, when I grew up, a dress cape, cane and top hat just like Mr March's. I realize now that this superbly crafted film, by far the best version of the story, is not only horrifying but surprisingly one-track-minded in the matter of sex, and therefore not at all a suitable entertainment for a boy of tender years; nonetheless what I most remember from that long-ago evening is how lustrous and dramatic it was to look at. Mum anxiously watched my reactions to the shock moments and, since I showed no ill effects, took me along a few weeks later to see the Lido's 'double thrill bill' consisting of re-issues of *The Old Dark House* and *The Invisible Man*. This time, to our astonishment, we were forestalled by the burly commissionaire in the second-hand uniform, who informed us between pursed lips that Children were not Admitted. My mother pointed out that both films had 'A' certificates, not 'H', and that she regularly took me to 'A' pictures, but argument proved useless, and we could only conclude that this was an entirely unofficial rule drawn up by the management either for the public good or (more likely) to drum up business during a dull week. Adamant, the commissionaire repeatedly tapped a hanging notice on which the words ADULTS ONLY had been inscribed in shaky green lettering. Although, he assured us confidentially, he had seen both pictures and wouldn't give you *that* (he snapped his fingers) for their horror content, he was powerless to help us, and could only suggest that we went round the corner to the Theatre Royal where *Old Mother Riley* was showing. His sister had described it as a real good laugh. Disconsolately, we took his advice; but I don't remember laughing much: the rather primitively filmed knockabout failed to capture the instinctive zest of Lucan and MacShane's crockery-smashing stage act which I had seen at the Grand on one recent Saturday night.

This same commissionaire had bad feet, and never tired of imparting this information, in a lugubrious voice, to the queues whose dimensions he strictly controlled. Mum and I shivered on many a wet evening by the Lido wall, under a long canopy too narrow to protect us adequately from the elements. We sympathized extravagantly with him, knowing that in the next breath he would bring out a joke or two to keep us cheerful and complaisant. ('Do you know who's in the navy? – Sailors!') He knew us well enough to be our ally. Sometimes he would round the corner shouting *Singles Only*! and wink at us as he passed. Mum would smilingly lead me to the box office and buy the tickets, and he would meet us inside to ensure that the usherette gave us the nice double he had found on the aisle. The Lido kept reducing the number of rows allotted to 'front stalls', but they were cheap enough at fourpence, though there was no half price. This was later raised to sixpence, with a threepenny half, so it made little difference.

We were very surprised indeed when *Wings of the Morning* played its first run at the Lido. It had been widely promoted as Britain's first Technicolor film, though there was nothing very British about it except the countryside settings and the Derby Day climax: the stars were Henry Fonda (American), Annabella (French) and the singer John McCormack (Irish). Apart from the colour, which seemed little short of a miracle, we described ourselves in a Lancashire phrase as 'not struck', and certainly not by the arbitrarily inserted Irish songs. Nor did culture impress us too much in the case of *Moonlight Sonata*, with the dowager actress Marie Tempest upstaging the Polish pianist and ex-prime minister Paderewski; but perhaps the truth was that we had already heard too much about the child star Binkie Stuart, unwisely touted as Britain's answer to Shirley Temple, who had been added to the mix of this curiously stilted production in order to add a dash of popular appeal. We much preferred the snickering villainy of Tod Slaughter, who made regular visits to the Lido in his reach-me-down productions of *Sweeney Todd, the Demon*

Barber of Fleet Street; *Maria Marten, or the Murder in the Red Barn*; *Crimes at the Dark House*; and *The Face at the Window*. Slaughter was the kind of larger-than-life character who was bound to be popular in Lancashire, and he so enjoyed his work that we always wished he could get off scot-free at the end. If he had dropped by, he would certainly have been pleased to see a whole cinema full of his fans, cheering loudly at each dastardly deed. He so loved to 'polish 'em off'.

Another cast-iron box office star who often appeared at the Lido, though in second runs of films which had already appeared elsewhere, was George Formby. Anything starring the lad from Wigan could be revived again and again in the town centre, for all the staff had to do was open the doors and stand well back, even on the third or fourth run. Mum and I were sitting one evening in the middle of the front row, waiting to enjoy once again his familiar antics in *Keep Your Seats Please*, a version of Ilf and Petrov's *The Twelve Chairs*. There had not been much in the way of a supporting programme, and for want of anything better to do we had even applauded the organ interlude. We felt the draught as the lush multi-coloured curtains swept together and obliterated Mr Liversidge from our view; but the house lights did not immediately dim as we expected, nor was a censor's certificate projected on to the curtains. Instead, just as we were beginning to wonder what had gone wrong, a rather gawky figure in a light grey suit stepped hesitantly through the curtains and stood there looking as bewildered as we were. It was – it couldn't be – it was, it really was, George Formby himself, standing there not ten feet away from me and looking as though he wished he hadn't come. And as soon as that startled audience realized the fact, he got one of the biggest cheers I have ever heard outside Burnden Park Football Ground. He grinned shyly – he really was shy – and finally said in his accustomed high-pitched gabble: 'I were just passing – that is, Beryl and me, we were coming through Bolton in t'car, and I saw you were playing me film. I thought, all them folk have paid good money to come and see me up on t'screen, so it seemed only right and proper to drop in and say how do, like.' Beryl was in the wings, he added, but she said she wasn't dressed up, so she couldn't come on. George then told a little story about Wigan Pier – it was only mildly funny – and seemed at a loss to continue. Somebody shouted for a song, but he said his ukelele was in the car, and we could hardly tell him to go and get it. After another pause he said, well, he had better go now, and leave us to gawp at yon feller on t'screen. Suddenly he was gone, the lights were down, the curtains were parting and the film beginning. We watched it in a gentle daze. It was the nearest we had ever been to a real film star, though Mum remembered once standing at the back for a personal appearance by Guy Newall and Ivy Duke, the stars of a silent melodrama which she thought was called *The Sound of Running Water.** I was surprised at how ordinary George had looked, not very tall, and rather like one of Dad's friends from the Textile Mill. On the way home Mum, who like the rest of us had heard the rumour that George was henpecked, chuckled and said Beryl was probably still telling him off for making a fool of himself. But, during the next few weeks, whenever George was mentioned in conversation, Mum and I smiled conspiratorially at each other, as though we had a proprietorial interest.

It was to the Lido that I ventured on my first solo visit to the pictures, which must have been in 1938 since I know I was nine at the time. My mother had been preparing

---

*It was in fact *The Lure of Crooning Water.*

nervously for this inevitable event, and one Saturday after-noon she packed me off to see *Owd Bob*, saying it did not sound like her cup of tea but I was bound to enjoy it as it was all about dogs. (We had owned a beloved Airedale called Peter, who mysteriously disappeared one winter while I was in bed with scarlet fever.) I wondered on the bus why she'd had tears in her eyes, and in fact I scarcely enjoyed myself at all because the Lido was cold and half-empty, Will Fyffe didn't even try to be funny, and one of the dogs got shot. Furthermore, because Mum was not there to stop me I ate too many sweets and was heartily sick when I got home. A trend, however, had begun. Just a few weeks later I was off to the Lido again, and although all I did was sit the programme through once, it was of such marathon length that when I got home Mum was just about to go for the police. Nor did it comfort her to hear my story of a man sitting close to me who had been taken ill and carried out on a stretcher. The oddly-contrasted bill that afternoon was another of the Lido's re-issue specials: *Floating Platform One* was an Anglo-German effort from 1933, with Conrad Veidt as the skipper of some kind of futuristic aircraft carrier; but it was *Imitation of Life*, a 1934 weepie, that really got through to me. Claudette Colbert and Warren William were among my favourite people in light comedy, but here there was nothing to laugh at at all. As the film grew sadder and sadder, I grew sadder and sadder with it, until at the death of the fat and lovable old black maid, renounced by her arrogant half-white daughter, I simply wept buckets, and could not be consoled all evening nor indeed for several days afterwards.

When at last the Odeon was ready, the family in its various ways prepared for the excitement of another première performance. We were all there, but I went with Mum and Dad and my sisters with their boyfriends. Report

had it that, over in Ashburner Street, there was a dogged
determination to outshine the Lido, which we thought
could hardly be difficult. Again a Saturday night was
chosen, and half our acquaintance dutifully put on best
clothes and trooped proudly into that vast auditorium,
having first made our choice of seats at sixpence, ninepence
or one shilling, and no half price. Memory suggests that,
despite arriving more than an hour early, we had to pay
ninepence, which must have been unique for us; at any rate
we sat a long way back, and although I couldn't see very
well I was prepared to put up with the handicap because
this was an *occasion*. But at the interval Mum miraculously
found three seats on the aisle, from which I had an uninter-
rupted view not only of the giant proscenium arch but of
several less fortunately placed friends near the front, to
whom I waved in an unforgivably superior manner. The
décor was undeniably sumptuous. My first impression,
after I got my breath back, was of rounded corners
everywhere, without a right-angle in sight. The immensity
of the red velour curtains; the cunningly concealed lighting;
the great golden honeycomb grills on each side of the
screen; the green octagonal clocks in which the letters THE
ODEON took the place of numerals; all these played their
part in the magnificence of that massive decorated space. It
was more overwhelming than being in St Mark's Church,
or even Manchester Cathedral. But as I later discovered to
be the case with all Odeons, the design was in fact simple to
the point of austerity. There was nothing that could catch
dust. The foyers and corridors were laid with rubber tiling
in green and black abstract designs, with just a touch of red;
and even the toilets had a smooth severity which counter-
pointed the general grandeur. Henceforth, Bolton's older
halls with their plaster cupids and decorated pillars would
seem tawdry indeed.

Each seat on opening night had a gilt-edged programme waiting upon it, and no sooner had we absorbed this dazzling piece of showmanship than a mammoth all-glass Compton organ rose from the orchestra pit, changing colour as it came and radiating 'The Entry of the Gladiators' through a dozen strategically placed loudspeakers. Where was the Lido now? The première attraction, following a Mickey Mouse and the news, was *Dark Journey*, a moderately adult spy melodrama with Conrad Veidt and a new young star called Vivien Leigh. There were absolutely no complaints about it, except that we would have preferred a happier ending, but some of us wondered why it had been chosen in preference to the great backlog of spectaculars which the Odeon was known to have held in reserve. But after this comparatively mild start, the spectaculars came at us in legions, with a colour film at least once a month. *The Trail of the Lonesome Pine*, *The Garden of Allah*, *Her Jungle Love*, *Vogues of 1938*, *The Goldwyn Follies*, *Jesse James*, *Hollywood Cavalcade*, these were some of the items which brightened our lives by their sheer splendour, even though Technicolor seemed oddly to drain their drama of vitality. However, we felt we had achieved a great bargain in getting full colour at no extra price. Very soft and lustrous the Technicolor was in those days, and its quality seemed always to be attributable to the talents of one Natalie T. Kalmus, who was invariably credited as colour consultant. (We discovered later that she was merely the boss's wife, and the boss probably valued a peaceful home life.)

There were, of course, some totally admirable colour films. The William Wellman version of *A Star is Born* was all of a piece and brilliantly satirical, its images of Hollywood being still recognizable in that studio town. I enjoyed all the vivid detail of life in a place I never expected to visit, though I was distressed by Fredric March's suicide. It was good to see him in better spirits in *Nothing Sacred*, a newspaper comedy etched in venom and printer's ink, achieving such moments of splendid invective as: 'The hand of God, reaching deep into the mire, could not elevate him to the depths of degradation.' That was the kind of language you didn't hear in Bolton. I also liked the scene in which Walter Connolly, as the irascible editor, tells Mr March, his hireling: 'I am sitting here, Mr Cook, toying with the idea of cutting out your heart and stuffing it – like an olive!' And one of the silent gems of my infant filmgoing is the moment when Mr March, a lone reporter in a hostile village, is suddenly bitten in the leg by a small boy who rushes out from behind a picket fence, performs the act and disappears immediately.

In black and white, but clearly very expensive indeed, was *Marie Antoinette*. As an MGM movie it should have turned up at the Capitol, and I don't know whether the Odeon bookers asked for it to add to their prestige, or found themselves landed with it because it was a commercial flop. Either way, I seem to remember queueing for it, and feeling hungry before the end because it went on for such a long time. Boltonians in those days relished costume drama, having flocked even to the ill-fated *Parnell*, a woebegone attempt to make a serious actor of Clark Gable. It was a time for historical biographies. The Capitol, with its MGM and Warner allegiances, had given us Garbo as Queen Christina and Marie Walewska, not to mention Paul Muni as Pasteur and Benito Juarez, while coming up were Edward G. Robinson as Reuter and Dr Ehrlich. The Odeon was not to be outdone. Spencer Tracy greeted Cedric Hardwicke with the famous words in *Stanley and Livingstone*; Tyrone Power was Ferdinand de Lesseps in *Suez*; Gary Cooper was Marco Polo; and it was the Odeon which came up with the most popular of them all, a royal one, *Victoria the Great*.

Locally there was great excitement at the prospect of a royal personage being impersonated by a mere actress; hitherto the matter had been almost as sensitive as the presentation of Jesus Christ on the screen. And the Odeon capped its own triumph in the booking of *Victoria the Great* by having its star, Anna Neagle, make a personal appearance on the first night. Mum and I were in the front row as she stepped on to the vast stage, wearing a soft pink gown and looking extremely modest. She was immediately presented with an enormous bouquet, and made a rather early exit after the briefest of speeches. (I gathered later that this was for her only one of four appearances in the area that night.) It was the closest we had come to cinema glamour, and we were duly awed. Later, as the film progressed, we could scarcely believe that the slim and quietly spoken girl we had seen in the flesh could possibly be the same person who, under layers of shrivelled make-up, portrayed the aged queen. *Victoria the Great* is not exactly a classic film, but it is a very carefully staged and enjoyable one. As we left the cinema we felt like relics of Victorian England – I suppose, come to think of it, my mother was – and the new orange sodium lamps of Thynne Street seemed even more futuristic and intrusive than usual. We recovered sufficiently to eat some chips on the way home, chips replete with salt and vinegar, and during their consumption I said, 'How different from the home life of our dear queen', a phrase acquired only that week from a book of jokes.

There was a certain amount of heart-searching on Mum's part when *Dead End* was shown. Great play had been made in the popular press of the heated discussions in America as to whether its depiction of New York low life, and in particular the antics of the Dead End Kids, were likely to corrupt the British young. However, the censor had blessed it with nothing more restrictive than an 'A' certificate, and of course I felt obliged to see it. My mother took some days to commit herself, but she did not like to miss anything in which Sylvia Sidney appeared, so finally, on a Friday afternoon (for this was during the school holidays, and it was raining) we turned up on the Odeon steps, only to be confronted by a notice 'recommending' that, in the considered view of the management, *Dead End* might be thought unsuitable for impressionable children. Mum stopped in her tracks for just as much time as it took to read the notice, then marched up to the box office, holding my hand, and said firmly: 'One and a half, please. He's a good boy and it won't harm him.' The cashier smiled, handed over the tickets in exchange for her coins, and gave me a lollipop. *Dead End* was a tense and exciting film, though even I could see that the set was impossibly stagey. We agreed on the way home that it pointed a very good moral, and that we should not have laughed so much at the Dead End Kids, who were a pretty reprehensible lot.

A favourite film which I first saw at the Odeon was *The Prisoner of Zenda*. Perhaps indeed it encapsulates everything I came to like most about the cinema: romance, suspense, comedy, skilled acting and courtly behaviour. I wanted to see it in the first place because it was packed with my favourite actors: Ronald Colman, Douglas Fairbanks Jnr, C. Aubrey Smith, Raymond Massey, David Niven, Mary Astor, Madeleine Carroll. They brought a literate flavour to an unlikely adventure story, which may well have been revived because of its topicality, for Edward VIII had just abdicated, and this was the story of a pseudo-king who gave up his throne despite his love for a princess. It fixed in my mind the desirable image of Ruritania right next to that of Shangri-La, and as soon as I could I borrowed the novel from the library and read it again and again. A measure of the quality of this 1937 version is that fifteen years later MGM made it over again, scene for scene and almost word for word but with a different set of actors, and produced a film wholly without lustre.

Almost as firm a favourite of mine, in a totally different genre, is *Destry Rides Again*, one of the very few westerns I cherish. In it a routine story, about a gunless sheriff ridding a town of baddies, was transformed into sheer magic by a group of fine professionals who not only possessed cinematic expertise in abundance but could tread the fine line between comedy and tragedy. It is Frank Skinner's evocative music above all which still rings in my ears, but in 1939 we paid it a visit largely because of Marlene Dietrich's much publicized mop-and-bucket fight with Una Merkel, and because the supporting cast contained so many people we liked: Brian Donlevy, Mischa Auer, Billy Gilbert, Samuel S. Hinds, Allen Jenkins and that fine old vaudevillian Charles Winninger. James Stewart, of course, also made an impression with his whittling and his constant ability to make a valid point by instancing a feller he knew once. We went again on the Saturday because we could remember no other film giving so strong an impression that all concerned had thoroughly enjoyed making it. And those wickedly sultry songs – 'Little Joe', 'That Look', 'See What the Boys in the Back Room Will Have' – were put across in fine style by a Marlene Dietrich who to me, after so many boringly glamorous roles, was a joyous revelation.

Four Odeon attractions are always associated in my mind with the physical thrill of pre-war cinema-going at its best. In each case we attended the last house after spending hours in a queue, which meant that the warm air of the auditorium, when the lights finally went down, was more than usually vibrant with anticipation. I don't know why else I should have derived so much enjoyment from *History is Made at Night*, except that in 1938 Charles Boyer and Jean Arthur, even in a stilted romantic pot-boiler, could do no possible wrong, and there was the added attraction of the exuberant Leo Carrillo going on about the female of the species being 'a-deadlier' than the male, which seems to have struck us as the very quintessence of wit. I think it was also the last film of that strange nervous actor Colin Clive, who had twice played Baron Frankenstein but, since those were for Adults Only, was new to me: I remember how uncomfortable it seemed to watch him on the screen when one knew he had already died, especially as he dies again in the film.

We had to be talked into seeing *Stagecoach*, because it was yet another western with John Wayne, and we associated him with second features at the Rialto; what he was doing at our gleaming new Odeon we could not imagine. We probably gave in once more because of the supporting players: cadaverous John Carradine, bald-pated Donald Meek, self-important Berton Churchill, and Thomas Mitchell as the alcoholic Doc Boone. But we adored it, not only because of the Monument Valley scenery (which Mum said was so unlikely that it must be artificial) but because of its central notion of assorted passengers facing danger on a journey, which had so delighted us in *The Lady Vanishes* and is still among my favourite recipes for a thriller.

Escape, by which I mean the MGM *Escape*, which appeared within a few months of war breaking out in September 1939, is almost a forgotten picture now, but on its first release it loomed as a very timely anti-Nazi melodrama, quite strongly propagandist when one considers that America was still neutral. Its distinguished cast made it a must: Norma Shearer, Conrad Veidt, Robert

Taylor and a celebrated actress from the past called Nazimova, who played a woman smuggled out of a concentration camp in a coffin. Two seats were found for us just before the end of the first house. As we came into the cinema, inevitably by a door beneath the screen, I glanced up as usual at the giant image and saw Conrad Veidt reacting in fury to the sight of an aeroplane in the sky, a sight which clearly meant that he had been tricked. A packed audience was cheering in enthusiasm at this climax to what had obviously been a gripping narrative, and the shot remains among my most vivid memories.

Finally, *The Young in Heart*. The title would not have attracted us, but the trailer did. It made clear that Janet Gaynor, Douglas Fairbanks Jnr, Roland Young and Billie Burke would appear as a family of amiable confidence tricksters, and there were also promises of an appealing dog, a charming old lady, a sensational new car called a Flying Wombat, and Henry Stephenson, that most avuncular of British character actors who had settled in Hollywood. All these elements did indeed find a place in a delightful film which kept its tongue firmly in its cheek, and the audience responded with especial warmth to the final shot in which the dog displays its puppies.

There was one Odeon attraction which I failed to see: a revival of *King Kong*. My mother refused point blank to take me: she had no objection to my going with someone else, but she said 'them things' would give her nightmares. I went down hopefully on my own, seeking strangers who might act as escort; but that very week the Odeon had acquired a brisk and hawk-eyed new commissionaire, who shooed me off at every attempt. I lingered by the still cases for an hour, gazing with an ache of despair at the 'artist's impressions' which were all that the canny distributors would allow in the way of pictorial publicity. But the attempt was hopeless, and eventually I hurried down Bradshawgate for a second taste of Laurel and Hardy in *Blockheads* at the Queen's. My father promised to introduce me to *Kong* on the Saturday, but came down with 'flu; and so more than ten years were to pass before I caught up with the great beast.

EIGHT

Around the Fleapits with a Hammer

On my now increasingly frequent solo excursions to the cinema, and because I missed the sense of my mother enjoying herself at my side, I began to take more notice of the people who sat around me, to watch them laugh at the slapstick, hold their breath at the suspense, and weep unashamedly at the sad bits: sometimes they were as entertaining as the picture. There was hardly ever a case of even minor misbehaviour, and so I became far more adventurous, both in my choice of films and in exploring the unknown regions which lay beyond the bright lights of the town centre. Nobody ever suggested that it might be dangerous for a small boy to explore back street routes through areas totally unknown to him, skipping at night from one pool of lamplight to another. 'He'll come to no harm,' said Mum once when the subject came up. 'Why, Bolton's as safe as houses.' And so indeed it always seemed, even in the slums of Virgil Street and Homer Street, which some Victorian alderman must have named in a fit of black humour: the only time I had a qualm of fright was once when I turned a corner rather hurriedly and ran smack into a policeman.

Come to that, a couple of the central cinemas had a poor reputation with the upper crust. The Embassy, formerly the Imperial Playhouse, held a fine position next to Boots and across the way from Woolworths. It advertised itself as 'Bolton's armchair cinema', but it was small and scruffy and the rumour ran that it was infested by rats; although I never saw evidence of them I was constantly on my guard for sharp teeth nibbling at my toes. There was no circle, but the stalls, following the slope of Bridge Street outside, were very steeply raked, so that a nipper like me could get a good view from almost any seat; I tried a good many, as until six o'clock threepence would entitle you to any seat in the house. If there was plenty of room I usually made for the back row, which consisted of 'lovers' couches' each wide enough for two people. In these I could curl up comfortably and lean on one elbow; but more than once the contraption snapped shut with me inside it.

Probably the best film I saw at the Embassy was *Pygmalion*, which I had missed at the Odeon because of scarlet fever. By the time of the second run Mum had been to see it on her own, so Dad (who was probably curious about the naughty language) volunteered to escort me on the Saturday afternoon. There were such long queues that the Embassy's management played a trick I never experienced again. They cut out all the supporting programme and even the intervals, playing nothing but the film itself, over and over again like a snake eating its own tail; no sooner had the end title appeared than it was followed by the opening credits. Knowing nothing about reel changes, Dad and I assumed that there must be two prints. I can still feel the shock of that audience when Wendy Hiller said 'Not bloody likely', and the minutes of incredulous laughter which followed, drowning half a scene of dialogue; but my favourite character was the dustman Dolittle (Wilfrid Lawson) with his wheezy laugh and his public bar rhetoric. 'I'm *willing* to tell you, I'm *wanting* to tell you, I'm *waiting* to tell you' was promptly added to my repertory of impressions.

The policy of the Embassy was to fight the Lido for second runs and re-issues, and usually the Embassy lost, but just occasionally it came up with a first run that nobody else wanted. This is the only possible explanation for its premièring *The Green Pastures*, on which even The ·Theatre had clearly asked to be excused. I popped in out of curiosity, and thoroughly enjoyed myself, but there were very few curious people that week despite Rex Ingram's performance as De Lawd, one of the great star achievements of the American cinema. I saw it on Tuesday, and meant to go again, meanwhile encouraging everyone I knew to follow suit. But few Boltonians had ever met a black person, and could clearly see little point in patronizing a simplistic black version of the Old Testament; so by Thursday the Embassy was advertising 'by public demand' a revival of Edward G.Robinson in *Bullets or Ballots*.

It was at the Embassy that a long-forgotten British quickie called *The Pointing Finger* gave me a night or two of bad dreams. It was set in one of those stately homes full of secret panels, and featured an ancestral portrait with removable eyes so that the villain could peep through. After that I went masochistically to as many mysteries and whodunnits as I could find, but I still remembered *Mystery of the Wax Museum* with a pleasurable mixture of fear and fascination, so what I really craved was the experience of a real horror film, one with oodles of gore. It was the Embassy which finally seemed to give me a sporting chance, with a re-issue double-bill of the original 1930 *Dracula* and the original 1931 *Frankenstein*. The reason for my optimism was that both films had been issued originally under an 'A' certificate before 'H' was introduced, and at least this might enable a nine-year-old boy to get in to see them if accompanied by his highly respectable-looking father. But the distributors, as a come-on, had had the films recertificated, and as we walked down Deansgate we could see the Adults Only banners waving about from the facade, so we had to compensate ourselves with Mr Moto at the Rialto. Very frustrating. I had even been cheated the previous week, when I patronized the Embassy's mediocre programme for the express purpose of watching the horror trailers. Imagine my disappointment when they proved to consist of nothing but the crudest animated lettering, 'daring' the public to see this 'monster' show and assuring them as an afterthought that members of St John's Ambulance Brigade would be in attendance at all performances. And the Embassy never splurged on still cases, so I was even foiled in this respect too. Indeed, the only satisfaction I derived from the whole affair was reading in the *Evening News* a story (no doubt invented) that five people had fainted during the first showing of 'the gruesome twosome'.

The Rialto advertised itself as 'the cinema where you meet your friends', which made me visualize it as a kind of introduction bureau. It was inconveniently situated next to the Baptist Chapel on the rather dreary St George's Road, which marked the most northerly extent of the town centre just as the Queen's marked the southern extremity. The Spinners' Union was up there, and the Palais de Danse, and the Co-op Drapery where my sister Edith worked, but I always disliked the steep hike up Bridge Street to the Rialto's level. The Rialto was owned by the same family as the Queen's, and occasionally showed a big film in concurrency, but as a venue it was never in the same class. It thrived on second features and 'B's, often from series and always in double-bills, such films being usually short enough to pack two plus the news into a programme which still ran no more than two hours and ten minutes. *Return of*,

Son of, *Strikes Back*, these were the phrases that whetted the appetite of the Rialto's patrons. The Jones Family, the Saint, Blondie, the Lone Wolf, Hopalong Cassidy, Dr Christian and Torchy Blane all celebrated their exploits there, as did the Charlie Chan impersonators: Warner Oland, Sidney Toler, and Roland Winters.

By and large, then, the Rialto's booking policy was aimed at the undiscriminating, yet oddly enough it used to advertise rather widely. At least three town-centre hoardings displayed massive 48-sheet posters, and I can still visualize myself absorbing the contents of the one at the corner of High Level as the 'N' tram hurtled down at it from the Crofters and seemed to swing left only just in time to avoid a collision. *Gentlemen Are Born*, *D'Ye Ken John Peel*, *Dusty Ermine*, *Lucky Jade*, *A Woman in her Thirties* and *Drake of England* are among the more obscure attractions on which the Rialto spent in this way. But I also associate it with minor comedians, especially Wheeler and Woolsey, to whom I never took at all, and the forgotten team of Slim Summerville and Zasu Pitts, a lugubrious couple who made several very mild comedies together, including one in which they played cook and butler and kept on saying 'No prunes' to each other. It was also in the Rialto's surprisingly elegant circle (which cost twopence extra), that Dad and I saw Sandy Powell in a low farce called either *Can You Hear Me Mother?* or *Leave it to Me*. It contained a slapstick scene involving a great deal of itching powder, and for some reason this began to make me physically uncomfortable. In the bus queue afterwards I was still scratching myself, and Dad was astonished that a mere film should have made such an impression. At home it seemed that I had a temperature as well, and when I refused black pudding and sliced peaches for tea Mum sent for the doctor. I had chicken pox.

Bolton Amusements Columns from the front page of the Bolton *Evening News* for a week in the summer of 1939. Just over a month later, war broke out

By the time the war came I had visited most of Bolton's suburban picture houses. Oddly enough there were none in our particular neck of the woods, a mile south of town. Great Lever was a pleasant enough district, keeping its mills at a distance; even so, it had nothing to be snooty about, and a cinema would scarcely have polluted its atmosphere, but it seems nobody ever thought of building one. The nearest in fact was almost into town and then a quarter of a mile west, a few steps from St Mark's Church, our family's place of worship for generations, though like most of its congregation we had moved out of its increasingly industrialized parish and thus suffered a long walk twice on Sunday (or four times if we felt particularly devoted). When the church was built in 1870 it had been set among rolling fields, but now the landscape was packed tight with snug little back-to-back houses, each with its earth closet down the yard, all in the sinister shadow of the mills which belched smoke up their chimneys from dawn to dusk.

Almost opposite the church in Fletcher Street, past Dyson's sweet shop, was the Atlas Cinema, later the Ritz, a tiny, rough-hewn building which was not considered very respectable. The local joke was that they loaned you a hammer with your ticket. On most family visits to church I managed to slip across the road to study the forthcoming attractions, and on one occasion Mum took a deep breath and agreed that we should pay the Atlas our first joint visit to see *The Blue Angel*. She thought it would do me good to see a foreign film, even though the advertisements made clear that it was 'entirely spoken in English'. But when we got there, either the print had failed to turn up or the management had thought better of its foolhardiness, for showing instead was an Errol Flynn comedy called *The Perfect Specimen*. Since it was raining, we went in anyway, and at least were able to enjoy the performance of Edward Everett Horton. My only other Atlas memory is of Edmund Lowe in the 1935 version of Phillip Oppenheim's *The Great Impersonation*. I had had a surfeit of spy stories (*Mata Hari, Dishonoured, I was a Spy*) and didn't want to go, because the heroines always seemed to end up facing a firing squad; but this one was filled with eccentric incidents including a madman trapped in a burning marsh, an image which has haunted me ever since.

The Atlas was incompetently run and maintained. The plaster rooftop sculpture of the man with the world on his back always looked as though it was about to fall apart: and there was a nasty crack running down Atlas's left arm. The auditorium certainly smelled, more in the front rows than the back because some of its less thoughtful patrons came straight from the mill and brought with them the sickly sweet odour of cottonseed oil. One could hardly complain when the prices ranged from twopence down to one penny; but filmgoers with high standards did better to cross the Fletcher Street railway bridge into Derby Street which, after a mile, became Daubhill (called Dobble) and later St Helen's Road. Near this turnpike lived several of my friends and relations, so naturally I had some acquaintance with its two cinemas. The one nearer to town was the Tivoli, rebuilt in 1937 on the site of the ancient Derby, which had been demolished as unsafe. It too came to smell of the mills, but when I first visited it soon after the gala opening it was a very clean, airy and pleasing auditorium in the new stadium design (no circle, but a steeply raised back stalls); it also had a long interior queuing corridor plastered with enticing posters of forthcoming attractions. I remember seeing a curiously chosen double-bill there in which both films featured Oriental detectives: Peter Lorre in *Mr Moto's Last Warning* and Boris Karloff as Mr Wong in *The*

Mystery of the Wentworth Castle. The *Wentworth Castle*, by the way, was a ship, and so far as I remember one never even saw it; for some reason the British distributors thought it made a better title than the original one, *Doomed to Die*.

The Majestic, formerly known as the Rumworth, had at one time been a skating rink and was all on one level, with no rake, so that the screen had to be set high. Even then it was impossible to see it if someone of even average height sat in front of you. The auditorium was precisely rectangular, with the screen absurdly placed in the middle of one of the *longer* sides, and all the seats in long, straight rows, so that many of the side ones did not face the screen at all. To suit the fire regulations there were frequent gangways, and if the house was full one was reminded of platoons of soldiers on the march. Luckily it was rare for more than a third of the 1,900 seats to be occupied, so a small chap could manage pretty well if he was prepared to do some adroit moving around. My mother once considered taking me to the Majestic for the silent version of *Ben-Hur*, which had been re-issued with a music track, but at the last minute she decided I wouldn't like it. We did see *She* there, and the dark spaces around me properly gave me the shivers at the sight of the mysterious African queen shrivelling in the flame of youth, though I determined not to say so in case other adventure thrillers should be denied to me.

Deane Road, the next western artery, runs from the bus station parallel to the Croale valley, through Victorian terraces designed to keep factory hands as near as possible to their place of work. It climbs to semi-moorland at a spot called Daisy Hill, descends in the general direction of Wigan, and peters out at a dull mining conurbation called Westhoughton, alternatively known as Keaw Yed City from the legend that a cow (keaw) once got its head (yed) stuck through a fence there. Towards the town end of Deane Road, on the flat and surrounded by mills, stood the Regent, a square, solid and unlovable little hall where, instead of tickets, they handed you heavy reusable metal checks in various shapes according to the price of the seat. The usherette collected them inside, and how one could subsequently prove what one paid is not clear to me. Here I saw an early Saint film in some discomfort from stomach ache, after eating green apples at a penny a pound instead of going for the riper twopennies; and I trekked there too to catch Annabella and David Niven in *Dinner at the Ritz*. Up the hill on the opposite side stood the small and spiritless Plaza, which one day had itself redecorated and came out as the Windsor. I can't remember which it was on the night I called, but for some reason its foyer was stacked high with basket chairs. I saw big-mouthed Joe E. Brown in either *Wide Open Faces* or *You Said a Mouthful* – it was the one in which he sails to the rescue of the girl on one of those old push-up-and-down railway trolleys.

Spa Road leads only to the gasworks and the cemetery; heaven knows where the spa was. Sitting low on it, where the ground shelves steeply to the River Croale, and just across the wide High Level junction which marks the western boundary of the town centre, was the Regal, previously the Olympia Skating Rink. (There must have been a lot of skaters in Bolton at one time.) It rather uselessly boasted the largest seating capacity in Bolton (2,200) until Oscar Deutsch built his Odeon; uselessly because the back stalls, though raked, were so far away from the screen that you needed a telescope to find out what was going on. Since it backed on to Queen's Park and there were very few residential streets nearby, the Regal attracted a sparse but lively mixed crowd of non-locals. It was untidy and uncomfortable and unpredictable, but you could not afford to ignore it altogether in case you missed something extraordinary. Strictly speaking a one-storey building, it did have a balcony of sorts, a wooden shelf which stretched down one side of its rectangular frame. This structure was popularly known as the orange box, for reasons apparent to all who frequented it; my mother would never allow me to ascend its rickety stair. As its seats faced directly across the hall instead of towards the screen, it was chiefly used by iron-nerved lovers who didn't want to see the film anyway. One day after the war it simply fell down. Luckily nobody was in it.

The Regal's greatest hour came in 1936 when it presented Bolton's first and only performances of the eccentric Warner production of *A Midsummer Night's Dream*, based on Max Reinhardt's staging at the Hollywood Bowl in 1934. In a zany bid for prestige Jack L. Warner (who never read a book if he could help it and probably knew about the production only from newspaper reports) had the whole production transferred to the screen with the help of William Dieterle's direction, Hal Mohr's photography, Anton Grot's sets and a list of Warner contract players none of whom was likely to spring to one's mind if one were listing possible interpreters of Shakespeare. There was Dick Powell as Lysander, James Cagney as Bottom, Mickey Rooney as Puck, Joe E. Brown as Flute, and Victor Jory as Oberon. The few people at the Regal on the night Mum and I attended had undoubtedly turned up in the expectation of seeing these stars play their accustomed parts. When only Shakespeare was offered, with a chorus of fairies, parts of the audience grew restive, and before long ice-cream cartons and any other weapons to hand were being thrown at the screen. Until this point we had not been much enjoying the entertainment either, but such behaviour put us firmly on the side of the film. Before I could advise against it, Mum rose to her feet and shouted 'Stop!' in such firm tones that most of the offenders actually did. Some walked out sheepishly; but by the time the *Pyramus and Thisbe* finale came on, the fifty or so remaining spectators were actually laughing *with* the film rather than *at* it.

On a later visit, to see Deanna Durbin in *Three Smart Girls*, my attention was drawn to three comic cut-out heads, giant size, which were attached by wires to the orange box. All were male; two had peculiar hair, and the third wore a hat which came to a point. I asked why they were there, and my mother said they were the Marx Brothers. From her tone I deduced that they were not a fit subject for polite conversation, but it turned out later that she only meant she personally didn't find them very funny, which was why she had not taken me to the Capitol to see *A Night at the Opera*. She now felt, however, that I should be put in a position to decide for myself, so a week or so later we found ourselves at the Regal again, watching *A Day at the Races*. I laughed intermittently, especially at the medical examination, the wall-papering, and the racetrack climax, but there seemed to be a great deal of irrelevant singing and romancing, so my loyalty to Stan and Ollie remained unaffected.

North-west of Bolton, where the upper classes resided, there were no cinemas save the Royal, a funny little place close in to town, just before the tram stopped at the Crofter's Inn. It had a fine mock-Tudor façade, but the interior was very seedy indeed, and the projection so appalling that on my only pre-war visit I, who had paid for my seat, actually walked out half way through the show, without having the nerve to demand my money back. Several mill terraces north, in Shepherd Cross Street, lay the Gem, the one Bolton cinema whose doorway I never darkened; and the Carlton, difficult to find for oneself but on the number 4 bus route. A barren-looking hall with a peeling stucco exterior, it ran the same three-day bookings as the Majestic – but at the opposite end of the week so that the same prints could be used.* I went there once to see a sub-Hitchcock train thriller called *Seven Sinners*, but the projection standards were lamentable and I scratched my thigh on a spring sticking out of the seat.

The next arterial road, leading north to Blackburn, once boasted three cinemas. Furthest out, on the corner of Belmont Road where the moors begin, was the Belle. Snuggled away behind a pub, it was a stone building, quite tiny, and low inside; apparently clean enough, but never without a dank smell. The front stalls uniquely consisted of backless wooden forms, riveted to the floor; not very comfortable, but for a penny one could hardly complain. I made the journey twice, feeling very adventurous: once to see Shirley Temple in *The Little Colonel*, and secondly to catch up with the Aldwych farce *Foreign Affaires*. As the latter had an 'A' certificate, my father volunteered to take me on Saturday afternoon, Tom Walls being a favourite of his. (He had once been introduced to him in a Blackpool pub, soon after the star's horse April the Fifth had won the Grand National.) But neither of us had read the advertisement properly, for Saturday afternoons at the Belle were reserved for kids. We found ourselves surrounded by screaming urchins, orange peel, and Ken Maynard, and I never did manage to see *Foreign Affaires*.

In the pre-war years the Empire had such a bad reputation that I never ventured closer to it than the corner of

---

*Although this practice was called 'bicycling', the Majestic used a conveyance which looked like a converted hearse.

Blackburn Road, from which one could glance up a side street for an oblique sighting of its red, white and blue posters. It seldom advertised its programmes, relying no doubt on local patronage for its second-feature double-bills, some of them passed down from the Rialto. Only a little less forbidding, but closer to town and on the main road, was the oddly dark and sinister Palladium. Difficult to imagine that it had once been the focal point of Bolton's movie entertainment, but yes, it was here in 1929 that *The Singing Fool* had opened, and awed stories were still told of the mile-long queues which had formed on that occasion. By the time I was a paying patron, however, the Palladium had been superseded; and I can recall seeing only two attractions there: Duggie Wakefield in *Spy for a Day*, a First-World-War farce which seemed funny enough at the time, and Claude Rains in *The Clairvoyant*, a fascinating melodrama about a man whose predictions of disaster prove only too accurate. Mr Rains, by end of the thirties, was a firm family favourite: Mum and I both admired the incisive command of his voice, usually in double-dyed villainy as when, in *The Adventures of Robin Hood*, as the perfidious Prince John, he enquires casually of his aide Sir Guy of Gisbourne: 'Any more objections to the new taxes, from our Saxon friends?'

Tonge Moor Road led under the railway viaduct, thence via a number of scattered moorland villages, to Burnley. At the Bradshaw end there had once been a cinema called the Picturedrome. Occasionally in my infancy I had noted scraps of torn posters for it still clinging to hoardings and telegraph poles – but apparently it had burned to the ground in 1930. Cinematically the highway remained featureless until 1937, when Crompton Way, which crossed it, was developed into one of the least used ring roads in Britain – until well after the war grass used to grow through the tarmac – and a brand new cinema called the Crompton was erected near the junction with Tonge Moor Road. In some excitement we attended the grand opening, but disappointment prevailed on the journey home. Both foyer and auditorium were very clean and functional, but gave the impression that there had been no money to spare for luxury trimmings or even for imagination. The attraction was decent enough, Robert Taylor in *The Crowd Roars* (second run following the Capitol; we had waited on purpose), but supporting it were *two* of those boring big band shorts, and no cartoon. We never went again. The Tivoli, closer to home, showed the same features but encased them in a more enterprising programme.

Next and last on my clockwise circuit of the town came the Palace, a scruffy little hall surrounded by back streets in the slum-like hollow below the Parish Church. For the uninitiated it was difficult to find, even though it lay only a few hundred yards from the bright lights of Churchgate. To it I hastened for a second experience of the Crazy Gang in *Alf's Button Afloat*, first enjoyed at the Hippodrome in company with a packed audience which laughed so loud that half the jokes were drowned. Despite a cut-about print it seemed even funnier at the Palace, especially the shipboard sequence when Bud Flanagan says 'Strike me pink!' in the genie's presence. Alistair Sim's sepulchral tones were never used to better advantage. 'To hear is to obey, O master,' he murmurs respectfully, but there is a slight misunderstanding, since Bud finds himself *striped* pink, like a stick of Blackpool rock.

Several Bolton cinemas were shuttered long before I could get to them. Thus the Beehive in Bark Street, which apparently thrived in the twenties but lost out when the Palladium, not far away, wired for sound first. Thus the Paragon in Bradshawgate, transformed by my time into a shopping arcade. Thus the Ideal in Silverwell Lane, a former warehouse whose walls still stand behind the Lido. Thus the Princess in Churchgate, incorporated during the year before I was born into the extension of the Theatre Royal.

Strictly speaking, the remaining five halls of my twenty-eight were in Farnworth, but until 1946 that sombre industrial wasteland (dignified at its railway station as 'Farnworth and Halshaw Moor', though patches of greenery were notable chiefly by their absence) remained part of the borough of Bolton and so came officially within my range. They were hardly palatial: the Palace, for instance, was a tiny barn in the middle of the food market, and you could hear meat being auctioned outside while the film was playing. But the Ritz, very curiously tucked away down a residential street, had some dignity when viewed from the circle, and was always used by the local amateur operatic society; while the architect of the Savoy, which stood in stately isolation on the southern side of a kind of by-pass called Long Causeway, clearly had ideas above his station when he designed the row of plaster cupids above the proscenium. The Moses Gate Hippodrome, though new in 1936, was so ringed about by mill chimneys, including those of the Textile where my father worked, that its fixtures and fittings quickly grimed over to make it the least desirable of the quintet; I visited it once to see the Dead End Kids on the screen, and found myself surrounded by their local equivalents in the stalls. Finally and confusingly there was the Farnworth Empire, which I visited once to see James Cagney in *The Frisco Kid*. A cheerless, double-gabled building with stone facings, it smelled curiously of stale beer, and its acoustics left much to be desired. In the fifties it was one of the first local cinemas to close, and I think it became a fire station.

Thus on my home ground I had a wide selection of cinemas, all quite easy to reach. But of course I also collected cinemas on holiday. How, when they were so frequently on the dole, cotton spinners managed to spend Wakes Week at the seaside with their families, I will never understand; but very few seemed to stay at home, and whichever resort we favoured, Dad always found work-mates with whom he could have a drink. Mum and I hardly minded, for our chief concern on reaching the unfamiliar station was to read the cinema posters and make our selection. There was that 1937 week in Southport when it rained all the time, thus enabling us to cram in Tyrone Power in *Lloyd's of London* at the Trocadero, Gracie Fields in *The Show Goes On* at the Scala, Deanna Durbin in *One Hundred Men and a Girl* at the Palladium, a revival of *Boys will be Boys* at the Grand, and Kay Francis at the Coliseum (was it *The White Angel*?). Finally at the Forum we caught a pleasing little small-town comedy-drama called *A Family Affair* which turned out to be the first of the Hardy Family series, though in this case Lionel Barrymore played the judge instead of Lewis Stone.

Most years, and sometimes twice a year, we managed to spend Wakes Week at Douglas in the Isle of Man, reached by a 56-mile, three-hour sail from Fleetwood. The cost was amazingly small, and Mum and Dad, between getting married and the outbreak of war, enjoyed more than thirty holidays there. Often the whole family went as a unit, though in later years the girls preferred to stay at different digs, thus gaining an illusion of independence. They still spent most of the long summer days with us, until an hour before the dance halls opened. The long-established family procedure was to book rooms by post with a Miss Edith Cannell who, when I knew her, was a sharp-faced, kindly person of about sixty. At her house in Mount Havelock, overlooking the bay from a high position reached most easily by cobbled steps, we had 'apartments', which was a Lancashire term for a very curious arrangement. We would pay for accommodation only, buying our own food, which was then labelled by Miss Cannell and cooked by her maid with great bravura. (There was an additional 'cruet charge' of sixpence per person per week.) The cheapness of this arrangement when compared with full board can scarcely have compensated for the immense confusion and waste of time which it caused for everybody. (I distinctly remember a weary-looking moustachioed gentleman telling his hostess, more in sorrow than in anger: 'Miss Cannell, I think you've given Mrs Orrell my black puddings'.) If our steamer docked at seven o'clock on a Saturday evening (and we never got there earlier because Dad had to work in the mill till twelve) we would grab a horse tram from the pier, hurry up the hill to say hello to Miss Cannell and deposit our luggage, then dash out *en famille* to queue at the local shops for bacon, eggs, bread, a Sunday joint and other comestibles, jockeying the while for position with hundreds of other groups on the same errand. The local retailers stayed open as late as was required in order to accommodate this insanity, but such frenzied activity left us too exhausted to do anything with the hour or so between supper and bedtime except loll in the window seat and watch the flickering lights from the funfair on Onchan Head. Next morning, however, I would be up and away, between breakfast and the open-air service at Kirk Braddan, for a quick survey of what the Manx cinemas had to offer during the week to come. Of course they had to jostle for my affections with the nigger minstrels on Douglas Head, the rock-making shop, Feldman's Singing Room (where we all joined in the choruses of *Oh! the Fairies* and *The Teddy Bears' Picnic*), the oyster beds at Port Soderick and the mountain railway to Snaefell; but on the whole I remained loyal.

One Douglas film I remember particularly vividly is George Formby in *No Limit*, because it was partly made on the island and the star is seen not only participating in the TT motor-bike races but emerging from his lodgings in a row of cottages which we instantly recognized. I remember, too, Laurel and Hardy in *The Bohemian Girl*, a disappointment apart from Stan's drunk scene and James Finlayson's belated appearance; Ronald Colman as *Clive of India*; and Roland Young in *The Man Who Could Work Miracles*, which made a deep impression on us. (We tried the magic passes repeatedly on the way home, but the moon remained obstinately in the same place.) When Chaplin's *Modern Times* came to the Gaiety, we were astonished to find that it had been booked not for the usual week but for the whole summer, and that it was necessary to secure seats in advance, a procedure quite unknown to us until then. Dad showed us the pink tickets over tea, and warned us that according to his understanding the film was silent, which caused Mum to remark that in that case the prices should have been reduced rather than increased. Naturally we all enjoyed ourselves, especially at the early scenes, but we didn't think much of Charlie's singing, and the movie as a whole was somehow less endearing than Chaplin's early shorts such as *Easy Street* and *The Cure*, which we had seen time and time again on 9.5mm at church bazaars. In *Modern Times*, of course, Chaplin was straining to make a socialist statement, and it hardly suited him, not with all the money he was known to have in the bank, to say nothing of those increased prices of admission.

Most memorable of our Manx movies was the Korda version of H. G. Wells's *Things to Come*, which had a prior-to-London try-out at the Crescent Pavilion, a massive

amphitheatre on the promenade. We had heard little about
the attraction except that it was 'different', which proved to
be the understatement of 1936. The impression it made on
that innocent, entertainment-seeking Monday night
audience can hardly have been less sensational than the
panic caused two years later in New York by Orson
Welles's famous radio broadcast of *The War of the Worlds*,
which caused millions of people to believe that Martians
had actually landed (and for which, incidentally, H. G.
Wells also shared the credit). From the opening titles of
Things to Come, with their monumental lettering in light
and shadow and the numbers 1940 rolling towards us over a
dark world, to that last lingering telescope shot of the
infinite universe, we were awed, gripped and frightened
(apart from a slow bit in the middle with Ralph Richardson
failing adequately to portray a gangster lord of the disease-
ridden future). War in 1940? Surely it wasn't possible. And
then everybody dying of plague? And people living in glass
buildings, and designing rocket ships which could fly
people to the moon?

Strolling uneasily afterwards along the darkened promenade, we all convinced ourselves that Mr Wells's ideas
were preposterous, and that we had been taken in by film-
makers' tricks: sets, lighting, models, and above all by that
insistent Arthur Bliss music. Dad finally gave an authorita-
tive cough and said I wasn't to worry at all about the future,
which would very likely take care of itself; but the film
persisted in our conversation and we were impatient to see
it again when it came to the Bolton Odeon the following
year. When a couple of years after that the war did come
along, pretty much on Wells's schedule, we were quick to
praise his foresight – and of course our own in championing
him.

The war put the Isle of Man out of bounds, except to

imprisoned enemy aliens. Our holidays were not the only enjoyments that ended, but I was at the best age to endure privation, if there is a best age. I was ten, and when the physical aspects of life in Bolton took a turn for the worse, I barely noticed, for I was living a rich, full life at the cinema. To myself I had the wisdom of Ronald Colman, the cockiness of James Cagney, the power of Charles Laughton, the dignity of George Arliss, the twinkle of Cary Grant, the cynical chuckle of Melvyn Douglas, and the blazing impudence of Clark Gable. They were more than enough to keep me going, through thick and thin.

I sometimes wonder whether I learned more from the cinema than from St Simon and St Jude's Elementary School. The information may have been a little twisted in the gleaning, but it usually stirred me to further enquiry. I distinctly remember following up my interest in ancient Rome, stirred by *Roman Scandals*; in the British Empire, stirred by *The Four Feathers*; and in the American Civil War, stirred by *So Red the Rose*. I was the librarian's pet. I learned about New York from *Dead End*, about Broadway from *42nd Street*, about the Ku Klux Klan from *Black Legion*. Science and exploration came vividly alive through a hundred different films. Emotionally, the strength of mother love was brought home to me by *Stella Dallas*, the horror of capital punishment by *Angels with Dirty Faces*, the wonder of great art by *Rembrandt*.

And so the well worn streets of Bolton came to seem like just another film location, one in which I was the leading actor. Our new house was almost the only disappointing part, never adequately furnished or thoroughly warmed, because semi-employment made it difficult even to keep up with the repayments. Oh, I snuggled happily enough by the fireside with my books, taught myself a tune or two on the old piano, and even played on my rocking horse until the

idea seemed absurd; but my real interests were outdoors.
Walking into town on a holiday weekday I would often
linger on Moncrieffe Street railway bridge to watch the
metal highways curling away in all directions, to Pendleton
and Bury and Manchester and even to London. What could
London be like? Were its trams more luxurious than
Bolton's, its roadways filled with cars? Did its policemen
wear gold helmets? I never really expected to find out.
Perfectly content with my junior lot, I would trot across the
high footbridge, dodging puffs of steam, on my way to that
holy of holies the central library; and very likely I might
have arranged to meet Mum later for tea and cakes in
Collinson's, a genteel balconied café on three floors, with
chairs of bright blue plush and a ladies' trio fiddling away at
Strauss and Mendelssohn. It really wasn't a bad life at all.

Nine

In the Event of an Air Raid...

... our programmes will continue. Unless, the posters hastened to add, enemy planes are directly overhead.

The outbreak of war caught me on one foot. I had barely understood all the newsreels about Munich and air-raid precautions, and the announcement brought down a curtain which seemed to separate me from my previous existence. When, at 11.15 am on 3 September 1939 we listened to Neville Chamberlain's voice on the wireless telling us that we were at war with Germany, our house was littered with evidence of the new public school career which I was due to take up on the following day: caps, football boots, gym shoes, shorts, emblazoned tie, shirts, blazer, all carefully purchased by my mother out of the maintenance grant allowed by the local authority. Each garment now proudly bore a Cash's name tape on which 'R. J. L. Halliwell' was embroidered in bright blue gothic letters, and I had been provided with a handsome wardrobe in which each item was to have its place. My mother's ambition that I should sit and win the scholarship examination for Bolton School at the age of nine had been realized. Awed thoughts of the unknown world to which that scholarship was giving me entrance had so distracted me that only now did I understand fully how ominous the newspaper headlines had been in recent months.

Despite the long history of Bolton School, dating back to 1542, its present buildings in red sandstone were begun in the 1920s and are still incomplete. Elegantly distanced by immaculate lawns from Chorley New Road, they were and are easily the most dominant constructions on the entire six-mile length of that splendid broad tram track with its multitude of dark Victorian mansions (not forgetting the Haslam Maternity Home in which I was born). The boys' division was joined to the girls' only by governors' offices over a simplified gothic arch; the ensemble was backed by playing fields descending in 'levels' towards the Croale, giving a nightmarish view of sixty-three mill chimneys and the slum streets of Deane Road. This backdrop, which would certainly have inspired L. S. Lowry, served me both as a reminder of my good fortune in winning the scholarship and a warning of the environment to which I must return should I fail to justify the confidence which other people had placed in me.

The year of the scholarship had been a tormenting one, for I knew what it meant to my mother. I was her last chance for family advancement. It was she who had somehow persuaded the education authority that my natural intelligence should not be ignored, that I should be allowed to sit for the examination under age. It was she who had proudly accompanied me to the headmaster's interview and stood up to the snobbishness of the other parents-in-waiting (one of whom, on eliciting the fact that we hailed from the poorer side of town, informed my mother that where she herself lived, it was 'all green, everywhere'). The headmaster, a leonine and immensely distinguished giant in a black academic gown and mortar board, was terrifying as the heavy oak door closed behind me and I stood nervously in the exact centre of his Turkish carpet. He surveyed me coolly from his swivel chair, and asked me what I would like to be when I left school. A barrister, please, I said, having recently seen some courtroom movie in which Francis L. Sullivan demolished the prosecution case with a few swift strokes. He raised his eyebrows and said that might be rather expensive, but if I came to Bolton School they would try to find me something cheaper and just as good. Then we talked briefly about some of the answers I had given in the tests, and I was outside again, answering Mum's questions as best I could. I never imagined I had won; but I had. There were predictable rejoicings in Bradford Road when the *Evening News* printed the list a month later, especially since so many friends had implied to my mother that she was mad to let me enter: it would turn my head, and we could never afford it, and anyway it was all fixed beforehand by the Freemasons. They should have known that, when my mother was determined on a course of action, contrary advice only put her back up.

The war certainly caused a hiccup in our plans. The start of term was put back for a week while air-raid shelters were completed. Gas masks were issued, and Mum made a neat black shoulder case for mine. Identity cards were queued for. Black-out curtains were hurriedly machined, and adhesive strips were placed across windows to reduce the effects of blast. Worse of all, cinemas were closed for a month. Nobody could sensibly explain why: it was probably to do with the danger of assembling in public places when bombs might fall. So that was the moment when radio really became the essential medium of wartime. And I never did see *The Saint Strikes Back*, which had been billed at the Odeon for the week of 4 September.

At last the day came. I took a ha'penny bus into town and a ha'penny tram with an 'N' on it from Trinity Street to Bolton School, finding it difficult to arrange myself comfortably with a satchel on one side and a gas mask on the other. At 8.45, 480 boys of various sizes filed into the huge hall, a copy of St Stephen's in Westminster, for morning assembly and prayers. The carved oak roof made it like attending service in a cathedral. Later in that fate-filled day I found myself learning the rudiments of French, algebra, geometry and physics, among other matters of which previously I had had no more conception than the man in the moon.

Though there was nobody at home to help or advise me, for a while I relished the strangeness and excitement of it all. Then, slowly but surely, I became a misfit. I was living in two worlds, neither having any connection with the other. My family was interested in what I was doing, but it was all too difficult to explain, especially since I was finding it hard to keep up. My mother tried to get advice for me from older boys in the district, but they were too busy to bother, and perhaps enjoyed watching me relive their own earlier traumas. At the end of the first term my old headmaster, Mr Pilling, professed himself disappointed when I came only ninth in a class of thirty. He had assured all concerned at Bolton School, he said, that he was sending them a boy whose progress would astonish them, and here was I letting him down. It was true that at St Simon's I had always come top of the class; moderately well behaved, I had also been something of a teacher's pet. Instinctively I knew that it was unfair of Mr Pilling to expect me to shine with equal brilliance when the competition was more intense, and also a little unwise of him to say so even if he thought it; but the damage was done. I retreated into frustration at my inability to keep up with all the new demands being placed upon me. I could not swim, and objected to being thrown in at the deep end by the form clown every time we went to the bath. I hated organized games. I found myself ill-at-ease with the fee-paying boys from wealthy families, who resented my getting something for nothing.

I did make one or two good friends, but we were the dull sort who enjoyed a walk into town after school or went for moorland cycle rides at the weekend. We strove to be ignored as much as possible, and it was not always possible. I suppose, too, that it upset me to be so quiet, since at St Simon's I had always been in the thick of whatever enterprise was afoot. Altogether, apart from some (but not all) of the actual lessons, I did not much enjoy public school life for two or three years, not until I was old enough to join some of the societies which were closed to the juniors.

This wholly unexpected period of depression in my young life, coupled with the slowly increasing privations and discomforts of the war years, turned me more and more to the cinema for solace. The difference now was that I brought to my filmgoing a more critical eye, as befitted a public school student who had spoken to the English master about Eisenstein and could translate *parlez-moi d'amour*. I ransacked the Central Library for books on film history, production methods and criticism: Alistair Cooke's *Garbo and the Night Watchmen* was my first primer, with C. A. Lejeune's *Cinema* a close second. Slowly, with help from my weekly copy of *Picturegoer*, for which every Thursday morning I queued between trams at Allanson's the newsagent's, I brushed up on all matters cinematic with the intention that in one subject at least I would still be top of the class. Even the headmaster, when I sat at his lunch table, had come to know of my special subject and occasionally asked me such posers as whether *Henry V* would come to Bolton or how he could get a print of *Les Enfants du Paradis*.

The pattern of my filmgoing naturally changed. The evening queues, which in peace-time had formed obligingly

enough for any attraction of merit, now formed at double
length for any old rubbish the management chose to offer.
The nation was desperate to be entertained, and the
cinema was the best way of accomplishing this. My mother
was increasingly preoccupied with affairs at home. Food
rationing meant that she had to preside over meals like a
dictator, and when I was sent to the Woodgate Street Co-
op to queue up for the weekly grocery order, I always made
for the assistant whom I knew to like films in the hope that,
after a cheerful chat about the current Gary Cooper or
John Wayne western, he might tip a little extra sugar into
the blue bag before sealing it up. Clothes rationing also
arrived, which meant that my mother had to spend more
and more time mending and making do. Coal shortage
involved frequent supervision of the grate, which heated
the oven and the hot water in the cistern as well as
providing warmth and a place to make toast or a cup of tea.
Then there was my homework, which could not be neglected, pictures or no pictures: two hours a night, five nights a
week. The solution which emerged was that I made most of
my cinema visits on my way home from school. I had to
come through town anyway, and a double journey would
have been a waste of time and money. With luck I could be
in my seat by 4.15 and home by seven at the latest, gulping
my tea as I spread my geography papers on the tablecloth.
This procedure had the added advantage that I got in at
matinee prices: at the Rialto, for instance, I sometimes had
the circle all to myself for fourpence.*

*There was one other keen filmgoer from Bolton School who had
obviously adopted the same system. I knew his name and that was all,
except that he was reputed to be a mathematical genius. We both made for
seats on the right-hand aisle, but although I would nod to him we never
spoke except to say 'Excuse me', or perhaps if we were close enough to
exchange a smile at some moment of hilarity. After I left school I never
saw him again.

In 1940 I began to keep film notebooks. From the school bursar I would buy for one penny a small feint-ruled brochure: the cover might be of rough wartime quality but the paper inside always had the smooth texture which invites careful penmanship, and my handwriting at that time was small and precise. Number one is now lost, but it was pale blue, and I did a title design in red crayon and outlined it in ink. I carefully allotted one page to each cinema programme, which left for each film only three or four lines of actual criticism if I stuck to my usual routine of sub-headings, which for a while I did. The first entry, I remember, went as follows:

RIALTO
Film: Nick Carter, Master Detective
Stars: Walter Pidgeon, Rita Johnson, Henry Hull
Studio: Metro-Goldwyn-Mayer
Verdict: Seek him out!

The 'verdict' was a self-conscious device borrowed from the critic of the *Sunday Chronicle*: I soon abandoned it, being quite incapable (see above) of concocting a capsule witticism for every occasion. There would follow a brief synopsis and my naïve little critique, beside which in the margin was a pictorial rating device, stolen this time from an American fan monthly, either *Movieland* or *Silver Screen*. It was the outline of a man's head wearing a topper, thus: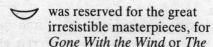

By the addition of a simple mouth, in varying expressions, I was able to express my approval or otherwise of the films under review.

⌣　was reserved for the great
irresistible masterpieces, for
Gone With the Wind or *The*

Wizard of Oz;

⌣ was more common, as I liked most
of the films I saw pretty well
but this side of idolatry;

— marked the average entertainment,
a time-passer;

⌢ demonstrated a genuine disappointment;

◠ was seldom used except for my pet
aversions of those days, war propaganda
pieces and second feature westerns.

All this was rather cumbersome, so I subsequently replaced the face by asterisks, from four down to one. This system was borrowed from *Picturegoer*, but I added a clover leaf – ♧ – as my heartfelt groan or lemon. These symbols of approval or otherwise preceded the film's title, which later on, as I acquired more journalistic skill, began to appear not as a headline but in the middle of the paragraph. I would then give my mini-essay a would-be witty title à la Lejeune: such as 'Angel Cake' for *Here Comes Mr Jordan*, and 'Tentacles of Terror' for *Reap the Wild Wind*. My judgements were of course wildly unreliable, and some of the films which I didn't take to then, such as *The Philadelphia Story* ('icy society cocktail') became great favourites later on when I was of an age to appreciate them properly. Nor could my reviews have been held up as models of prose style; but I slowly improved and, more to the point, I enjoyed myself. I kept the notebooks going in one form or another for nearly ten years, until I was reviewing so many films for a university paper that they began to seem an unnecessary extra call on my time when I could keep the press clippings.

As Bolton's cinemas became more and more popular (MEMBERS OF THE ARMED FORCES ADMITTED FREE was displayed less frequently than FREE LIST ENTIRELY SUSPENDED FOR THE CURRENT ATTRACTION), so their number diminished. Quite unexpectedly in 1939 the Hippodrome had announced a summer season of live repertory by the Lawrence-Williamson Company, which had made occasional visits to the Grand with such popular standards as *Rookery Nook* and *The Barretts of Wimpole Street*. This time they came for six weeks and stayed for twenty years; my beloved Hippodrome never showed films again. However, the atmosphere of low comedy and high melodrama was not entirely lost, for the amiable T. C. Williamson, who was in charge, loved to alternate *Turkey Time* and *Are You a Mason?* with *The Terror*, *The Bat* and *The Thirteenth Chair*. Name any lowbrow commercial play written since 1900 and the Hippodrome probably played it, twice nightly at extremely popular prices, with a new attraction every Monday.*

This establishment of a rep in Bolton resulted directly from the need of actors to find a safe base for the duration instead of dodging bombs in their more accustomed haunts. Number one tours began to take number two spots, and since even Manchester could no longer be considered a safe haven, our long-neglected Theatre Royal came briefly into its own again as a showplace for the lively arts. 'Bolton Becomes Show Town', announced the *Daily Express* to our delight as we goggled at a line-up of star attractions which

---

*A few years after the war it even put on one of mine, a farce on the Aldwych model called *Make Your Own Bed*. As so often, the prophet was without honour in his own country, which does not surprise me when I look at the script, of which the following is a typical exchange:

'I'm Mrs Moore.'
'Ah, one of the Yorkshire Moores?'
'You say that because I'm so open and healthy.'
'No, because you're so wet and windy.'

included the Ballets Jooss, the D'Oyly Carte Opera, the Carl Rosa Opera, and an assortment of dramatic ventures ranging from Ernest Hemingway's *The Fifth Column* to *No Orchids for Miss Blandish* and *The Hulbert Follies*. We never got Sybil Thorndike in *The Trojan Women*; but I did manage to see George Formby again at close range.

My mother had somehow been persuaded, after meeting a mysterious Mrs Wilkinson in a cinema, to join the Anglo-Russian Aid Committee, which arranged functions at the Town Hall under a well-liked Labour mayor called Alf Booth. I went along to one of these, a tea party to which each adult had to bring as a minimum contribution a pair of socks to be sent to the Eastern Front; and Alf Booth persuaded George Formby, who was an old pal of his, to attend as guest of honour since he was topping the bill that week at The Theatre. I nearly sank into the floor when Alf brought the great star over to our little group for conversation. 'Ee, George,' said the irrepressible Alf, 'it mun be a great thrill to see your name up in lights outside yon Theatre. Good luck to you, son. But tell me this, how is it that when *you* come to see us, the prices go up?' There was a moment's pause which might have been embarrassing, and George swallowed hard on his tinned salmon sandwich. Then he gave us his shy grin. 'Well,' he answered guilelessly, 'Beryl says, if they want to see me, they mun pay!'*

It was heartening to see the Theatre's regal corridors thronged with our local nobility as never before or since. I

*Stories about George being under Beryl's thumb were legion, and she supervised every day of his filming so that she could be sure he did not kiss any of his leading ladies either on screen or off. It was only in the fifties, after her death, that he revealed in public how unhappy they had been, and gave his plans to marry again; but it was not to be, for a heart attack claimed him.

usually took my share of culture from the back of the gallery, but I found ways of mingling with the mighty during the intervals. It was certainly a great time for Bolton. The Victoria Hall frequently opened its doors to the Hallé and the Liverpool Philharmonic, and even the Lido, with its cramped backstage area, went semi-live, presenting ciné-variety and the occasional all-star pantomime. Flanagan and Allen; Vic Oliver; Afrique; Albert Whelan; Norman Evans; Robb Wilton; and Forsythe, Seamon and Farrell all appeared there at one time or another.

The war had more emotional effect on me in screen terms than in reality. Nobody I knew was killed or injured during the entire six-year period, and only a handful of bombs fell within the corporation boundary, although the sirens sounded with monotonous regularity and at home we all crouched under the kitchen table whenever planes were heard overhead, even if we thought they sounded like our own. The Anderson shelter provided by a thoughtful government was a hideous corrugated iron excrescence in the middle of the back lawn, waterlogged for most of the year and far too cold and damp during the remainder.

If the sirens sounded during a cinema performance, however, we all stayed put. Rather stupidly its audiences instinctively believed in the absolute impregnability of the Odeon, and in any case it was unthinkable to exchange the delights of Deanna Durbin or Donald Duck for the miseries of a communal shelter. A packed audience seemed almost to enjoy the little frisson of excitement which we could sense when the wail of the siren was faintly heard outside. We would look round at each other, mutter 'Them again!' or some stronger imprecation, and return defiantly to the business of being entertained. No doubt about it, the cinema was proving a great morale booster as well as the nation's most effective weapon of propaganda; during this tense period it gained respectability even in the eyes of fervent detractors who had previously characterized it as a corruptor of innocence. We were all addicts, but we did not want reality. We put on our rose-coloured spectacles as we took our seats, and removed them only to go home.

Until 1943 or so, when such brilliant war documentaries as *Fires Were Started* and *Western Approaches* made the Ministry of Information trade mark, which had previously been the cue for sporadic booing, quite popular, the nearest we wanted to come to truth about the war was *Mrs Miniver*: glamorized, middle-class, cliché-ridden, full of hope and glory and Dover's white cliffs. As an MGM production this epic of a Hollywood-imagined home front, written by a woman who had hot-footed it to America for the duration, was presented at the Capitol for an unprecedented fortnight's run. Seeing it became as obligatory as going to church, and queues formed every day before noon for the 2 pm performance. The Halliwells, sensing an occasion, turned up *en famille* and waited two hours to get in. It did us a world of good, we thought. How could it fail, indeed, with all that starry-eyed optimism and rose-gardening? But since it was set in the south of England, we had no real idea whether it offered truth, caricature or downright lies. We didn't actually know people who behaved like Greer Garson or Dame May Whitty, but perhaps in Tunbridge Wells or Bexhill that was the way they were. Either way, we would still have applauded with tears in our eyes as the bombers flew over the ruined church during Henry Wilcoxon's final sermon.

In addition to 'Film Notebooks' I began to keep 'Amusement Guides'. These were week-by-week records of the films playing at Bolton's town centre cinemas. Each Saturday night I carefully ruled enough spaces to fill two

pages of a standard-size notebook; the attractions were
arranged in order of merit, the lettering was designed as
carefully as my abilities permitted, and the poster-like
results were filled in with coloured crayon and an occasional ink sketch. I was hopeless at freehand drawing
('That wouldn't improve sales much,' said the headmaster
once as he passed a poster for *Player's, Please* which I
designed in art class) but not too bad at visual composition,
and some of my lettering still pleases me mildly: classical
for epics, shaky for horror, higgledy-piggledy for farce.
Lest it be thought that I merely frittered away my
adolescence in these vain pursuits, I should add that the
'Guides' were only a pastime for restless fingers while my
mind concentrated on the radio. Saturday was Edith's
night out with her girl friend; Lilian was married in 1940;
and Mum and Dad had temporarily re-acquired the habit of
spending Saturday nights together on the town, which
meant that one week she would reluctantly accompany him
to the saloon bar of the Nag's Head, and on the following
Saturday he would take her even more reluctantly to the
Hippodrome. Rather to their surprise I was delighted to be
left on my own. As soon as I had the house to myself I
would lock the back door in case of burglars, draw up my
armchair to the fire, lay my drawing board across it, switch
on the radio and set to work. I was busy in this way with pen
and ink through 'Music-Hall' at eight o'clock, the news at
nine, and Saturday Night Theatre thereafter. Woe betide
the family if they returned in conversational mood before
10.45 when the play ended. If they did, my only recourse
was to abandon the fireside and lie on the sofa with one ear
to the radio until the final curtain fell, after which I was not
only willing but eager to discuss what they had all seen and
done, and perhaps to shoot along to the chip shop for a
tasty supper.

By now the theatre was challenging the cinema as my primary interest. I had always been prominent in the St Simon's school concerts, reciting bad poems like *Snow in Town* or playing one of the three wise men at Christmastime. Now, for the St Mark's Youth Club (an after-evensong group which met in the church house and so first enabled me to learn how to play snooker), I produced and appeared in Saturday night entertainments to accompany the traditional potato pie suppers. There was a minstrel show (with me as interlocutor and Jolson impersonator). There was a school sketch (with me as Will Hay). There was a farce called *Oh! Aunt Agatha*! with some mild undressing in it. More ambitiously there was a pantomime for which I adapted W. S. Gilbert's *Mikado* lyrics to fit the story of *Aladdin*. I played Widow Twankey myself, lifting my voluminous skirts to reveal a sign which read *For Export Only*, and when in the finale I marched off to wedded bliss with Abanazar, we both sang:

> Our cup of joy will be a big 'un;
> We'll have our honeymoon in Wigan!

More serious undertakings were bound to follow. In 1943 the Bolton School play was revived after a three-year gap because of black-out problems in the vast hall with its high casemented windows. The solution was to stage the plays in June and start them promptly at six-thirty. The platform was augmented into a genuine stage complete with proscenium, orchestra pit, rich drapes, side scenery, steps, a lighting switchboard, the lot. Year by year I worked my way up from Fourth Servant in *She Stoops to Conquer* ('My place is to be nowhere at all, so I'se to go about my business'); to crusty Uncle Jeremiah in *Gallows Glorious* ('Sentimental rubbish!'); D'Estivet in *Saint Joan*

('I am the promoter, sir'); Bolingbroke in *Richard II* ('Exton, I thank thee not') and the King in *Hamlet* ('O, my offence is rank'). In preparation for *Hamlet* we went to see Donald Wolfit's version at the Manchester Opera House; it was one of his last performances in the role, and the line 'He's fat and scant o'breath' really came into its own.

At church, another style of show business, I was altar boy, cross bearer, lesson reader and I even preached a sermon on Youth Sunday. At school, as well as the Dramatic Society, I belonged to the Film Society, the Literary and Debating Society, the Philatelic Society and the Chess Club. All these pursuits enabled me at least to become a person of sorts, though I was still oddly shy except with people I knew well, to whom I was unforgivably bossy. Gradually my multifarious school activities enabled me to command some kind of tolerance and even respect from those who had initially despised me as an intruder into their closed society. I was the only boy who dared to act in a play produced by the Girls' Division, and the entire form came along to cheer me for it. It was *Elizabeth Refuses*, a scene from *Pride and Prejudice*, and I enjoyed myself as the prissy Mr Collins. That was the year I was a prefect, a librarian, and an editor of the school magazine. It was also the year of Higher School Certificate, in which my subjects were history, French, and English literature.

The school film society, which had flourished briefly before the war to show GPO Film Unit documentaries which were made available to schools at no charge, resurfaced during hostilities and was operated initially by Mr Higginson, the art master, who loaned his 16mm projector for shows in the library after school, and taught me to operate it in case he got bored. The first film I saw as a member, and my first wholly foreign film ever, was a silent Russian documentary called *Turksib*, about the building of the Turkestan-Siberian Railway, with trains letting off steam in unison at the end. A dull beginning, perhaps, but luckily the taste of Miss Waterhouse, a physics mistress who succeeded Mr Higginson, was nothing if not catholic, and among the attractions she booked were *The Lady Vanishes, Victoria the Great, Sabotage, Dr Syn*, and *South Riding*, a rather splendid British bunch. I cannot imagine how *A Cuckoo in the Nest* came to be included; and when the headmaster chanced to look in with some visitors, and found forty teenage boys laughing hysterically at the sight of Ralph Lynn running round Yvonne Arnaud's bedroom in his nightshirt, that was very nearly the end of the Film Society. We earned a reprieve because our attraction for the following month was D. W. Griffith's epic *The Birth of a Nation*. As treasurer and chief assistant projectionist I had cast my vote in favour of this ambitious booking, which was to be shown in the evening because a few parents and teachers had said they might come, though there had been a marked lack of enthusiasm among the boys for a silent film which ran three hours and was more than thirty years old. Our maximum attendance was usually fifty people, but on this occasion we thought forty chairs would be ample, and planned a relaxed academic evening about whose joys we could be snooty to all those who had refused to support us. To our astonishment more than two hundred people stormed the doors, including the local press and teachers from other schools. We had to move the projector back through the double doorway and consequently endure a smaller image; even then people were practically sitting on other people's knees. The performance went like a bomb, with cocoa at the reel changes, though few of us quite understood how Griffith could see the Ku Klux Klan as the heroes of his picture, or why the dastardly negroes were played by white men in blackface. It was a superb print; and the evening was filled with beautiful compositions.*

At the ripe age of thirteen I began to write letters about films to newspapers and magazines. Such practice was officially against school policy unless specific permission had been granted, so I adopted several *noms de plume* of which my favourites were Nicholas Kent and Hilary Hunt. It was a red-letter-day indeed when *Picturegoer* sent me five shillings for a gobbet of doggerel, my contribution to a discussion in their columns about horror films:

> I love to see monsters, and things that go bump;
> There's an eerie delight in one's heart going thump.
> Although they're not handsome, I'm fond of each one,
> Of Boris, and Bela, and Basil, and Lon.
> In the movies these ghouls make me gaze open-eyed . . .
> But I have no desire to meet them outside!

But usually it was the *Bolton Evening News* which tolerated my outpourings. I defended the cinema, for instance, against the attacks of Miss Jones of Farnworth, who considered it a disturbing influence on juvenile morals; I made several ineffective pleas to independent exhibitors for more foreign films; I complained bitterly about talkative usherettes, about the sale of ice cream during the feature, about the proliferation of screen advertising, and about the shoddy supporting programmes which became all too familiar during the war. On the matter of revivals I was especially eloquent. 'The attitude,' I wrote, 'of a person

---

*Later on the school bought a new Bell and Howell projector, of which I had charge, though whenever anything went wrong I had to run for help to the nearest science master. To get our money's worth out of the machine we instituted a series of lunchtime documentary sessions in the music room, which meant setting up, screening and dismantling all within forty minutes.

who refuses to see an old film again is mere foolishness. He would be willing to hear a piece of music or read a gem of literature many more times than twice, and some films, like good wine, improve with age. It may not be going too far to suggest the foundation in Bolton of a special cinema to show re-issues only, at bargain prices.' We can all dream.

Throughout the war *Picturegoer* was my bible. Before its amalgamation with *Film Weekly* in 1939 it had been a dull, flabby film magazine in hazy shades of brown, making intelligent communication with nobody but surviving on its advertisements for cheap cosmetics. *Picture Show* was even less professional, but I saw more of it because my sisters relied on its beauty advice and fashion notes. Its articles and gossip column came straight from the renters' press releases, and the entire farrago was edited (as I came to know later) by two old biddies who wore feather boas, knew little or nothing about journalism or the art of the film, and thought Mary Pickford was still the world's sweetheart. In pre-war days the magazine had a bottle green cover with a circular picture on it, like a medallion: I remember one of Robert Taylor in *His Affair*, all curly hair and flashing white teeth (Edith said the latter had to be 'pot'). Around 1940, however, *Picturegoer* took the lead and began to show a new liveliness and responsibility. Its regular credits for new films provided just the reference I needed, and so my collection, augmented weekly, was neatly stacked on top of the meat safe, with a 'Keep Off' notice adorning it.

Picturegoer's resident reviewer then was Lionel Collier, and it was his star system that I borrowed for my notebooks, though we invariably disagreed on the number to be awarded. He was particularly mean, I recall, to the *Road* films and to *Blithe Spirit*. His vocabulary seemed curiously stilted: he was overfond of such words as *stereotyped*, *transpontine* and *peripatetic*, which must have foxed many of his readers. 'The film possesses full romantic values,' he might say, 'but the mixture of comedy and drama does not jell.' 'It would be impossible in the space at my disposal' was a favourite opening gambit, and he was frequently condescending to 'those who appreciate the art form of cinema'. His one obsession with which I sympathized was that all films were too long. 'I do not know any story,' he would pontificate, 'which could not be told well on film within sixty minutes.' Presumably he had not read *War and Peace*.

In addition to Collier's weekly double-page spread, covering up to a dozen new attractions, *Picturegoer* featured The Dentons, contributors of a weekly 'Film-goer's Diary'. They purported to be, and perhaps were, a sprightly young couple telling us just what they personally thought of the movies, and the presentation, at their local cinema. Their style was infectiously gossipy with just a touch of sophistication. There were drawings to point up the funnier bits, such as Ralph dropping an ice cream into somebody's hat on his way back to his seat. They might inform us that 'from our corner of the balcony *Northwest Mounted Police* didn't seem quite up to de Mille's gold standard', or 'we watched Jack Carson the other week having a whale of a time with a bit part, and we're glad to see him cropping up in bigger roles'. The real secret of the Dentons' success with me was that we seemed to choose the same films and to hold identical views about them.

Picturegoer was sound, reliable and friendly. Apart from its ever-more-pleasing layout and sensible informative articles (it even ran one on *Ivan the Terrible*), it had a reader service which personally and comprehensively answered questions on receipt of a stamp, filling its column with replies to those who had not sent the return postage.

('Van Johnson's eyes are blue. Barbara Stanwyck is not married at present. Sorry, we do not give out stars' addresses.') Editorially the magazine was all for quality despite an addiction to frivolous headlines such as 'Veronica Lake's Careless Curl Career'. I could hardly wait to become a *bona fide* contributor and sent in several rather lame pieces. Most were promptly returned, but on a certain Thursday, towards the end of my schooldays, I found one of them in print under a headline I had not invented, *Do We Need Plots in Musicals*? It was credited rather surprisingly to someone with my surname but different initials, which worried me until the second post brought a cheque for six guineas. I celebrated by taking my mother out to tea at Collinson's Café, followed by Bing Crosby and Fred Astaire in *Blue Skies* at the Odeon. A couple of years later, when my school friend Jimmie Beattie was serving in the Dental Corps in Kenya, he sent me a page from the Nairobi *Daily Post* in which my article appeared in full. I forwarded it to the editor of *Picturegoer*, who replied apologetically that this kind of thing often happened, but African newspapers weren't worth suing.

In 1940 I had finally extended my geographical horizons. Impetuously and perhaps foolishly, for it was of course the summer of the Battle of Britain, my mother decided to visit her newly married daughter Lilian in Surrey, and to take me as her escort. For some reason she was recommended to take the night train. There was an air of strain about the house on the day we left, and since we were all packed by lunch time she took me to the Lido in the afternoon to see Ralph Richardson in *On the Night of the Fire*. It was a dim, depressing little drama which did us no good at all.

Carrying minimum luggage, we arrived in Manchester in good time for the midnight departure, but the total black-out meant that I had to hold Mum's hand on the walk between the stations, and to tell her when she was nearing a step up or down. (At last, I felt, I was in a Hitchcock film!) The train from London Road Station started on time, and we were reassured by the sight opposite to us of a bespectacled young man who had his nose in *The Forsyte Saga*; but on Stockport Viaduct we stopped for two hours while bombs fell on the adjacent city. It was like a horrifying firework display, and we were very nearly involved ourselves when a stray incendiary fell close to the railway line. As we finally shunted away I fell asleep, to wake up as we passed the Heinz factory at Wembley. The sign reading '57 varieties' was to me as cheerful a sight as the Emerald City in the Land of Oz. At Euston my first descent 'Underground' was a thrill, and there was another when a fellow passenger screamed just as the train moved that she had left her bags on the platform. At Waterloo we settled into a clean compartment and found ourselves, amazingly, once again opposite the young man reading *The Forsyte Saga*; while at Weybridge the first thing we saw was a dead body in the road, the result of a road accident just before our arrival. All in all, it was a most memorable trip, especially since the Surrey climate was as balmy as I had expected, and most of the local cinemas had a cool modernity to which I was unaccustomed.

In Walton, I saw Alistair Sim as an unlikely MI5 man in *Cottage to Let*, a spy comedy-thriller which sprang a real surprise by casting young John Mills as the villain; also Flanagan and Allen in *Theatre Royal*, and Henry Fonda in *The Ox-Bow Incident*. Weybridge itself had a curious town-hall building which had been turned into a cinema called the County. I was astonished to find it playing a ribald North Country comedy starring Frank Randle, the one in which he turns up on army parade sitting on a donkey. 'What do you think you're doing?' thunders the brigadier.

'I'm sitting on me ass, sir,' is the reply. I was ashamed for my Northern shire. I would have laughed at home, but it did not seem proper to sink so low in Weybridge.

The Odeon in Weybridge, a sleek and modernistic little cinema just by the cricket ground, is the only cinema I know which has become a Catholic church. It was comfortable and sweet-smelling, and had the kind of screen which easily converts dross into gold. I enjoyed every film I saw there in the 1940s: Joseph Cotten in *Journey into Fear*, with Orson Welles as the sinister Colonel Haki; Sidney Howard in *Once a Crook*; Ginger Rogers and Mr Cotten again in *I'll Be Seeing You*; Douglas Fairbanks Jnr in *Sinbad the Sailor*. It was half a mile from the centre of Weybridge, but on the way you could stop for a snack at Mrs Grundy's Tea Shoppe, and the return route was all downhill with the sweet smell of Surry pines to refresh one's soul. At last, I thought, I have found Shangri-La.

TEN

The Baron, The Count, and Their Ghoul Friends

Only once was I genuinely frightened in the cinema. The film bore nothing stronger than an 'A' certificate, and I was taken to it by Bolton School's junior history master.

Early in the war, British National Studios turned out an abysmal propaganda film called *This England*. In it, against cardboard sets, John Clements, Constance Cummings and Emlyn Williams played Britishers through the ages, stoutly resisting the threat of invasion. The history master clearly did not read the reviews, and when the movie turned up at the Lido, that haven for lost causes, he thought it might make a pleasant change for those who could afford the threepence admission and did not mind missing games for once. It might even, he suggested, improve our historical perspectives.

And so, after school lunch, a score of us were escorted by tram to the town centre, and filed into the Lido just as the main film was starting. Even the history master roared with derisive laughter at the inept and extremely boring goings-on, and as soon as *This England* was over he said he had had enough and was off, but if we liked we could stay and see the cartoon or whatever. He must have been either very short-sighted or a sadist; for if he had read the posters outside he would have known that those of us who stayed would shortly be watching *The Mummy's Hand*. *We* knew, of course, and chuckled at our own cunning in not letting on, but seventy minutes later some of the green from the opening floodlights had rubbed off on us as we warily made our lonely ways home through sunlight which now seemed eerily bright. We gave all shadowed alleyways a wide berth in case a marauding mummy might be lurking there, brought to nauseous life by an overdose of tanna leaves after three thousand years in an Egyptian tomb. Looked at in the cold light of a later day, *The Mummy's Hand* is mostly innocuous banter, and the monster moves so slowly as to be a creature of hilarity rather than horror, but it touched a raw nerve in a twelve-year-old schoolboy.

Cheap second-feature horrors were a part of Hollywood's wartime output, but they were not the charnel house nightmares which later became popular. The best of them were fairytales for grown-ups; the worst were comic-strip adventures for mental incompetents. It was perhaps natural, as the casualty figures rose on the fighting fronts, that there should be an increase of interest in life after death and the supernatural generally. (Similarly on the radio, *Appointment with Fear*, with Valentine Dyall as 'The Man in Black', drew a huge audience every week, and there seemed to be a dramatization of *The Monkey's Paw* several times a year.) Light comedies about angels and devils, after the unlikely success of *Here Comes Mr Jordan*, poured forth from every studio, and Boris Karloff and Bela Lugosi came back into steady employment. The British censor did what he could to stem the tide of these conveyor-belt ghoulies, usually by neatly removing the climax, or occasionally banning a film entirely until the war was over; but quite a number of them did get through, and I went to see as many as I could.

Officially one had to be sixteen in order to gain admission

to any film bearing an 'H' certificate, but even at thirteen I found it easy enough at most cinemas. If, say, *The Monster and the Girl* was showing at the Lido, I would wander along at a quiet time, inspecting shop windows until an opportune moment presented itself for consultation with the commissionaire (he of the bad feet) as to my chances. Critically and conspiratorially he would look down his nose at me, take sidelong glances both ways along the road, then mutter: 'Give us your tanner and take that cap off!' We both knew our parts after that. He disappeared into the front entrance, I down the side alley; a crash door opened; he emerged to thrust a ticket into my hand and whisk me inside. Once safe in the darkness, he would wink broadly at the nearest usherette and install me in the remotest corner of the back row.

It was even easier to gain admission at the Theatre Royal, which by now did not seem to care if it lost its licence. I got in with no subterfuge at all to see *A Child is Born*, which had an 'H' certificate; but I wished I hadn't, for the film was a cheat. It contained no horror at all, being a melodrama of the maternity wards. The Boris Karloff specials then being produced by Columbia varied between 'A' and 'H'; either way the Theatre displayed Adults Only cards but would probably have admitted unaccompanied infants providing they were ambulatory and could pay fivepence. There was one very odd Karloff film about frozen cancer therapy: the American title was *The Man with Nine Lives* but we saw it as *Behind the Door*. Boris played a lot of mad doctors around this time, in *The Man They Could Not Hang*, *The Devil Commands*, *Before I Hang* and *The Ape*; I saw them all, and marvelled at his silky menace, except in an item called *Black Friday*, when he affected a stiffly unattractive hair-do and acted as though he had been eating alum. The honours were easily stolen in that case by an under-appreciated actor called Stanley Ridges; and Bela Lugosi, who was also in the cast, had nothing to do but look on and submit to strangulation. Karloff and Lugosi appeared together in revivals of *The Invisible Ray*, *The Black Cat* and *The Raven*, all of which were tolerable without providing any real excitement, though the last of them had a splendid scene with multiple mirrors. Weakest of all the Karloff films was a spoof called *The Boogie Man Will Get You*; but even in this his charac-ter erred in a just cause, which seemed to be an essential feature of any Karloff performance.

An 'A' certificate horror film with a surprising amount of lustre turned up at the Lido in a badly balanced double-bill, with a piece of forgettable romantic frivolity called *Moon over Her Shoulder*, starring Lynn Bari, who was a mildly fashionable leading lady, or 'other woman', of the time. It was *The Wolf Man*, starring Lon Chaney, Jnr, as the unfortunate lycanthrope Lawrence Talbot. After this suc-cess Chaney dropped the 'Jnr' and had himself billed as 'the screen's master character actor'; at the same time his acting talent, modest in the first place, left him entirely, and his supremely wooden performances ruined a good many promising horror feasts. His father would have been ashamed. *The Wolf Man* ran only 71 minutes and was set in an absurd Hollywood conception of a Welsh village, with dry ice rising from every open space in sight. It was slow, and its transformation scenes cheated, yet it started a series. Perhaps its fans are still puzzled as to why so strong a cast was hired to go through such feeble motions. Claude Rains, Warren William, Patric Knowles, Ralph Bellamy, Bela Lugosi and Evelyn Ankers were all involved in a futile search for speakable lines, and only the marvellous Maria Ouspenskaya made a lasting impression as the gypsy Maleva, who warns early on what is going to happen to our stalwart hero:

> Even the man who is pure in heart
> And says his prayers by night
> May become a wolf when the wolf bane blooms
> And the moon is pure and bright.

Chaney was happy enough: 'The Wolf Man was my baby', he used to say later. He starred too in the sequel *Frankenstein Meets the Wolf Man*, a doom-laden saga which had plenty of style despite its then risible title. In this chapter, Frankenstein was a woman, played by Ilona Massey, and Bela Lugosi finally got to play the monster, having turned down the role in 1931. He did it rather badly, but the performance you see on the screen (I later discovered) was not entirely his fault. This is the film in which the monster first stalks around with outstretched arms, because when the film was shot he was supposed to be blind; but for some reason all reference to this was removed in the editing.

If technical trickery had permitted it, Chaney might well have played both monsters: for a year or two he seemed to do everything at Universal Studios but build the sets. In three lukewarm scare sessions – *The Mummy's Tomb*, *The Mummy's Curse*, *The Mummy's Ghost* – he nominally took over from Tom Tyler the role of the 3,000-year-old man, but under the bandages it might have been anybody, and sometimes was, though Chaney was always billed above the title. In *Ghost of Frankenstein* he had already played the monster, very badly indeed; and to my astonishment he turned up also as a much-too-well-fed *Son of Dracula*. (As the sombre story, set in a Louisiana bayou, unrolled, it became clear that the sinister Dr Alucard – spell it backwards – was none other than the old Count himself, but this hardly mattered at a time when most audiences confused the Frankenstein monster with its creator.)

When the law of diminishing returns persuaded the studio that the box office required a whole gallery of monsters in the same film, Chaney insisted on reverting to lycanthropy, allowing John Carradine to assume the Dracula job and Glenn Strange to don the Monster make-up. Two films were made by this trio before Abbott and Costello turned the creatures into figures of fun. In *House of Frankenstein* Boris Karloff returned to play the stately but homicidal Dr Niemann, who breaks jail during a thunderstorm and with the help of his hunchback assistant, played by J. Carrol Naish (a ubiquitous character actor who, originally Irish, played on the screen everything from Red Indian to heathen Chinee, ending his career on television as Charlie Chan), murders the proprietor of a travelling Chamber of Horrors. Exit George Zucco, another fine, thin-lipped horror actor, originally hailing from Manchester. The hunchback falls futilely in love with a gypsy girl who, in her turn, loves the Wolf Man in his Talbot persona but is eventually murdered by him when the moon is full. Meanwhile a dagger is removed from Dracula's bones, and the Count grows back on them like the Invisible Man when he needs a new injection. He however is melted by the rays of the morning sun after doing no more harm than can be caused by a few hypnotic passes. As for the monster, he has been found in an ice cavern and revived, but when the villagers attack with their flaming torches he drags the doctor to what he thinks is a place of safety but turns out to be the local swamp. (All good Bavarian villages have one.)

House of Dracula, which followed, was even more absurd, with the kindly doctor getting a dose of Dracula's bad blood and turning into a regular Jekyll and Hyde. But at least Larry Talbot was allowed a happy ending and even got the girl, after having his complaint diagnosed as over-active hormones stimulated by mental obsession. If only the scriptwriters had possessed a sense of humour to match their inventiveness, this could have been a fine spoof; but alas, they did not. Meanwhile the Invisible Man was also spawning sequels, each in a different mood from its predecessor. *The Invisible Man Returns* was a fairly serious and even a solemn piece set among the North British coalfields; *Invisible Agent* was a cheap farce in which an untrained hero far too easily outwits both Nazis and Japs; in *The Invisible Man's Revenge* the drug turned its taker into a crafty homicidal maniac, but the script and treatment were too stodgy for anyone to care, despite the novelty of an invisible Great Dane.

Horror elements also crept in to Universal's updated Sherlock Holmes stories, in which Basil Rathbone, after two satisfactorily traditional outings at Twentieth Century-Fox, was given an eccentric haircut and set to fight Nazi spies.* *The Scarlet Claw* was a variation on *The Hound of the Baskervilles*, with a vengeance-crazed murderer stalking the foggy moors of Quebec and killing with a garden handfork. *The Pearl of Death* introduced the grotesque Rondo Hatton, a real-life victim of acromegaly, as the

*A feature of the series was the patriotic speech with which Rathbone used to close most of the stories. The speeches stemmed from the fact that the first episode was an adaptation of 'His Last Bow', and used the peroration from that story: 'There's an east wind blowing, Watson, such a wind as never blew in England yet . . . a good many of us will wither before its blast. But it's God's own wind, nevertheless, and a greener, better, stronger land will lie in the sunshine when the storm has passed.' In the next story Holmes delivered himself of the John o'Gaunt speech from *Richard II*: 'This blessed plot, this earth, this realm, this England . . .' And later on he grew misty-eyed at the sight of Washington, of Canada, and of a self-sacrificing heroine: 'There's a new spirit abroad in the land. The old days of grab and greed are on their way out.'

Hoxton Creeper, who kills on command by snapping people's backs. In *Sherlock Holmes and the Secret Weapon* Moriarty was prevented only in the very nick of time from draining Holmes of every drop of blood. And so on. Only fragments of the original stories survived, and the art director must have used *Broken Blossoms* as a guide for the London settings, but what mattered was that Rathbone and Nigel Bruce were just about perfect as Holmes and Watson, while in support was to be found a repertory company of English expatriates including Henry Daniell, George Zucco, Reginald Denny, Lionel Atwill and Miles Mander. Yet another Universal series was *Inner Sanctum*, which disguised very poor mystery plots behind a rather splendid opening sequence narrated by a misshapen head inside a crystal ball on a boardroom table. Titles such as *Dead Men's Eyes*, *The Frozen Ghost* and *Weird Woman* gave a clue to the level, but the only real interest of these cheap-jack enterprises was to discover whether Lon Chaney would be hero or villain: he liked to alternate.

Very different in style from Universal's were the occult thrillers produced by Val Lewton for RKO. Some audiences could have found them too morbidly depressing, and a couple were banned until the late forties, while others had already impenetrable stories made even more obscure by senseless cuts. They usually found their way into double-bills at the Lido or The Theatre, and proved well above the heads of the average audience. They were simply too determined to be different. *Cat People*, though it boasted a couple of superb suspense sequences, refrained from showing its monsters; *Curse of the Cat People* had no monsters at all, being a fable about a child's imagination. (Lewton, it seems, was set on the story, and the studio was set on the title, so a mismatch was inevitable.) Anybody capable of explaining the plot line of *The Seventh Victim*, about devil

Author as Baby   My mother, at
44, introduces her afterthought to
the backyard of No 12 Parkfield
Road

Author Going Up in the World
In 1934, a garden to sit in at 166
Bradford Road

Author on Holiday   With mother
and two sisters (Edith and Lilian)
collecting heather at Point of
Ayre, 1935

Author on Holiday Again   With
father and mother in Douglas, Isle
of Man: to be precise, outside 18
Mount Havelock; probably 1936

The Queen's Cinema, Bolton   Site of the author's first encounter with the silver screen. The forward car on Station Hill stands close to the projection booth, the door of which was so often open. The photograph was taken in the sixties, but the fabric remained intact. The building has now been demolished, and the site serves as a car park

The Hippodrome Cinema, Bolton   Formerly, as the facade suggests, a music hall called the Empire and Hippodrome. Site of the author's first encounter with British low comedians. In 1940 it was taken over by the Lawrence-Williamson Repertory Company, and until its demolition in 1961 it remained 'the people's popular playhouse'

The Odeon Cinema, Bolton The town's most magnificent modern structure, seating 2,600 people; here photographed in 1937 during its first week of public performance. The attraction is *Dark Journey,* with Conrad Veidt and Vivien Leigh. The building is now closed except for bingo nights

The Odeon An interior view showing the modernistic décor (including clock), with colour-changing Compton organ and pictorial inner curtain

The Rialto Cinema, Bolton   It was backed by Bolton's poorest streets, but a little dignity was added by the *palais de danse* across the road and by the Co-op drapers next door. Here, in 1936, the double bill comprises *Gambling* and *Once in a Blue Moon*. The building still stands, but derelict

The Theatre Royal, Bolton   Its truly impressive interior was belied by its cramped and antique facade. The photograph seems to date from 1930, when the attraction was *Interference,* starring William Powell

The Lido Cinema, Bolton   Pictured during 1937 when it was in course of hasty erection. Visible through the girders is a garage workshop which was once (1907-16) a cinema called the Ideal

The Lido   An interior view which does not quite manage to include the Venetian scene on the proscenium frieze but gives an idea of the otherwise muddled décor. The Christie organ did not change colour but boasted a phantom piano attachment

Author as King Bolton School's 1946 production of *Hamlet* had me second-billed as Claudius (right). I always thought of the film connection when I spoke the line 'O my offence is Rank . . .'

Author as Editor *Varsity* rewarded me for seven terms of hard work, but I was happiest writing 'Next Week's Films'

Author as Sergeant But only in the Royal Army Education Corps. The stripes were valued as a means of escaping boots and rifle drill. The beret simply wouldn't stay on my head

Author as Groucho A 1951 college revue was the excuse for startling the chaplain and pulling the legs of a few dons

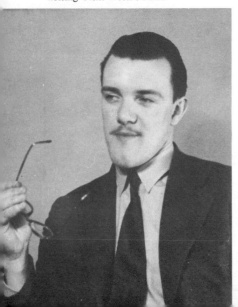

The Rex Cinema, Cambridge I never wanted to be reminded of the unaesthetic exterior. This photograph seems to have been taken in the late sixties, when the neon sign has fallen down and Miss Cleaver's pay box has been brought forward from the foyer to the main steps. The visible windows are the toilets, which never worked. But the stills cabinets have been renewed: George Webb probably put a penny on every seat to cover the cost

The Kinema, Cambridge Formerly Sturton Town Hall, and partly occupied (in the sixties, when this photograph was taken) by the Gladstone Liberal Club. The actual auditorium is a good fifty feet back: this facade merely covers the entrance to the pink-stuccoed passageway which came to be known as the Tunnel of Love

Author as Caricature This amusing drawing was started and finished within twenty minutes by an undergraduate friend whose name, alas, I can no longer remember. It should not be taken too seriously: even the Rex could not run on candle power

Author as Manager A cod photograph dreamed up for Varsity. Tuxedos were not *de rigueur* at the Rex

George Webb, Esquire Owner, dictator, and general handyman of the Rex. He was 33 at the time (repeat, 33), and the category board was almost the only aspect of the cinema which functioned efficiently

worshippers in Greenwich Village, would have won a lot of wagers in 1943. *I Walked with a Zombie* was a remake of Jane Eyre, set in the West Indies with some eerie moments but no real intent to frighten. And so on. By the time the studio forced Lewton to tell a straightforward story straightforwardly, in a version of R. L. Stevenson's *The Body Snatcher*, it was too late to recapture the lost audience, even with Karloff and Lugosi heading the cast, but being smartly upstaged by that superbly chilling actor Henry Daniell as the anatomist.

The most subtly chilling film I saw during the war had no more than an 'A' certificate and was basically a romance with supposedly genuine ghosts. *The Uninvited* starred Ray Milland and was set in a clifftop house in Hollywood's idea of Cornwall. It had a young girl possessed by the evil spirit of what was thought to be her father's mistress but was finally proved to be her own sinister mother. It sounded so unusual that I travelled to the Manchester Odeon to see it, and I was not disappointed, for it alternated a light touch with moments of genuine fright, and the mystery was unravelled with the aid of a character clearly modelled on Mrs Danvers in *Rebecca* and played by an American stage actress, Cornelia Otis Skinner, who for some reason I felt privileged to see on the screen, even though she was not very good. The national critics had unanimously congratulated the producers of *The Uninvited* for daring not to show the ghosts in some conventional misty way but to leave them to the viewers' imagination. Years later, when the film was shown on television from American prints, I discovered that the ghosts were in view, all right, and very frightening too: the British censor in 1944 had cut them out in order that *The Uninvited* might escape an 'H' certificate!

The original *Frankenstein* had still not come my way, nor

had there been any chance of my gaining admission to *Son of Frankenstein* when it played during 1939 on a three-cinema concurrency in Douglas. But I somehow got into a re-issue at the Regal in 1942, and found it to be an expensive-looking piece full of robust barnstorming from actors who are upstaged throughout by massive gothic sets. Honours were for once taken by Bela Lugosi as Ygor, the malevolent shepherd, who had been hung once already and can therefore have no further crime laid at his door. In one early scene the innocent young Frankensteins are returning by train to their gloomy inheritance. 'Just look, my dear,' cries the ubiquitous Basil Rathbone, drawing attention to a stunted and gnarled tree which is just passing by, 'at this depressing country, this warped vegetation.' Unfortunately the conversation carries on for another couple of minutes, during which time the same tree passes by at least three times on the studio's rotating cylinder.

One evening about a year later, Jimmie Beattie and I approached the Rialto rather tentatively and were admitted without question to a double-bill comprising the 1936 *Dracula's Daughter* (which has pleasant moments) and the 1935 *Bride of Frankenstein*, surely the finest horror film of them all. Designed by Englishmen in Hollywood as a diversion for a hot summer, it plays more as a black comedy with horror asides, and is narrated, in an eighteenth-century drawing-room during a stormy night, by Mary Shelley, explaining to her husband and to Lord Byron how a sequel to her famous tale might run if Frankenstein were blackmailed into creating a mate for his monster. My favourite scenes concern the skeletal Dr Praetorius, the baron's old teacher and evil genius, who can create mannikins of perfect proportion but has been defeated by size. A little grave-robbing is indicated, therefore, a fresh female corpse is unearthed, and the doctor's assistants demand their recompense since they very much wish to be off. The doctor's role was originally intended for Claude Rains, who would have had waspish fun with it without being able to top the actual performance of that animated gargoyle Ernest Thesiger (who in his spare time wrote books on embroidery). In this famous scene he pays off the men and glances around him. 'Oh, very well,' he says. 'I think I shall stay here for a while. I find the atmosphere congenial.'

Using a tomb slab for a table, piling up some bones and a skull to hold his candle, and humming a merry tune the while, he sets out his lunch: an apple, a packet of sandwiches, a bottle of gin. As he munches away happily, raising his glass to 'a new world of gods and monsters', the scene cuts to the mouldering churchyard above, where the misunderstood monster, having accidentally set fire to a blind hermit, is being pursued by the familiar pack of villagers with the inextinguishable flaming torches. Stumbling into an open grave, he finds himself in a series of low caverns, only a few steps behind the carousing doctor. We watch over the monster's shoulder as he ominously approaches his potential victim. The music wells up into heavy chords. It seems that the role of Praetorius has run its course when suddenly Mr Thesiger glances over his shoulder, recognizes his unexpected visitor, raises an eyebrow and says blithely: 'Oh. I thought I was alone. Would you like a cigar? They're my only weakness.'

In a supposed horror film, there can be no answer to that.

Eleven

There'll Always Be an England

The war did Hollywood no harm at all. Despite the closing off of enemy markets, movies amply repaid their costs by causing eager queues throughout a glamour-starved free world. A war also tends towards the raising of culture levels, because people feel the need to be inspired; and so, in addition to the dopey Betty Grable musicals and the idiotic anti-Nazi action melodramas, we were offered during those years the best comedies of Preston Sturges (and if I especially treasure the memory of *Sullivan's Travels* it may be because Veronica Lake was the first film star for whom I felt the pangs of adolescent love). John Ford impressed us with the power of *The Grapes of Wrath* and to a lesser extent *How Green Was My Valley*. Ernst Lubitsch raised period romance to a high level in *Heaven Can Wait* and brought off a bitter wartime farce in *To Be or Not to Be*, which had such magnificent running gags as 'So they call me Concentration Camp Ehrhardt?' In *The Maltese Falcon* and *Across the Pacific*, John Huston showed Hollywood new ways of making villainy fascinating; Humphrey Bogart and Sidney Greenstreet were in both, and Bogart followed these up as the romantic cynic Rick Blaine in *Casablanca*, sticking his neck out for nobody but doing the honourable thing in the end and setting out for an unknown future with the comic-villainous Vichy official ('Round up the usual suspects') played so superbly by Claude Rains. 'Louis,' says Bogart to him a little ambiguously, 'I think this is the beginning of a beautiful friendship.'

Ingrid Bergman, who co-starred in *Casablanca* along with Greenstreet and Peter Lorre and Conrad Veidt, provided throughout the war years the highest standards of beauty and intelligence, and her name alone was enough to draw immense queues to such disparate films as *For Whom the Bell Tolls*, *The Bells of St Mary's* and *The Murder in Thornton Square*, the last-named winning Oscars but seeming to me an overblown version of its British original, *Gaslight*, in which Anton Walbrook as the mad husband had chilled my blood. There was Somerset Maugham's mordant *The Moon and Sixpence*, and a visually satisfying film version (by William Wyler) of his short story *The Letter*. Wyler also made memorable films of Emily Brontë's *Wuthering Heights* and Lillian Hellman's *The Little Foxes*; he never seemed happy without a sound literary basis. Billy Wilder, on the other hand, rose to the fore with cynical modern classics like *Double Indemnity* and *The Lost Weekend*; while the overpowering melodrama of Henry Bellamann's *King's Row* was brought to the screen in a version stunningly designed by William Cameron Menzies. (As the publicity claimed, it 'made no concessions to nitwits'.) And of course there was *Gone with the Wind*, which opened in Bolton three years after its London première but proceeded to run for twelve incredible months.

One week I was vastly intrigued at the Lido by a trailer in which a young man named Orson Welles, surrounded by chorus girls and unfamiliar actors, stood by a piano and assured us that his film *Citizen Kane* was well worth seeing even though the girls were there only for the purpose of 'ballyhoo'. However, when on the Tuesday of the follow-

ing week I expectantly turned up with my fourpence at the
ready, it was to find that the film had been taken off after a
disastrous Monday, and it took me ten years to catch up
with it. Perhaps *Kane* was too strong a medicine for a time
when Frank Capra was still sentimentally celebrating the
common man in *Mr Smith Goes to Washington* and *Meet
John Doe*; but on our way through London to see my sister
Mum and I did catch up with another milestone in our
cinematic education. This was Walt Disney's animated
concert *Fantasia*, for which we occupied one-and-tenpenny
seats at the New Gallery; it seemed cheap at the price. Back
in Bolton our sights were kept high by the ladylike Greer
Garson, who after playing Mrs Miniver was *Mrs Parking-
ton* and *Madame Curie*, without even bothering to change
her diction. It was quite a shock when in *Random Harvest*,
while helping Ronald Colman get his memory back, she
donned a short kilt and did an impersonation of Harry
Lauder. Whatever Bette Davis chose to do invariably
caused long queues; the pity was that so much of it was
pitched at soap opera level. However, even I had to admit
the power of *Now Voyager*, with its Walt Whitman quotation, its ugly duckling turning into a swan, its trick of two
cigarettes lit at once, and its final line of romantic sacrifice:
'Oh, Jerry, don't let's ask for the moon, we have the stars.'

All these films had a grain of adult seriousness and truth,
and I had now reached an age at which I was capable of
appreciating them. I took their points at first acquaintance.
Perhaps later on I understood them even better, but I
already sensed that I was living through a golden age of
cinema, a time when filmgoing had become an occupation
not merely to pass an evening but to stimulate the mind. My
general knowledge came to be constructed almost entirely
from the subjects of films that interested me. Not that mere
frivolity was in short supply: quite the contrary. Deanna

Durbin was still Little Miss Fix-it who burst into song at Universal's command, and Judy Garland fulfilled the same function for MGM. All-star musicals were in vogue: *Star Spangled Rhythm* and *Thank Your Lucky Stars* were especially enjoyable since they spoofed Paramount and Warner Brothers respectively, and were mostly shot inside the studios. At Fox, Alice Faye, Carmen Miranda and Betty Grable held sway; Eddie Cantor and Joan Davis gave us a whiff of vaudeville in *Show Business* from RKO, the studio which was nurturing Frank Sinatra; and Jimmy Cagney had the time of his life playing George M. Cohan in *Yankee Doodle Dandy*, while Errol Flynn buckled his swash in *The Sea Hawk*. Comedians, too, came at us by the carload. Bob Hope was at his peak in comedy-thrillers like *The Cat and the Canary*, and teamed with Bing Crosby and Dorothy Lamour for the *Road* films. Abbott and Costello were top box-office throughout the war period; Danny Kaye was a bright new star who seemed to possess all the talents; Olsen and Johnson had a hit in *Hellzapoppin*; the Ritz Brothers were still clowning around. Fantasies proliferated, from *The Wizard of Oz* to *Topper Returns*. They were great years for Hollywood, and good, too, for a maturing film-goer in an industrial landscape on the other side of the Atlantic.

The blossoming of British films was equally remarkable. About a year into the war, we all began to realize that something was happening. For one thing, the words *A British Picture* started to appear in large type on the Odeon showcards which hung in Mrs Wood's chip shop. In pre-war years that would not have been an inducement, for the vast majority of British films had been stiffly artificial, their unreal and posh-talking characters bathed in a silvery hotel-bedroom gleam by directors who had scarcely learned the grammar of their profession. There were reasons, or excuses, for this. Since World War I the Americans had maintained a stranglehold on world film production, and although they expected to sell their films abroad they refused to buy British films in return, preferring to lure the best British talent over to Hollywood and Americanize it. British producers could not afford to spend big sums of money because they had no export market; their costs had to be earned at home. Since 1934 Britain had indeed been producing as many as two hundred features a year, but in the main these were second features, 'quota quickies' bred of short-sighted government legislation to ensure full employment in the industry by insisting that exhibitors show a high proportion of British product without regard to its quality. Indeed, however bad a British film might be, these laws gave it a money-back guarantee. It was small wonder, therefore, that few local producers aimed even as high as competence. Many came into the studios with the intention of marketing films just as they would have marketed soap; which was one reason why Alfred Hitchcock put *Jamaica Inn* behind him in 1939 and sailed for Hollywood and a fat Selznick contract. We minded not a whit, since the mesmerizing *Rebecca* (which played two whole weeks at the Lido) was the first result.

But there are exceptions to every rule. Low comedy deriving from the music-halls had often been presented with vigour and skill; directors like Walter Forde and Marcel Varnel knew the tricks of this particular trade. Victor Saville produced a few solid, sincere entertainments: *The Good Companions*, *Friday the Thirteenth*, *South Riding* and the Jessie Matthews musicals. Herbert Wilcox's meaty if often unimaginative biographies were carefully mounted as showcases for Anna Neagle, his wife-to-be. MGM's short-lived British studio produced three international winners in *Goodbye, Mr Chips*, *The Citadel* and *A Yank at Oxford*, before the war put paid to the venture. Alexander Korda was the great enigma, a Hungarian who used other Hungarians to make superior British films, and did not always bother to put his name on the films he financed or otherwise arranged, despite the fact that it meant almost as much to the public as the stars he created. *The Private Life of Henry VIII*, *The Scarlet Pimpernel*, *The Four Feathers*, *The Thief of Baghdad*, *Rembrandt* were just a few of his unchallengeable masterpieces, though he made some stinkers too. A combination of native genius, cosmopolitan cunning, organizing ability, creative vision and abject foolhardiness, he left many fascinating projects unrealized when in 1940, for controversial reasons, he was driven to Hollywood along with such continental stars of British films as Elizabeth Bergner and Conrad Veidt.

Each of these producers had his own coterie of talent, outside which there was little chance for young directors to learn their craft, let alone make a mark. Thorold Dickinson, Carol Reed, David Lean, Anthony Asquith were all working in the thirties, but their light was hidden under a bushel. Documentaries were the best training ground, but I saw far more of these at school than in a cinema, which suggests that the producers of feature films may never have seen them at all. Oddly enough the war brought the documentary movement into sharp focus, every Odeon programme being suddenly filled with snippets labelled *Do It Now*, *Food Facts*, or *What to Do If the Germans Come*. They gave opportunity to film-makers with visual imagination, who could make dramatic points without expensive sets. For example, a little piece called *Miss Grant Goes to the Door* was directed by Brian Desmond Hurst and ran six minutes. In that time it told an entertaining little spy story which, forty years later, still provides vivid sidelights on

Britain at war; the immobilization of motor cars, observation of the blackout, not grumbling about the food ration, spotting enemy planes, and listening for strange accents which might give away a German parachutist.

Some of the official documentaries, which gradually aspired to feature length, became classics: *Western Approaches*, *Desert Victory*, *San Demetrio, London* and *The True Glory* were studied and appreciated by cinéastes the world over, while Humphrey Jennings in *Listen to Britain* and *Fires Were Started* brought to the cinema a form of poetry. More to the immediate propaganda point, a ten-minute film called *London Can Take It*, showing the city under the blitz and powerfully narrated by an American, Quentin Reynolds, was credited with helping to bring the United States into the war. It was these suddenly revealed skills of documentary observation, coupled with a realization of traditional English values and the need for all classes to fight the war side by side, which within twelve months earned for British films an unprecedented and totally unexpected place in world-wide esteem. Fiction films had already begun to use real backgrounds. *Turn of the Tide* described lobster fishing; *The Edge of the World* concerned itself with life on the remote Scottish island of Foula; sheepdog trials figured largely in *Owd Bob*; coal mining was the subject of *The Stars Look Down* and *The Proud Valley*. As the war got under way, Ealing Studios were planning *Convoy*, a tribute to the Royal and Merchant Navies, and John Baxter, who in 1932 had made *Doss House*, was busying himself with what turned out to be a commendably raw and urgent version of *Love on the Dole*. (In Bolton we queued for it because it was set just down the Manchester road and might well have been photographed in the dingy cobbled streets surrounding the Textile where my father worked.) Korda's propaganda feature *The Lion*

Has Wings, on the other hand, was a sad look-back to the bad old class-ridden and stilted days of British film-making, its one effective scene being Flora Robson's Tilbury speech lifted from the 1937 swashbuckler *Fire Over England*.

What we now noticed about the new British films was that we were being made to look at ourselves in a fresh way. In them the spirit of wartime Britain still comes to life, though when analysed in the cold cynical light of later years they can be seen to have glaring deficiencies of content and characterization as well as technique. Classical music is often spread over them like a universal pacifier, and the famous British stiff upper lip is grossly overworked. The strains of command, and the natural humour of the working classes, were familiarized until they bred contempt. But after years of muddling through, the British at last had a cause and a leader, and this was what showed and what mattered. These films told us what we were fighting for and made us care about it.

Once started, the parade of famous titles kept coming. *The Next of Kin*, intended as an army training film, dramatically demonstrated the dangers of careless talk. *The Lamp Still Burns* doubled as a recruiting poster for the nursing profession. *Millions Like Us* took audiences into the factory assembly lines. *This Happy Breed* and *Salute John Citizen* explored life in the suburbs. *The Bells Go Down* eulogized the London firemen who fought the blitz. *49th Parallel*, under cover of an exciting chase story, showed us how Canada viewed the war. *In Which We Serve* (for which Noël Coward was writer, star, producer, director and composer) fictionalized the sinking of a ship under Mountbatten's command, and treated all hands as of equal importance. Aircraft carriers were treated in *Ships with Wings*, escape through the Dutch underground in *One of Our Aircraft is Missing*, the Polish air force squadron (with a background of the 'Warsaw Concerto') in *Dangerous Moonlight*. *The Big Blockade* was an all-star semi-documentary, *A Yank in the RAF* morale-boosting pulp fiction. *We Dive at Dawn* was about submarines, *The Gentle Sex* about the women's army, *Tawny Pipit* (just to show that the British had not lost their spirit of gentle self-mockery) about the fuss over a pair of rare birds nesting near an English village. What might have to happen if the Germans should invade just such a village was shown with surprising savagery in *Went the Day Well?*. *The Way Ahead* followed the fortunes of nine raw recruits from enlistment in the army to their first taste of fire in North Africa. Finally in 1945 came the dying fall of *The Way to the Stars*, a film about the British and US air forces in which scarcely a plane was seen, though the daily concern among the women at the hotel near Ha'penny Field was whether their men would come back. One who didn't return (Michael Redgrave) left a poem instead, and for months almost everyone you met could recite it:

> Do not despair
> For Johnny Head-in-air;
> He sleeps as sound
> As Johnny under ground.
> Fetch out no shroud.
> For Johnny-in-the-cloud;
> Best keep your head
> And see his children fed.

The keynote of the film however, was perhaps not John Pudney's verses but a line which before the war would have been unthinkable: 'You Americans and English, you're all the same.'

The new impetus which created these war films had its effect also on the more obviously escapist material. As early as 1939 Carol Reed, in Hitchcock's shadow, was working on a cracking comedy-thriller called *Gestapo*, which was released as *Night Train to Munich*; and Thorold Dickinson started off the trend for period nostalgia with *Gaslight*. Others in the latter vein were Reed's *Kipps*; Dickinson's *The Prime Minister* (with John Gielgud as Disraeli); Wilfred Lawson as *The Great Mr Handel*; and the notorious Gainsborough melodramas from *The Man in Grey* through *Fanny by Gaslight* to *The Wicked Lady*.

But there were some more thoughtful pieces which had reference to wartime discontents. The Boulting brothers gave us *Pastor Hall*, about the refugee priest Niemöller, and *Thunder Rock* which, through a ghostly maritime fable, warned of the dangers of isolationism. *The First of the Few*, a biography of R. J. Mitchell who invented the Spitfire, had a long sequence about how the rest of Europe had preferred not to notice that Germany was re-arming. There was iron propaganda, too, beneath the deceptive lightheartedness of *Pimpernel Smith*, in which Leslie Howard transposed Baroness Orczy's fiction to Germany under Hitler, and gave us as a modern Chauvelin a Gestapo buffoon who was trying desperately to understand the British sense of humour. Powell and Pressburger's *The Life and Death of Colonel Blimp* was a self-mocking epic which Winston Churchill tried to suppress because it had a good German as hero.* In fact, the upper-class British general played by Roger Livesey, even in his absurdity, seemed

---

*Powell and Pressburger, who called themselves the Archers, had a curious partiality for stories in which the British were bested by superior Germans or Austrians. Thus the use of Anton Walbrook in this film, in *The Red Shoes* and in *Oh, Rosalinda*; the nobility of Langsdorff in *The Battle of the River Plate*; the cleverness of the German general in *Ill Met by Moonlight*; the superiority of Conrad Veidt in *Contraband*, Eric Portman in *49th Parallel* (although he was bested by Raymond Massey's 'freedom' speech), and Esmond Knight in *The Silver Fleet*. Oddly enough, nobody seemed to notice while the war was on.

more lovable in the end.

By the war's end no purely patriotic reason need be sought for watching a British film: Powell and Pressburger's *A Matter of Life and Death* was spectacular Hollywood moonshine with a welcome dash of vinegar; *Dead of Night* offered four intelligent ghost stories in a classy binding, while *Henry V* was the most instructive and delightful treatment of Shakespeare yet seen, and its transition to stark reality for the Battle of Agincourt was breathtaking. British films had reached maturity, and I felt I had done so along with them. My notebooks reinforced this impression. 'Excellent entertainment with a moral, and made at little cost,' I wrote of *Waterloo Road*. 'It is a pleasure to come upon a British picture which is so technically competent and correct in its minute detail,' was my view of *A Place of One's Own*. As for *Blithe Spirit*, I considered that 'although the film is essentially a photographed play, camera and dialogue are used to such effect that this passes almost unnoticed'. I was generous to American films, too. *The Woman in the Window* was 'a superlative thriller, taut as a wire, with skilled dialogue and skilled direction'. *A Tree Grows in Brooklyn*, I thought, 'abandons glamour and action to tell a real human story with obvious sincerity, allowing of course for freer American self-expression'. 'Besides being rattling good melodrama,' I opined of *The Picture of Dorian Gray*, 'the story has a strong moral sense and provides plenty to think about.'

All these activities were taking place while I was working my way up the academic ladder. As I reached the fifth form my earlier feelings of being a misfit seemed to evaporate. I was taking an active part in several after-school societies, and was virtually assistant producer of the school play. The producer was the senior English master, an unassuming chap called Frank Greene, who usually walked into town with me through Queen's Park and after a series of intense conversations fixed my sights on a university scholarship. At first I thought the idea absurd, but he made it seem sensible. If a boy from the wrong side of the tracks had contrived to win a scholarship to Bolton School, why should he not repeat the pattern and go to Oxford or Cambridge?

I gave in, and Frank Greene arranged everything, in the autumn of 1946. I was lucky at my third attempt, but before I could take up this new challenge I would have to suffer two years of national service; before then, while continuing to help the family by doing part-time jobs (usually in the Post Office or on the buses) I was determined to enjoy my last few months of liberty.

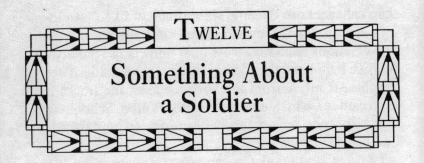

TWELVE

Something About a Soldier

Now the cinema had to share my time with other activities. I joined Bolton Little Theatre and played a number of small but lively parts, from a blackamoor slave in *Spring 1600* to a fawning courtier ('You amaze me, ladies') in *As You Like It*. My hour of glory was as the March Hare in *Alice in Wonderland*; for this I adopted a maniacal chuckle which was alleged to have perforated a few eardrums. For another amateur group I had the gall to play the leading role of eccentric 76-year-old Martin Vanderhof in Kaufman and Hart's *You Can't Take It With You*. Heaven knows how I got away with that final dinner table prayer which had even foxed Lionel Barrymore in the film version:

Well, sir, here we are again. We want to say thanks once more for everything you've done for us. Things seem to be going along just fine. Alice is going to marry Tony, and it looks as though they're going to be very happy. Of course, the fireworks blew up, but that was Mr De Pinna's fault, not yours. We've all got our health, and as far as anything else is concerned, we'll leave it up to you. Thank you.

For St Mark's Church I staged a Victorian music-hall, played the extremely boozy chairman, and sang a rude song or two. These were also my big years in the school play. For the part of Bolingbroke in *Richard II* I wore a fine swashbuckling purple cloak, and coped as well as I could with that impossible final couplet:

> March sadly after; grace my mourning here
> With weeping after this untimely bier.

(At each and every rehearsal the assembled cast would then sing in unison 'Beer, beer, glorious beer', which made it difficult to get through the first night with a straight face.) Irving Wardle, now dramatic critic of *The Times*, was the ill-fated king, and in the following year I was Claudius to his Hamlet. We had an argument then as to which of us in our final death throes should be allowed to roll down the throne steps; I won by the spin of a coin, and on most nights contrived to have my crown roll off and fall into the orchestra pit, which brought the audience aghast to its feet.

This theatrical activity led me into a spate of theatre-going. The Hippodrome repertory company was still thriving on its diet of *Moonlight is Silver, Autumn, Living Dangerously, The Sign on the Door, Young Woodley, Seven Keys to Baldpate, The Queen Was in the Parlour, The Naughty Wife, Daddy Long Legs, Outward Bound, Berkeley Square* and *Dangerous Corner*; but Jimmie Beattie and I were now also venturing regularly to the Manchester Opera House, where Ralph Richardson was a frequent visitor in such plays as *Royal Circle* by Romilly Cavan; and on one later occasion we found ourselves sitting behind Laurence Olivier as he watched Vivien Leigh play Blanche in the European première of *A Streetcar Named Desire*, which widened our horizons with a vengeance.

My holidays at this time tended to be informal affairs, since the government was still encouraging people to spend them at home. Walking on the moors (Auntie Flo had a favourite route known locally as The Jumbles); taking day trips to Blackpool and coming home late after the pictures;

venturing by bus as far as the Brontë house at Haworth (on which occasion I twisted an ankle on Saddleworth Moor and had to spend a night in a cell at Todmorden Police Station); cycling to Southport or Chester; and planning days among the fleshpots of Manchester, ostensibly to study in the John Rylands Library but more truthfully with second-hand bookshops and cinemas in mind. (One programme at the Gaumont stands out: Paulette Goddard in *Standing Room Only*, Johnny Weissmuller in *Tarzan's Desert Mystery*, and the news on the giant screen.) I even attended a school farm camp, which my family thought a tremendous joke as they did not normally associate me with hard labour. It poured with rain, and we spent three days in the pig styes, playing pontoon for halfpennies. Twice a week I would struggle into Kirkham, the local town, and see whatever was on at the Co-op Cinema (the only one I have come across to be owned by that well-intentioned but joyless body). One of its programmes was strangely ill-constituted, comprising two indifferent romantic comedies each starring Fredric March: *There Goes My Heart* and *Trade Winds*.

The highlights of the summers of 1944 and 1945 had been visits to the Worcestershire parish of the ex-vicar of St Mark's who, having prepared me for confirmation, taken me to sex lectures in the town hall, and introduced me to the ghost stories of M. R. James, forsook us for the hilltop church of Areley Kings, on a hill overlooking the Severn. It was my first experience not only of the gentler English countryside but of a house two hundred years old; I saw a ghost in the latter and became a lover of old churches, winding lanes, country driving and unexpected views. The cinema, however, was not forgotten. In nearby Stourport-on-Severn lived a suburbanite who had converted his ample garage into a tiny 16mm cinema. For a modest fee one could ring up and book a comfortable seat, and the projection standards were impeccable. The whole arrangement filled me with envy when I was taken along to enjoy Tom and Jerry, Our Gang, and Spencer Tracy in *The Seventh Cross*.

The years immediately after the war were a watershed for Hollywood, marking the last fling of the big studios. Disillusionment after the war had something to do with it: romances and melodramas were filled with war veterans who had been shabbily treated by society, and this led less typically to the inspirational mood which ended William Wyler's *The Best Years of our Lives* than to the cynicism and squalor of the *film noir* cycle, as instanced by *Kiss of Death, The Big Sleep*, and *Dead Reckoning*. There was a longish hangover period when the stockpile of war films kept on being released to diminishing returns, and some unexpectedly delightful months in 1947 when a Board of Trade embargo on imports brought forth a flood of grade-A re-issues, often in delightful double-bills. Meanwhile we were welcoming back ex-service stars such as David Niven and James Stewart and Robert Taylor, wallowing in bright comedies which no longer hinged on restrictions or soldiers chasing girls, and exchanging evil Nazi villains for devious communist ones.

The most successful movies of 1946, so far as Bolton was concerned, were in the pre-war tradition of slick, hard-hitting entertainment: *Wonder Man, The Spiral Staircase, The Jolson Story*. I adored *The Jolson Story*. I had not been expecting too much: the critics considered it beneath them, Jolson himself did not appear in it, the cast was virtually unknown, and Columbia had declined into a cheap studio relying on fifth-rate hokum. But I pottered along to the Rialto, which was showing the film in concurrency with the Queen's, and slipped into my seat about twenty minutes

from the end of the first house, just as Larry Parks and
Evelyn Keyes were singing and dancing 'Around a Quarter
to Nine'. I immediately liked the low-key style, the discreet
sentiment, and the off-beat ending, and by the time I had
seen it through again, and listened to Jolson's voice singing
thirty-odd songs, it was already among my favourite films
despite the show-business clichés, of which it is a veritable
compendium. I was not alone: word-of-mouth made it an
enormous hit, and it was held over for a second week,
during which of course I went again and learned the words
of some of the choruses. Over the next couple of years I saw
it six or seven more times: in Bury, in Yeovil, in Salisbury,
in Glasgow, and back in Bolton again when I took my
mother to see and enjoy it at the Tivoli. And in every case I
had to queue to get in.

During the late spring of 1946, my father came home
from a Co-op meeting and rather uncharacteristically chatted over supper about the evening's agenda. Among the
national events to which his committee had been invited to
send a representative, it seemed, was something called a
Film Study Course at the Co-operative College near
Loughborough. My ears pricked up. The Committee had
not thought the matter important enough to warrant a
reply, but five minutes later Dad was promising to recom-
mend me as Bolton's delegate. Much to my surprise the
scheme worked, and I spent a delirious week that summer
at Stanford Hall, a sort of small-scale Xanadu, once the
property of industrial millionaire Sir Julien Cahn. There
was a gadget-filled gymnasium in the attic, and a lion pit in
the grounds. The bathrooms had sunken marble tubs, and
hand-carved mirrors adorned the bedroom walls and ceilings. Three hundred people could be seated in the luxurious private theatre, which possessed a brand new projection suite and everything backstage that a master showman

could desire. Since the takeover, however, the spirit of the Co-op had cast a pall over the place: the food and service were of Lyons' Tea House standard, and my fellow delegates did not boast a cinéaste amongst them. I shared the King Charles Room, for instance, with an elderly greengrocer from Walsall and a communist engineer from Huddersfield. We got along pretty well, since neither knew the first thing about films and I was more than pleased to enlighten them, whether between sessions, in bed, or during an unexpected game of croquet. There were lectures every morning by distinguished guests. Paul Rotha came along, and Miles Malleson, and Dilys Powell, who signed my current Amusement Guide and talked for a long evening about 'The Film as a Narrative Art', taking her illustrations from *They Knew What They Wanted* (in which Charles Laughton made a very fanciful shot at an Italian accent). On five out of six evenings there was a film show: *Henry V, The Blue Angel* (at last!), *Land of Promise*, the British Film Institute's documentary compilation *Film and Reality*, and an exceptionally boring parade of silent avantgarde experiments. On my return to Bolton I gave a lecture about it all to the Co-operative Men's Guild, who kept heckling me about the cinema's contribution to juvenile delinquency. I also wrote a report for my father's committee, but whether anybody read it seems doubtful.*

June 1947, when I was due to report for army duty, was looming on the horizon. It was to be the end of my regular

---

*Busy as I was in 1945 and 1946, I also found time to sit for several university examinations. In Oxford I was attacked by a bat in a Magdalen cloister, which put me right off. In Cambridge on a chill December night I felt very lonely indeed, having been allocated in Jesus College an unheated room with bars on the windows and a grate in which there was coal and paper but no wood. Next day I spent six hours writing on unlined paper at the very furthest desk from the solitary fire. I had not been quite so uncomfortable during the whole of Bolton's war.

contact with Bolton's cinemas, but I continued to keep an eye on them from afar. They dutifully followed the pattern set by the rest of the country, their decline being accelerated by the advent of television. Their décor got tattier and their seats less and less reliable; this was the age of post-war austerity, and by the time their owners were permitted to renovate them, they could no longer afford to. The only remarkable event of these years was that our dingy Empire, the notorious fleapit off the Blackburn Road, was taken over by a Pole with advanced ideas. He had recently opened a continental cinema in Preston, and now the *Bolton Evening News* announced, in tones of some surprise and to the accompaniment of muted trumpets, that next week at the Empire the attraction would be Marcel Carné's *Les Enfants du Paradis*, and that other subtitled films would follow. I remember being slightly irked, as I had recently paid four shillings to see *Les Enfants* at the Manchester Deansgate, and the Empire's prices were fourpence to one-and-three. Naturally, in a spirit of moral support, I went again, and found the projection pretty good and the audience most congenial (which was not surprising, since it consisted almost entirely of masters and mistresses from the secondary schools, plus a sprinkling of journalists). During the next few weeks the Empire allowed me to catch up with *La Fille du Puisatier*, *Quai des Orfèvres*, *La Femme du Boulanger*, *Frou Frou* and *Les Visiteurs du Soir*. Down at the front we could usually see up to a dozen bemused locals and sometimes their kids; we held our breath at times lest they should grow restive and start to wreck the joint, but only once, during the long-drawn-out climax of *Les Portes de la Nuit*, when Serge Reggiani walks endlessly to his death along the railway line, was there a mass exodus, and that was dignified and silent enough. I went off on holiday reluctantly, feeling that the Empire would miss my support. When I returned ten days later I heard at once that the Pole had gone bankrupt, and that the Empire's new management was offering an array of irresistible re-issues, including *Devil on Wheels, One Night in the Tropics*, and *Old Mother Riley's Circus*.

Ironically, after eighteen years of strait-laced Sundays devoted to church and homework, I left Bolton just as the Sunday licensing of cinemas came in. The proprietors, alas, treated the much coveted permission when they got it as a means of making a fast buck. Separate Sunday programmes consisting of whatever re-issue prints happened to be available were booked in at the cheapest of flat rates (as opposed to the normal weekday programmes which were charged at a proportion of the box-office take). I felt a little cheated; on the other hand there were plenty of re-issues which I would want to see. But the only Sunday show I recall seeing in Bolton, at the Odeon, was a very curious one indeed, both films having been dredged from the vaults of RKO. There was *Farewell My Lovely*, a fairly new film (1944) by Sunday standards and a good one, with crooner Dick Powell taking over a tough guy role as Raymond Chandler's private eye Philip Marlowe. In support was an older RKO film, *The Falcon Takes Over*, with Tom Conway, the brother of George Sanders who had previously also played The Falcon. What the distributor had failed to notice, however, was that this was also based on the same Chandler book, so that as the evening wore on we were subjected, even though the names were different, to two Marlowes, two Veldas, and two Moose Malloys; but out of more than a thousand people I believe I was the only one who noticed. At any rate, nobody around me seemed able to understand why I was laughing so hysterically.

I was then weedy, long-chinned and bespectacled: not a good bet for the army. I was all for doing my duty, but roughing it has never been in my line, and although in theory a simple, healthy, regimented life has its attractions, it would have needed to offer more in the way of physical compensation than was available at Bury Barracks, home of the Lancashire Fusiliers and the scene of my primary training. I hated every minute. Not that the routine was harsh: indeed, during the first six weeks we were allowed, if we wished, to go home for supper. But half a day within the blackened walls told me that it was going to be an alien world, and my uniform seemed to symbolize this. When I presented myself at our front door in a massive greatcoat that seemed to weigh a ton, and a floppy beret which refused to stay on my knobbly head, my mother took one glance and burst into tears.

In army life, I quickly found, three items were stressed too heavily: rifle-cleaning, boot-and-button polishing, and drill. So I needed no encouragement at all to lighten my load by becoming what the army called a skiver (or malingerer). Through a childish habit of tying my shoelaces too tightly, I had acquired early in life two little lumps of hard skin, like mild warts, on the upper part of my feet. Consulting the Medical Officer, I informed him soberly that these very tender protruberances must have been caused by the wearing of army boots. The MO was a vacuous-looking young man, like the vicar in *Dad's Army*. He studied my feet in bewilderment, prodded the lumps once or twice, and seemed satisfied when I winced. (All that amateur acting!) He put me on light duties only, which meant helping in the library, and said I should not wear boots again for the time being. He even gave me a chitty to this effect: I was the envy of the entire platoon. However, after a week of comparative bliss the MO called me back to say that he had consulted with a colleague who was familiar with my condition, and who thought that the lumps should be surgically removed. I reminded him that within three weeks I would be moving on. He nodded sagely and gave me a note for the MO at my next camp, where I would have a longer stay. I smiled obediently while already planning my next set of delaying tactics.

The Personnel Selection Officer asked me what I wanted to do in the army. I diffidently mentioned Intelligence, but he only smiled and shook his head, which I took as an implied insult. He said they needed drivers. I pursed my lips: it would be a useful skill to acquire, but I could not see myself grubbing about in a truck's insides. 'Of course,' he added, 'the other thing we need, as you've no doubt noticed, is Education.' I had indeed noticed. The great surprise of my first day in the army was that half my platoon was incapable of writing home on the stamped postcard provided. Some were even incapable of writing their own names, though all had presumably attended school until the regulation age of fourteen. Unable to resolve this contradiction, I accepted the PSO's suggestion with genuine fervour, especially since it meant that, after the next eight-week period of corps training, I would hand in my rifle and boots for ever.

Bury's chief claim to fame is as the home of black puddings, which consist of blood, brains and other offal, and are best eaten boiled with as much hot mustard as the palate will stand. In 1947 it was among the grimmest blots on the Lancashire landscape, a ragbag of rough streets converging on a triangular junction and market place called the Rock. Its only conceivable merit was that per head of population it boasted more than its due share of cinemas, and although for the most part undeniably scruffy, they reflected life at a somewhat higher level than did the army barracks. It was in a draughty old barn called the Palace that I caught up at last with *The Old Dark House*, which lighted my life at least momentarily. I was already subscribing to the British Film Institute's *Monthly Film Bulletin*, whose reviewer had held the re-issue at arm's length as though it bore a bad smell: 'an unpleasant thriller which had been better left in the vaults from which it was resurrected'. That taught me never to trust reviewers, for here, apart from a couple of soppy romantic moments, was a splendidly consistent sardonic comedy grouping together half a dozen eccentrics on a stormy night in a Welsh madhouse. According to J. B. Priestley, who wrote the original novel in 1929, the Femms stand for various types of post-war pessimism, and some of this still percolates through a minor classic made at one of the more commercial Hollywood studios by a clique of slightly mad Englishmen. I walked back through the drizzle to my billet, practising the while Eva Moore's dismaying shriek: 'No beds! They can't have beds!'*

It was not easy to enjoy films in Bury: the place seemed to taint them. At the clean but boring new Odeon, oddly constructed to face into a maze of back streets, I sat glumly through the Ealing version of *Nicholas Nickleby*, which later seemed to me full of good points. According to my notebooks, I only mildly enjoyed Hitchcock's smooth and cunning *Notorious*. Betty Grable's *The Shocking Miss Pilgrim*, in which she played a turn-of-the-century typewriter (*sic*), seemed tame indeed. A friend and I spent one

---

* The Old Dark House immediately assumed a place towards the bottom of my 'top twenty', and something went out of my life a few years later when it could no longer be shown because the literary rights had lapsed. When, in 1982, I began to buy films for Channel Four I negotiated its British television première; but meanwhile something had happened to the negative, and it seems that *The Old Dark House* can never again be seen in a print which glows so beautifully and with such satisfying depth, turning faces into gargoyles and shadowed corners into areas of tingling terror, as the one I saw, and saw again, in Bury in June 1947.

desperate evening in search of a remote fleapit which was allegedly showing Paul Muni and Claude Rains in *Angel on My Shoulder*, but finished up catching instead the last performance of Disney's utterly unlikeable *Song of the South* at a musty museum-like hall called the Art, which seemed to have been frozen in time between 1898 and 1914. Aspidistras dotted the auditorium, the heavy velvet drapes smelled of mothballs, and there was, uniquely for that time, a strict policy of separate shows at 6.15 and 8.30.

After Bury, our next posting for corps training was Park Hall Camp near Oswestry. The camp routine was not exactly arduous, at least not for those with curious lumps on their feet. These afforded me a couple of trips to Chester Military Hospital, where I was able to defer the prospect of an operation by assuring all concerned that the mysterious molehills were responding well to my 'excused boots' treatment. As a celebration of my success I went to see Ronald Reagan in a long, dull film called *Stallion Road*, in which an outbreak of anthrax was narrowly averted in time for the regulation happy ending.*

Back at base, the army did its best for new recruits by providing compulsory sport and religion along with weekend dances and free contraceptives. I was shocked when I discovered that the latter items were freely available in the little hut by the guardroom; but the idea of sport was even more repellent. The Oswestry cinemas involved a two-mile walk each way. Even so, on my first spare Sunday

---

*The supporting feature was a British re-issue called *Thursday's Child* which had a fairly good critical reputation at one time for being rather more sensitive than the usual run of family dramas. But in 1947 I was not impressed; according to my notebooks: 'It is surprising that this film was made as recently as 1942, because it creaks considerably in most respects – one of those cheap products which the British film industry is now trying hard to forget.'

I marched off in eager anticipation to see Will Hay in the five-year-old *The Black Sheep of Whitehall*, but was disgusted to find the print so cut about, with barely a sentence left intact, that it ran only fifty-four minutes instead of the expected seventy-two. Incensed, I made a formal complaint to the manager, but he seemed less than interested: 'What do you expect on a Sunday night?'

I felt very homesick at Oswestry, and in a curious way that made me more assertive and adventurous in my picture-going: eccentric, even, in my choice of a nuthatch picture called *The Chase*, with Michele Morgan, Peter Lorre and Robert Cummings, none of whom seemed to have any idea what it was about; effete in the case of *The Man Within*, which tried to make a period action melodrama out of a Graham Greene novel about a novice smuggler (Richard Attenborough) who betrays his captain in a fit of spite, and lives to regret it. (Even the one-line synopsis sounds boring.) However I did enjoy an all-star MGM musical called *Till the Clouds Roll By*, and Herbert Lom as twins in a circus melodrama, *Dual Alibi*. I made half-day trips to the picture palaces of Shrewsbury, Wrexham and Welshpool. Rough-hewn army ways could make one more than usually grateful for the comfort and luxury which a well-run cinema provided in those days. It was the next best thing to home. I rejoiced in the familiar nationwide smells of ABC's rubber flooring and Gaumont's thick carpets, in the smoke extraction and the foam-filled seats; while it was reassuring to know that the same trailers, the same ice-cream advertisements, the same newsreels would also be playing in Bolton very shortly, and taking a little of me home with them. In retrospect, however, such thoughts seem more than a little ridiculous, since by hook or by crook I managed to get back to Bolton every second weekend. If I could neither afford the fare nor fiddle a travel warrant, there was always the upraised thumb, which might get me there quickest of all, although I once began the journey in a milk float and finished it learning to drive a horse and cart.

On one of these fleeting visits my heart missed a beat when I learned that Laurel and Hardy, in person, were coming to Bolton as part of a British music-hall tour. I promptly wrote to them for an interview, which Stan most obligingly granted, and the red-letter day was fixed for a Saturday three weeks ahead. I had visions of a respected *Sight and Sound* article which would cause Stan and Ollie, then neglected, to be rediscovered. Even a book might result. So I still find it hard to forgive the army for what happened next. At the time of the proposed interview I was home on a week's leave, prior to a further posting. Suddenly, with three days to go, the posting was brought forward and the rest of the leave cancelled: a telegram on the Wednesday morning said I must be back in camp that night. Fighting back my fury, I wrote to Stan in bitter apology, and left the note with the Lido commissionaire on my way to the station. Stan sent me a sympathetic handwritten letter and a photo, the latter with 'Hello Leslie' on it and the signatures of Ollie and himself. At the time it barely compensated for my loss.*

Our next stop, for those of us aiming to be army 'schoolies', was Loch Lomondside, or to be specific Buchanan Castle, former residence of the Dukes of Montrose. It sits on an eminence just four miles from the

---

*I have since been shown several letters which the obliging Stan sent to his fans, each with the same signed photo, and there must be hundreds in existence. It is pleasant to know that, in the 1970s, his home town, Ulverston, founded a permanent Laurel and Hardy museum, and in 1984 the international Laurel and Hardy fan club called the *Sons of the Desert* held its convention there.

lake's eastern shore, and had been taken over by the army, first as a military hospital and then as the training head-quarters of the Education Corps. As the comparatively cushy life of this select body of men involved a quick jump to the rank of sergeant (the lowest rank in which one could be a member of the RAEC) as well as the end of rifle practice and drill, we were now made to pay for these future benefits by undergoing a three-month course of rigorous training under the Welsh Guards, at this remote spot where our cries of anguish could not be heard by civilized beings. The odd bit of teacher training was thrown in, but the accent of the course was unmistakably military. Furthermore, our visit coincided with the unprecedented cold snap of October 1947, and since army regulations did not permit winter to begin until 15 November, we had to suffer a month without heating. Even when the switches were allowed to be pulled, the primitive system quickly broke down, and for weeks we were roused at five each morning in order to go for a run and get the circulation going. It was a lot less amusing than any army comedy I had seen at the cinema.

Warm or cold, most of our entertainment had to be provided within the castle itself, though once a week a group of us thought it worthwhile to splurge on dinner at the luxury Buchanan Arms in Drymen, a mile and a half down the lonely drive. Here for a couple of hours we might imagine ourselves to be gentlemen of leisure. Glasgow itself was an hour's journey from the castle gates by the little local bus which on the Saturday return run was always packed with red-faced farmers singing 'I Belong to Glasgow'. We were frequently warned by Drill Sergeant Vonk, a terrifying man who stood six feet five in his socks, and wielded a vicious-looking pace stick, not to go near the Gorbals on any excuse whatsoever, nor, on pain of instant retribution, to be seen in Sauchiehall Street eating fish and chips out of newspaper.

'Oi shall be walkin' round, every weekend, lookin' for ya,' he said. 'And then, when Oi find ya, where will ya be?'

'On a charge, sergeant.'

'That's *right*!' (The last word was always bellowed at the very top of his resonant voice.)*

Vonk had no objection, luckily, to our visiting the Glasgow cinemas. Unfortunately it proved not much of an autumn for filmgoers. I did enjoy an unpretentious John Mills 'suspenser' called *The October Man*, but it was lost in the wilderness of a multi-thousand seater called Green's Playhouse. *Song of the Thin Man* surprisingly contained a feeble joke about Somerset Maugham, but was otherwise a tame end to a declining series. I might have better enjoyed James Mason in *The Upturned Glass* if it had made clear the meaning of its own title. *Golden Earrings* was sheer lunacy, with Marlene Dietrich as a gypsy who helps Ray Milland to be a spy. And Larry Parks in *Down to Earth* proved a major disappointment, for he was still playing Al Jolson, as though it was his only trick, in a dispirited entertainment which was little more than a musical rehash of *Here Comes Mr Jordan*. One highspot of this period, however, came during a weekend in Edinburgh where, in an unlikely cinema called Poole's Synod Hall, I was reintroduced to the Marx Brothers in *A Day at the Races*. What a difference a full house makes, even in a converted chapel where the circle seats face each other instead of towards the screen! I can't remember hearing such helpless and continuous laughter in any cinema before or since, and I staggered

---

*Thirty years later I was taken to lunch at the Directors' Club in Belgrave Square. The door was opened by a very tall uniformed flunkey. There was no doubt about it: it was Vonk. 'I knew you in the army,' I said. 'Sir?' he bellowed.

away trying to memorize the Tootsie Frootsie ice cream sequence.

Buchanan Castle was by design a hive of extra-mural activity. We were, after all, supposed to learn how to keep the other ranks amused in camps which might often be very remote indeed. Enlisting the aid of some local nurses, I practised organizing a dance, but blotted my copybook by falling heavily on my partner during an attempt at the Dashing White Sergeant. I also took part in an extremely poor revue, contributing my rendition of 'Albert and the Lion'; and I was able, with the avuncular aid of one Colonel Cullimore, to start a Castle Film Society. Unfortunately the committee took too many meetings to agree on the films to be shown; two ordered through the Army Kinematograph Corps failed to arrive; and by the end of my stay all we had achieved was one showing of *Dragonwyck*, with several unscheduled intervals when the projector broke down. Meanwhile Colonel Cullimore had unfortunately become convinced, with paternal solicitude, that I had one shoulder higher than the other, and needed a week's intensive battle training to straighten me out. I was speechless with horror, but as this was obviously fate's comeback for my excused boots period, I accepted it as philosophically as I could. Nevertheless, after five days of ten-mile runs, obstacle courses and Tarzan-like swinging through the trees, I decided to steer clear of officers for a bit.

As part of our training we were divided into small groups, each of which had to contribute a 'project report' on a subject involving local research and practical investigation. I found myself in charge of six apathetic chaps, and persuaded them to plump for the professional theatre in Glasgow. With the co-operation of the staff of Messrs Howard and Wyndham, we wandered happily backstage during Michael Redgrave's production of *Macbeth*, and sat in a box watching the D'Oyly Carte Company in *The Mikado*, before settling for our intensive research on a prior-to-London tour at the King's of Patrick Hastings's courtroom play *The Blind Goddess*. At the first night I had a seat in the wings followed by a drink in the dressing-room of the star, Basil Radford, who though amiable enough seemed a good deal less amusing in the flesh than when teamed on screen with Naunton Wayne as a pair of bumbling English gentlemen abroad. I do not remember writing a report, but if I did, I am sure nobody read it.

The weather became so bad that we wanted to do nothing all day but wrap ourselves in the thickest blankets we could find. We all cheered when the BBC finally announced, towards the end of November, that warmer air from the Azores was on its way; but when it arrived, some freakish element in it caused every last panel of brown paint to turn temporarily blue, at which those of us who had read Conan Doyle's *The Poison Belt* fully expected to fall into a deep coma. It was lucky that we did not, for our postings came through with only a day's notice. Pausing only briefly in Bolton so that my mother could sew my sergeant's stripes on straight, I headed south for Salisbury Plain.

THIRTEEN

Carry On, Sergeant

Figsbury Barracks, where I spent the next eight months, was built on the slopes of a Roman barrow, not too far from a scattered village called Winterbourne Dauntsey, five miles from Salisbury by way of a left fork off the London Road. The barracks, which had housed many and various inhabitants, was shared in 1947 between the Army School of Chemical Warfare, the Southern Command School of Physical Training, and the Southern Command Headquarters of the Royal Signal Corps. The Signals unit, to which I was attached, had had dumped upon it eighty-five GD privates whom no other camp would take in. GD stood for general duties, that is to say men at the lowest standard of literacy and ability, capable only of keeping the camp tidy and (presumably) being killed in action should the requirement arise. An RAEC sergeant had been requested for the sole purpose of keeping the 'GD wallahs' occupied.

It was no sinecure. When the problem was explained to me, I spent an evening worrying about it in my billet, as I sat on my iron bedstead with its three hard 'biscuits' doing duty for a mattress. Then I split my unwilling and somewhat obstreperous pupils into three groups and worked out a timetable. As I was not prepared to teach more than six periods a day, each man was under my supervision for little more than seven hours a week, which to me seemed too much but to the CO better than nothing. What I filled their heads with, neither he nor anybody else seemed to care. As the majority could not even spell the four-letter word they used most frequently, it had to be something simple. I stuck firmly to the basics of arithmetic and English, jazzed up and sugar-coated according to the instruction booklets provided by the Army Bureau of Current Affairs (ABCA). The flaw here was that the booklets assumed a willingness to learn which my pupils did not possess. After a frustrating ten days, however, we reached a workable compromise. I would talk for a maximum of ten minutes, then ask questions on what I had been saying, with high points and a modest prize for those quickest with the right answers. Finally I left ten minutes for general discussion on the subject they most wanted to talk about, which invariably turned out to be either sex or the pictures. They soon discovered that, while on the former subject they were way ahead of me, on the latter I was something of an authority, and this led to the most successful aspect of my army teaching. I would invite the lads to name any film they could think of, and if I failed to name one of its stars I would pay out threepence. It was too easy, for the same titles kept coming up over and over again; they did not have the wit to look up more obscure ones in the reference books. I would occasionally keep boredom at bay by reversing the process, i.e. asking for the name of a star for whom I would then name at least two films. I never paid out once, but the placidity with which they endured the rest of the lesson in order to get to 'the film bit' was quite touching. The CO passed by the closed window one afternoon as I was enumerating the stars of *Rebecca*, and told me afterwards how impressed he was by the rapt enthusiasm for knowledge which was evident on the faces of my men.

I hated Figsbury at the time, but day by day, apart from the regrettable waste of effort, it probably was not too bad a life. Cheap drink and snooker in the mess, cycle rides to Old Sarum and Stonehenge, weekly play readings and leathercraft at nearby Bulford, even AKC film shows in the camp itself. (I saw *Dillinger*, which was popular enough to be repeated a month later, and *Without Love*, which was not.) There was plenty of time for writing (I was at work on a derivative bedroom farce called *Twice Two Are Five*, which I later turned into a murder comedy-thriller by simply killing off the original hero; neither version has yet faced the footlights). On many days, by some forgotten wangle, I contrived to finish work before lunch, so that by two pm I was waiting at the church for the infrequent, privately-owned Silver Star bus into Salisbury. I liked Salisbury then. Apart from its nobler assets of cathedral close, ancient buildings and second-hand bookshops, it boasted clean and delicious-smelling cafés, in one of which I became such a regular that they used to keep for me a cream meringue, rare in those days of rationing. It had a reasonably enterprising Arts Theatre, an enormous purpose-built Naafi Club, and various literary societies which were open to the public when guest speakers came down. (I was first in the queue to hear Ernest Lindgren on 'The Art of the Film'.) I joined an amateur drama group and was immediately collared to play the naval commander in *French without Tears* and Captain Rattray in J. M. Barrie's *Seven Women*: odd, since I had never seen myself as the officer type. But chief in my eyes among the cathedral city's merits were its three impeccably-run cinemas.

The continuing embargo on new Hollywood films enabled me during this period to take a crash course in famous movies which I had missed, to consolidate my appreciation of long-established favourites, and to take a fresh look at others which I had dismissed as a child but might appreciate as an adult. These plums were arrayed before me in double-bills of staggering value. The ABC house, for instance, offered *In Which We Serve* with *Lady Hamilton*. The latter, for purposes of shortening, had been sadly shorn of its opening and closing flashbacks, but the programme suited Salisbury down to the ground and caused longer queues than most new films could have managed. The Warner gangster thrillers came back with both barrels blazing; *Public Enemy* with *Little Caesar*, *The Roaring Twenties* with *Brother Orchid*, *The Petrified Forest* with *G-Men*. *The Beast with Five Fingers* was new and disappointing, despite Peter Lorre's bravura performance as the haunted librarian; luckily it was supported by *The Man Who Came to Dinner*, at which as always I laughed till I ached, envying Monty Woolley's way with invective. For example, in reply to his nurse who tells him that in his condition he should not eat chocolates, the hirsute invalid replies: 'I had an aunt who ate a box of chocolates every day of her life. She lived to be a hundred and two, and when she had been dead three days, she looked healthier than you do *now*!'

Most of the other new films were disappointing, too. *Pursued*, with Robert Mitchum, was a western which seemed to take place entirely in the dark, and the only interest of a thriller called *Cry Wolf* was to show the world what Errol Flynn looked like in spectacles. However, it was supported by a revival of Will Hay in *The Ghost of St Michael's*.

Although efficiently managed, the Regal, like most ABC halls, had little personality except that of a chilly rectangular box in pink and pale blue, at its best with the lights out. The Rank cinemas in Salisbury, however, were a pleasure to sit in, their atmosphere compensating for many

an indifferent film. The Picture House was a futuristic-
looking place in which one might well have staged scenes
from *Things to Come*. Its stadium-type auditorium, the
circle only slightly raised behind the stalls, was reached
through a long, wide, softly illuminated tunnel in shades of
orange and turquoise. Simply to enter it made one feel like
a star actor, and it was the happy possessor of one of these
very large, limpid, restful screens which made second
features look like epics. I saw *The October Man* again at the
Picture House, and relished the accuracy of its suburban
boarding-house full of petty jealousies; coupled with it now
was that delightful twenties semi-musical *Margie*, full of
college students in raccoon coats. *The Naked City*, allegedly the first crime thriller to be shot on the teeming streets
of New York, was a new one that slipped through, in a
strange combination with a revival of that most British of
comedies *Quiet Wedding*. Betty Grable in *Song of the
Islands* made an equally unlikely but happy coupling with
Noël Coward's *Blithe Spirit*; while the two satirical com-
edy-dramas *Nothing Sacred* and *A Star is Born* seemed
made for each other. *Lost Horizon* and *It Happened One
Night* were marvellous value for the price of one ticket, but
the show ran so long that I missed the bus back to camp and
had to walk five miles, reciting such lines as I could
remember under the moonlit sky.

The Gaumont had a cramped and flat auditorium, with a
screen set deliberately high so that one could see it above
the heads in front. It claimed the major films because it was
a unique showplace. The shell of the building was a
medieval residence known as Ye Halle of John Halle, and
the main foyers and gallery had been preserved almost
intact, with armour, swords and pikes adorning the walls.
The façade was half-timbered and the interior replete with
linenfold panels in carved oak – you felt that they should

have made a separate charge simply for the use of the building. This unique décor made the Gaumont highly suitable for any attractions with a classical air; and so it was able to announce *The Red Shoes, Carnegie Hall* and *Monsieur Verdoux*, for all of which I happily queued. Even *A Double Life*, with Ronald Colman as an actor who, during a run of *Othello*, could not prevent himself from strangling the ladies of his real-life acquaintance, seemed perfectly at home there. However, watching Peter Ustinov's Victorian lark *Vice Versa* in these surroundings was rather like meeting a bishop in a nudist camp, although I sat most of it through twice for the sake of hearing James Robertson Justice as the fearsome headmaster bellow: 'Boy! You will write out the word "transubstantiation" three-hundred-and-sixty-five times, spelling it both forwards *and backwards* on each occasion!'

American comedies such as *Sitting Pretty*, however, found the going especially hard, apart from the well-advertised scene in which the eccentric male baby-sitter (played by Clifton Webb) at breakfast teaches the naughty infant a lesson by tipping a bowl of porridge over its head. Also, one curious habit of the Gaumont was to play along with its Grade-A features some of the poorest conceivable seconds, among which I retain to this day the most painful recollections of *Little Iodine, Gasoline Alley, Black Memory*, and a resurrected weepie from the early thirties called *Road to Happiness*. Only once during my stay did it follow the current fashion for re-issue doubles, when it presented that splendid pair from Paramount, *The Miracle of Morgan's Creek* and *The Cat and the Canary*.

At Figsbury Barracks I contrived to persuade the army to sponsor several 'cultural' excursions. I forget precisely whose funds I plundered when Mrs Lee's bus took twenty-five of the livelier sparks up to London on a 'project', but we had a full day. In 1948 the nation was still grateful to the army for services rendered, and red carpets were rolled out at the drop of an army beret. We enjoyed an hour at Isleworth Brewery, with selected samples, before going on to Ealing Studios for a buffet lunch. We were shown various processes involved in the making of *Another Shore* and *Scott of the Antarctic* – I remember crumbling in my fingers a block of artificial snow – but this first visit to a film studio did not, curiously, fill me with any longings to get behind a camera and shout instructions through a megaphone. I marvelled at the technical trickery but was appalled at the waste of time involved, and my resolve henceforth was to be a critic rather than a creator.

The later part of the afternoon was spent backstage at the old Winter Garden Theatre, where the current attraction was a Ben Travers farce called *Outrageous Fortune*. I had written a personal letter to Ralph Lynn, that superb farceur, and was invited to chat with him in his dressing-room while my charges enjoyed themselves in the pub across the road. His features had sadly aged, his skin was leathery, and his voice had become a croak, but the gestures were still there in abundance. I learned later that his famous limp-wristed technique, by which he seemed able almost to fling his hands off the ends of his arms, was conditioned by the fact that his limbs were riddled with arthritis, so that he could gesture in no other way. He said that he was still stage-struck and always would be; I could believe it, for as he plastered on the make-up he seemed to come alive, and by the time he finished it was the dapper and monocled Ralph Lynn of *Rookery Nook* who stood before me. Robertson Hare popped in, I swear minus trousers, as we were saying goodbye; he had just come from seeing Gielgud's production of *An Ideal Husband*, and hoped that gracious events of that kind might in future be seen more frequently than the dingy sex-obsessed melodramas which seemed then to be in vogue. The two elderly gentlemen smiled sympathetically at each other, and shook their heads as they prepared to satisfy the audience's craving for belly laughs. We all stayed for the show, but it seemed a hollow entertainment in a theatre less than one-third full.

The post-war army looked benignly on any attempt by its members to better themselves. Thus I had only to murmur in the right ear that Urchfont Manor, an adult education centre near Devizes, would shortly run a two-week course in twentieth-century literature, to be invited to enrol. At first my main pleasure was to be wearing civilian clothes again, but it was no bad thing, in preparation for Cambridge, to be discussing Wordsworth and James Joyce with the likes of novelist John Wain, poet Kathleen Raine, and critic John Heath-Stubbs. However, what beneficial effect the army thought this might have on the teaching of sub-literates I can only conjecture. In this helpful climate it came as only a mild surprise to read in Part One Orders that Southern Command was forming a Drama Team to tour camps with a blend of entertainment and instruction in the theatrical arts. My application, though uninvited, went in on the very same morning; and to my astonishment, after a hurried interview at Didcot (after which I saw Edward Rigby in *Easy Money*) I was instructed to join the team at Bovington in mid-July.

The summer of 1948 was a splendid one. There had been rain enough in the spring, but now we were treated to a succession of hot cloudless days. The team's territory included Wiltshire, Dorset, Somerset and Devon, the gentlest counties. At around midday on Friday we would arrive by truck, eight of us. Having unpacked our minimal scenery, we were not required again until Monday evening, when there was a pre-arranged discussion during which I had to ask two questions and deliver one opinion. Unless there was something to rehearse, all the days were free. On Tuesday evening there was a 'cod' rehearsal showing what mistakes the amateur producer should avoid; in this I had half a dozen lines. Wednesday brought our two one-act plays, *Scenario* by L. Du Garde Peach and *The Seventh Man* by Michael Redgrave: I was a messenger in the one and a rent collector in the other. On Thursday there was an open forum, but we always had to keep it going ourselves; the audiences came in only because we were free and they were broke. Come Friday morning, usually with a hangover from too much scrumpy, we threw ourselves and our belongings into a truck and trundled away to the next camp. Needless to say, the odd film cropped up along the way. At Yeovil's high and imposing Odeon there was Anna Neagle in *Spring in Park Lane*, an ideal entertainment for those dejected post-war years. During a thunderstorm in Torquay I took refuge with *The Winslow Boy*, good straight theatrical stuff with a resourceful cast; and in Sidmouth there was *The Woman in White*, a muddled stab at Wilkie Collins's convoluted plot but with Sidney Greenstreet in fine form as the treacherous Count Fosco.

One Sunday in Shaftesbury I walked a mile or so south in the still of the evening to the military mental hospital, where there was to be a 16mm showing of *King Kong*. Simply to catch up with it at last, to make one's first obeisance, was a relief for which I gave thanks. But what a revelation it was! What splendour had been hidden from me by that doorkeeper at the Bolton Odeon! The delightfully creaky opening gave little indication of the wonders to follow; we even laughed uneasily at the first sight of Kong himself, with his back fur rippling. But Max Steiner's music was slowly exerting its grip, and after the wrestling match with the triceratops, and the sinister encounter with the amphibian in the oily lake, and the quick despatch of the pterodactyl, we were all Kong's slaves . . . as I am still.

The tour concluded in September with the unexpected bonus of a week at Salisbury's Arts Theatre, which must suddenly have been short of an attraction, as we hardly provided value for money. We gave the one-act plays every evening and filled up with a dramatized reading from *Saint Joan*. We would all have been happier if admission had been free, for when placed in a professional setting our show was no good, and we knew it. A fortnight's leave followed; I spent the time in and around Bolton and returned light at heart, even after sitting through *Forever Amber* and *I Remember Mama* in one day; but a nasty shock was in store. Our plan was to reassemble for rehearsals of *Macbeth*, followed by a tour; but the Scottish play must have worked its legendary evil magic, for when we reported back to Chisledon, near Swindon, we found the camp was being evacuated and that a newly appointed head of Southern Command had ordered the immediate disbandment of the Drama Team as an utter waste of time. None of us would have contested this judgment, but equally wasteful were the weeks during which we now sat around awaiting posting. A few nights in Swindon were my only solace, once at the local rep when the villain split his tights during the last scene of *A Murder Has Been Arranged*, and once at Ealing's rather doleful film version of *Saraband for Dead Lovers*, from which I treasure one single image, of raindrops making a madonna in a stained glass window appear to weep at an unhappy wedding.

The army could think of nothing better to do with me than to send me to Aldershot for a teaching refresher course; but at least the garrison town was only a few miles from Guildford's second-hand bookshops, where, with Cambridge less than a year away, I began to stock up on such items as *Bradley on Shakespeare* and *Metaphysical Poetry from Donne to Butler*. Meanwhile Aldershot's glossy new Naafi Club had film shows most evenings, but the air in the packed theatre was always sweaty and oppressive, and a ribald reception was invariably accorded to any entertainment which did not involve cowboys and Indians. What happened to Leslie Howard and Norma Shearer in *Romeo and Juliet* can easily be imagined, and as a result it is a film that I have never again been able to take seriously. That was the same evening on which I gave up and went across the way for the last performance of *The Body Snatcher*, which had some pleasant acting from Henry Daniell and Boris Karloff but made no sense because the British censor had cut the climactic twist in which the supposedly dead body in the sack appears to change its identity. Other highlights of my three-week stay were two re-issue bills: Will Hay in *The Goose Steps Out* (the one in which he persuades Nazi schoolboys to give Hitler the V sign in reverse) with George Formby in *It's in the Air*; and *The Seventh Veil* coupled with a sadly abbreviated version of *The Life and Death of Colonel Blimp*.*

The remaining eight months of my army service I spent with the Ordnance Corps in Portsmouth. The barracks had a rambling but well-organized education centre where four of us sergeants lived under the direction of a seldom-seen second lieutenant who spent most of his time squiring the CO's daughter. It was, on the whole, a happy time, for

*It was BBC Television who, more than thirty years later, finally located the missing 'bookends' from *Colonel Blimp* and transmitted a restored three-hour version. Several longish films were shorn this way in the late forties in order to make double-bills, and in some cases it was impossible later to restore the cuts. An example of this, ironically, is the material from *Lady Hamilton* which shows her final downfall and was inserted in the first place to please the censor; it is not missed dramatically, but without it the beginning and end of the film seem extremely abrupt.

within easy reach of North End Barracks were more cinemas than even I could cope with. Portsmouth proper had more than twenty, of all shapes and sizes, though of course several of them doubled up on programmes. I developed a special regard for the Troxy, a large barnlike independent on the Fratton side of Southsea. Starved for more commercial product, it showed some arty newcomers (John Ford's *The Fugitive*, Ben Hecht's *The Spectre of the Rose*) in addition to a welcome run of re-issues. What particularly commended it to me was its policy of using old Laurel and Hardy shorts to round off the programme, and it was here that I first made acquaintance with some choice items originally issued before my filmgoing time: *Helpmates*, *Chickens Come Home*, *Men o'War*, *Hog Wild*. Portsmouth also had a Classic, which like the rest of its chain put on nothing more classical than Jean Harlow and the Marx Brothers; it did however show a beautiful colour print of *The Blue Bird*, the Maeterlinck fairy play in its haunting and undervalued version starring Shirley Temple. Gale Sondergaard as the black cat seemed an example of perfect casting, and the concept of the lands of the past and future both chilled and fascinated me. Yes, Portsmouth was a happy hunting ground: I felt like a caliph submerged in gold pieces. I even saw my old favourite *Lost Horizon* ('George, haven't you ever wondered what's on the other side of the mountain?') on two consecutive days at different cinemas in order to compare their comfort and efficiency.

Gradually, however, I grew lazier, and concentrated my attention on the first-run halls within walking distance of the barracks. These, in Cosham on the mainland, played concurrent with London release, and it was here that I found the new British films taking giant strides forward while Hollywood lapsed to a standard of mediocrity which a couple of years previously would have seemed unthinkable. *The Bride Goes Wild, This Time for Keeps, You Gotta Stay Happy, You Were Meant for Me, The Sainted Sisters* – these were all uninventive variations on themes which were already too well worn, no match for Somerset Maugham's *Quartet* or David Lean's *Oliver Twist* or Carol Reed's *The Fallen Idol*. I remember emerging from the last of these, both a suspense thriller and a character study, in a glow of elation at a good job well executed, and even feeling excited about it during breakfast next morning. This state of affairs lasted for a few months and was then abruptly reversed. Britain offered misconceived technical experiments like *Warning to Wantons* (in 'Independent Frame') or tedious family comedy like *Here Come the Huggetts*, while Hollywood climbed right back on to the band wagon: Paramount with Billy Wilder's *A Foreign Affair*, MGM with the joyous musical *Easter Parade*, and Goldwyn with Danny Kaye in *The Secret Life of Walter Mitty*, which caused queues so long that I had to find ways and means of attending a matinée. A little comedy from RKO, *Mr Blandings Builds His Dream House*, produced wit and wisdom from the tribulations of New Yorkers buying a house in the country, and earned a place right up in my 'top twenty'; while Bob Hope in the western spoof, *The Paleface*, delivered that marvellous feeling of wondering whether two thousand people roaring with laughter at the same time might actually raise the roof or split the walls.

Many of my weekends were spent with my married sister, who now lived ten miles up the road in Fareham, a straggly town saved by the more westerly of its two cinemas. Both were owned by the Shipman and King circuit, both were set in the High Street within a few yards of each other, yet the contrast between them was striking, and my sister was well aware of it, for she would never willingly go to the Savoy. Square and unfinished-looking, the building was covered in white emulsion paint which was always peeling; the auditorium was draughty, depressing and uncomfortable, and I didn't enjoy a single film in it, certainly not Errol Flynn and Eleanor Parker in a dismal remake of the old Elisabeth Bergner classic *Escape Me Never*. The Embassy, on the other hand, was one of the few really attractive modernistic buildings: cleverly styled in brick, softly lit inside, and with excellent sight lines from any seat in a relaxing auditorium which tapered gracefully towards a simply decorated proscenium arch. It seldom played run-of-the-mill supports, preferring old but durable comedies, and the result was a number of richly enjoyable shows: the exciting *Sleeping Car to Trieste*, with Laurel and Hardy in *Way out West*; *London Belongs to Me*, with the Crazy Gang in *Gasbags*; *Miracle on 34th Street* (Anglicized as *The Big Heart*), with *The Jones Family in Hot Water*. (A few years later I made a return visit to see how the hall coped with CinemaScope, the attraction being Sophia Loren, agreeably wet, in *Boy on a Dolphin*. The answer was, admirably, but Fareham is a long way to go to see a wide-screen film properly projected.)

At around this time, via day excursions, I began to patronize London's West End cinemas, mainly in order to say that I knew them all. I caught Olivier's *Hamlet* at the tail end of its run at the Odeon, Leicester Square, and was dismayed to find it rather boring. (A current joke had it that the statue of Shakespeare in the adjacent gardens was heard to mutter: 'O this offence is Rank, it smells to heaven.') *The Queen of Spades* at the Warner I visited on its opening day, but there was no sense of occasion, and despite its intense acting and overpowering décor the supernatural story somehow failed to catch fire. Incredibly, the supporting programme consisted of *two* community

singing shorts, during neither of which was a single voice
raised in the auditorium. I am not sure what I expected
from the West End, but certainly not this. Gilt-edged
screens, perhaps?

The Empire in Leicester Square suited the image better:
here you got not only Clark Gable in *Command Decision*
but Tom and Jerry and an elaborate stage show, all for a
shilling if you slipped in before midday. Nor did I starve
myself of culture, seeking out *Paisa* and a revival of *Quai
des Brumes* at Academy prices: The atmosphere was
charged with quiet appreciation, but the seats could have
been more comfortable. I also wormed my way into some
of the British Film Institute's archive shows, then being
held in a cellar beneath the ugly Ministry of Education
building in Curzon Street. One way or another, Harold
Lloyd in *Safety Last*, Lillian Gish in *Way Down East* and
Buster Keaton in *The General* all managed to cheer my
evenings before I caught the milk train, but I could find
little to say in favour of a silent film called *Polikushka*, set
among Russian peasants and concerning states of mental
depression which spread right out into the audience. The
print was on tinted stock: yellow for sunshine, green for
rain, and blue for night. When we came to the scene in
which the hero hangs himself in a barn, it was printed in
good old black-and-white!

In January 1949 I discovered that I had accumulated a
total of thirty-one days' leave, which I would lose unless I
took it before the end of March. (In fact I had had most of
it, but it was not marked up in my pay book, and national
servicemen were seldom troubled by conscience.) I was
also entitled to a warrant for travel to my home town, so in
a fit of adventurous madness, for which luckily I was never
called to account, I filled in my home address as 19
Waverley Road, Stornoway, and set off for a winter

holiday in the Outer Hebrides. It is a longish way from Portsmouth. I called at Bolton to assure the family that I had not entirely taken leave of my senses, then caught the night train from Wigan to Perth and changed for Inverness. Arriving at this northern outpost in a snowstorm, I leaped into the 11 am train for Kyle of Lochalsh – a wild and thrilling journey, though the rain was pelting down as we crested the Highlands at Achnasheen and began our descent to the rugged West Coast. Skye loomed sombrely from across the narrow water as I heard someone say that there was a bad storm in the Minch and it looked like being the worst crossing of the winter. A few held back, but I could see no attraction at Kyle save an extremely expensive hotel, so I strode aboard MacBrayne's boat just before it lurched into the heaving waters for a supposed six-hour voyage. Snug in my army greatcoat, I refused a kipper tea and gripped the top deck rail determinedly while my travelling companions huddled miserably below. I stood there for four hours, watching the infrequent flickers of light, first in gloaming and then in darkness, until it occurred to me that should I slip and fall overboard, nobody would know a thing about it. As I went below I began to whistle *Over the Sea to Skye*, and wondered why I got such sour looks.

Thanks to all that fresh air, I seemed to be the only person aboard not to be violently sick, and it was nearly one o'clock in the morning when we moored at Stornoway. Since I had booked no accommodation I had visions of spending the night in a dockside shed surrounded by barrels of herring, and was astonished to find myself in a well-lit and bustling community of ten thousand people, with twenty-six churches, a Burton's, a Woolworth's, and two cinemas, not to mention a fleet of buses waiting to take my exhausted companions on to whatever portion of Lewis or Harris they cared to nominate. I made for a modest hotel by the quayside, and found myself the only guest: next day they got out the silver service and cooked me a special haggis.

Most of my time during the next few days seemed to be spent refusing offers of hand-woven Harris tweed from chaps in pubs, in cafés, and on the streets; but I did go to the pictures once, to a little hall in a shopping arcade, and very professional the presentation was. *Crime Does Not Pay* was followed by a cartoon and a two-week-old newsreel, and the main attraction was Korda's slightly flat post-war comedy *Perfect Strangers*, in which a boring marriage is transformed by war service into a relationship that is fresh and vital. It seemed to me to speak only to the South of England, but to my surprise the islanders lapped it up.

Restricted by the wintry weather, I gradually made my way back to Bolton and spent the rest of my leave anticlimactically in the reference library, making what little I could of Chaucerian English. ('Whan that Aprille with his shoures soote . . .') The cinemas on my home ground were already showing signs of wear and tear, spiritual as well as physical. Attendances had fallen off, and the old sense of occasion was sadly lacking. Most of the halls now saw little future for themselves. Their heyday was certainly gone. Built or renovated for the coming of sound, they had survived fifteen or more years of hard use, plus the privations of a world war, and they now needed attentions and repairs which nobody could afford, even if government permission had been obtainable. Gradually other means were being found of keeping the sites profitable. In the town centre, the aromatic Embassy became a chain store. Then, one by one, the fleapits died, in most cases without even an *In Memoriam* notice. The Odeon's projectors clearly needed new mirrors, and its auditorium now smel-

led fusty. The Lido shrieked neglect, and ran only cheap
exploitation programmes; the commissionaire with bad
feet had either retired or died, no one seemed to know
which. But during this last winter leave, and in the following summer between my quitting the army and making my
first journey to Cambridge, I tried to ignore this inevitable
decline as my mother and I doggedly revisited the scenes of
our former pleasures. We smiled comfortingly at each
other and pretended that we were both ten years younger;
but we knew that the old magic was on the point of
evaporation.

At the cinema the age of elegance had long gone:
everything had to be as gloomy and meaningful as life itself,
and it was useless to sigh for satins, pearls and tuxedos in a
world where existence was still dominated by rationing.
One had only to look around Bolton to see a town past its
peak of interest. Mills were closing for lack of orders, and
the old personally-managed shops were giving way to the
new chain-operated supermarkets. As I gazed at the grimy
buildings I remembered the low point of the war, January
of 1944, when we had to burn furniture in order to keep
warm, and there was so little food that we struggled daily
through the snow to be first in line at the Co-op Restaurant
for a plate of potato pie ($3d$) followed by rice pudding ($2d$):
a whole meal for less than 2p in modern money. We
suffered all that because propaganda had given us the will
to win; but now, four years after the war ended, nobody
seemed able to tell us why we were still suffering the same
privations. Within the army's disciplines I had been, in a
way, cosseted and well fed, but this was a grim, drab,
exhausted reality. Nothing had been painted for ten years.
The older people I knew as a child had begun to die. There
was still a fuel shortage, and I queued twice a week at the
gasworks for bags of coke. Mum never seemed really well,

complaining drearily of headaches, and swollen ankles, and something unspecified to do with 'ladies' insides'; her relationship with Dad was more strained than ever. Of the whole widespread Halliwell clan only I seemed to have before me the possibility of a shining future, and that meant deserting the sooty streets where life had had most meaning. The impossible Venice of *Top Hat*, the caricature Ireland of *Oh Mr Porter*, the unattainable land of Oz, the cloud cuckoo suburbia of Laurel and Hardy, the Shangri-La of *Lost Horizon*, had all been reached by me through the shadowed back streets of my home town. But that sort of magic was totally lacking in the current output from both sides of the Atlantic. In retrospect 1949 can be firmly labelled the nadir of film art. Directors and stars alike gave us their poorest films: Ingrid Bergman as Joan of Arc, Hitchcock's *The Paradine Case*, John Ford's *Three God-fathers*, Preston Sturges on the decline with *Unfaithfully Yours*, Humphrey Bogart in *Knock on any Door*, Astaire and Rogers making a dismal comeback in *The Barkleys of Broadway*. The few films which pleased the critics, whose barometers were set for storm, flooded our screens with gloom, doom and cynicism: *The Snake Pit*, *Champion*, *We Were Strangers*, *Force of Evil*. Of course, there remained in the pipeline little flurries of optimism: the glory days of Gene Kelly and Alec Guinness were still to come. But incurable optimists like my mother and me were swimming against the tide, and we knew it.

All the same, we spent an unexpectedly enjoyable afternoon at the Theatre. Only in desperation, as can be imagined, did we go to a boxing film; but we agreed afterwards that *The Set-Up*, which was based rather incredibly on a poem, was exciting and well made, with plenty to say about people. And in support was *Variety Time*, one of RKO's lively compilations from its old comedies and musi-

cals, with Mum's favourite Leon Errol given due promi-
nence. There was even a Donald Duck for good measure.
We sat through that twice, and on the way home called at
the UCP to get a pound of honeycomb tripe for tea.

FOURTEEN

Ah! The University

My years as an undergraduate at Cambridge, from 1949 to 1952, coincided with the most momentous upheaval in cinema history. In America, vivid and popular entertainment was already available from the box in the corner of the living-room, and all around the world, as instanced by the decline I had seen in the Bolton cinemas, movies were losing out against the competition of better living standards, cars, international travel, and more exciting things to do with one's evenings. The bread-and-butter picture no longer made a profit: only size and sensation sold tickets. Stars, producers and directors all helped to kill the system which had worked so well for so long: thinking they deserved a bigger slice of the profits than a studio contract could give them, they demanded ever higher percentages, and when these were refused, set themselves up as independent production companies and rented studio space as required. In the old days the MGM lion had stood for every bit of quality that a huge studio and careful promotion could give; now it more often masked a shoddy piece of goods which happened to have been shot on the MGM lot or had been picked up for distribution after completion elsewhere. As Billy Wilder later complained, 'We now spend eighty per cent of our time making deals and only twenty per cent making pictures.'

But to me in Cambridge, that joyous intellectual back-water, Hollywood had temporarily taken a back seat while my eyes were opened to the whole precious expanse of international film culture. Scarcely a film of note, whatever its age, was not screened somewhere in the town during my nine terms. The difficulty was finding time to fit them all in. I had, after all, come there to learn about English literature, and it took me the whole of my first term to get acclimatized. I had to settle in lodgings, learn the college traditions, decide what lectures to attend, plan my reading courses, and cycle out to Cherry Hinton twice a week to discuss my essays with my supervisor. I missed the discipline of both school and army, not yet feeling ready to select my own star and follow it.

But amid the uncertainty there were manifold compensations. Urgent political discussions over coffee at the Venetian or tea at the Dorothy: bachelor beer parties which ran far into the night on chat about Proust or Hemingway or Aldous Huxley; star performances from lecturers to whom visits were really unnecessary because they had published all their papers in book form; but a number of them were irresistible actors. I recall my own senior tutor, Tom Henn, with his deep Anglo-Irish brogue, coming into his first lecture on Shakespearean criticism and asking me to hand out a stack of four-page leaflets impeccably printed by the University Press. They listed about 150 books, of which I had read one and a half and heard of a dozen or more. When the buzz died down, Tom lazily wiped the blackboard with the tail of his gown and growled: 'Well, gentlemen, the books in the first section, as you've no doubt recognized, are those which you have already read and digested at your schools. The rest, of course, are those which you *will* have read and digested by the end of this term.' The man next to me was petrified, but I had caught the twinkle in Tom's eye, a twinkle he did not bother to hide when he launched into his favourite lecture, on the geography of *The Tempest*. This had little to do with Shakespeare, but was a brilliant *jeu d'esprit*. From clues which he professed to find in the text, most of them based on puns, Tom drew on the blackboard, in glowing colours, a detailed map of Prospero's island, complete with bays, cliffs, caves, currents, and mermaids offshore. I wish he had published that.

Cambridge offered a life of bewildering richness. You could join more than a hundred societies. You could debate in the Union with the great names of the day. If you possessed a comfortable bank balance, you might think of joining the Pitt Club. You could row, of course: you could play any outdoor game you fancied. You could marvel at the exhibits in the Fitzwilliam Museum or follow your literary inclinations in the new University Library (which most people said looked like a cross between a jam factory and a crematorium, and was wisely kept hidden from view on the far side of the river). Abhorring most forms of organized activity, I found myself taking a good many lonely cycle rides in between my stabs at drama and journalism; but whatever else happened, I managed to fit in four or five movies a week.

The Cambridge University Film Society, embracing both town and gown among its one thousand members, was a particular joy. Its principal meetings were on Sunday mornings in the Central, a delightful venue which I instantly counted among my favourite cinemas. It had a vast, airy circle and a compact stalls area tapering down to the width of the screen, which was generous. Sunday became an indispensable ritual. One enjoyed a leisurely breakfast and got to the Central soon after ten. By twenty past, the entire circle would be alive with the rustle of newsprint as six hundred undergraduates struggled with the *Observer* or the *Sunday Times*. At 10.25 there was a tendency to turn to the beautifully printed booklet of programme notes, and promptly at 10.30 the Secretary of the Society would cough discreetly into the stage microphone as preface to any necessary announcements. The lights would then dim, and for the next two hours and a quarter respectful attention would normally be paid to the matter in hand. By these means was I introduced to the earliest, purest examples of Marxism: the *Duck Soup* Marxist, I mean, the one who said 'Brush the crumbs out of my bed, I'm expecting company', and 'Remember, men, we're fighting for this woman's honour, which is probably more than she ever did.' Here too I claimed acquaintance with the idyllic *Partie de Campagne*, the worthy *Kamerads-chaft*, the pallid *Hôtel du Nord*, the overpowering *Ivan the Terrible*; and with *Storm over Asia*, which arrived without subtitles and thus became something of a strain on the imagination, though there filtered through, surprisingly, the odd English phrase such as 'Bird's Custard' and 'Winston Churchill'.

Only twice was the even intellectual quality of these occasions disturbed. *The River*, made in 1938, is a poetic documentary about the Mississippi, conceived by the American writer and critic Pare Lorentz as a series of beautiful images accompanied by a rolling, almost onomatopoeic commentary which employs a good deal of poetic repetition:

> They took the top off Minnesota
> And sent it down the river.
> They took the top off the Alleghenies
> And sent it down the river . . .

And so on. I was fond of the film, knew it backwards from

school lunchtime sessions, and had always found it to work perfectly; but at Cambridge it provoked outbursts of hysterical laughter from the rear stalls, and a group of medical hearties began chanting their own ribald version of the lines. Cries of 'shush' only made matters worse, and *The River* staggered to its dying fall amid scenes of semi-uproar, almost as though the entire audience had seized upon it as a means of getting rid of some quite irrelevant frustration.

The second cause of trouble was also a documentary, Georges Franju's *Le Sang des Bêtes*, which takes its audience on a twenty-minute tour of a Paris slaughter-house. The programme notes firmly warned that the film was not for the squeamish, and the message was underlined by a stage message from the Honorary Secretary who added that, both before and after the film, there would be a one-minute interval with the lights up for the convenience of any members who might wish to leave and return. This announcement, predictably, was greeted with howls of derision, and when the time came nobody moved at all; in the circle at any rate there was not a single empty seat when the film started. About five minutes in came the killing of a horse, followed by a clammy silence in the auditorium, then the scuffling sound of someone about to be violently sick. I began to feel rather warm myself, and was not helped by the slaying of the oxen or the rows of struggling sheep having their throats cut. When the film mercifully ended, about two-thirds of the original audience filed back shamefacedly from the foyer, most of them still looking rather green. When I got back to college for lunch, there was no way I could touch the cold veal and ham pie, and since dinner that evening offered jugged hare, I went hungry until the Koh-i-Noor opened and I could seek the benison of a vegetable biryani.

The Society's midweek sessions were sparsely attended, being held in a remote and cheerless engineering laboratory. The prints were sub-standard, and there was little enough mystique about the presentation, but a film buff has to learn. Here I caught up with Ruttman's *Berlin*; Dreyer's *The Passion of Joan of Arc* and *Vampyr*; and all the standard *avant-garde* titles such as *Menilmontant*, *Rien Que Les Heures* and *The Seashell and the Clergyman*.* For some reason John Ford's tribute to the US Marines, *They Were Expendable*, also turned up at a midweek session and was roundly booed: the Americans were none too popular at that time, and certainly not when they were shown winning the war single-handed.

Another addict's paradise which normally demanded a weekly visit was the Arts Cinema in Market Passage. Formerly the Cosmo, it took the form of a little square box seating two hundred people, was kept going by the non-profit-making Arts Trust and managed by a graduate, which was supposed to give it class. Its separate performances, still a rarity in those days, ran as close to two hours as could be achieved, which usually allowed for a couple of carefully selected shorts, there being neither newsreel nor trailers; its principal defect, resulting from lack of space, was a curious projection system by which the image was projected up from a cellar and bounced off a mirror to hit the screen from behind, giving the oddest finish as though one were watching the picture through butter muslin.

I was still feeling my way with the current continental cinema, and the Arts Cinema, by its prompt showings of

---

*Of *The Seashell and the Clergyman* the British censor, in refusing a certificate, is reported to have made the comment: 'It is so obscure as to have no apparent meaning. If there is a meaning, it is doubtless objectionable.'

the films like *Bicycle Thieves*, *Day of Wrath*, *Orphée* and
La Ronde, helped me to understand the Sunday reviews.
La Ronde had been such a *succès de scandale* in London
that it was booked for an unprecedented fortnight, which
prompted *Varsity*, the undergraduate newspaper, to run a
story under the headline *Naughty Nights, for Fourteen
Days*. Equally important, the Arts offered a chance of
reappraising such lighter diversions of the past as *The
Thirty-nine Steps* (in which a Sunday-night audience, who
in order to get at it had to sit through Vigo's baffling *Zéro
de Conduite*, found even more *doubles entendres* than
Hitchcock intended); *The Private Life of Henry VIII* (in
which only the bedroom scene still worked); *Ninotchka*
(after which we all tried to sound as cynical as Melvyn
Douglas); and *The Philadelphia Story*. This splendid comedy of the American upper classes ('with the rich and
mighty, always a little patience') had seemed to me, at the
Bolton Capitol eight years earlier, rather stodgy, cold and
talkative. Now, a friend and I saw it at a thinly attended
matinée, and laughed till we ached. We went again on the
following evening, taking three other friends with us; and
by Thursday, so strong were the word-of-mouth recom-
mendations, every seat was booked for the rest of the week
and the startled management had to promise to bring the
film back next term. For weeks parties thrived on such
affectionately remembered lines as 'I understand we
understand each other' and 'C. K. Dexter Haven – what
kind of name is that?' and 'No mean Machiavelli is smiling,
cynical Sidney Kidd' and 'Good Golly, why didn't you sell
tickets?' In a vein not dissimilar, the Arts also revived from
the earlier thirties two brilliant comedies directed by Ernst
Lubitsch, *Trouble in Paradise* and *One Hour with You*.
Shiny evocations of an age of brittle romantic make-believe
though they were, they did not draw the crowds of *The*

Philadelphia Story; but they were instantly recognized as gems and cherished by the *cognoscenti*.

For all its tiny capacity, the Arts did remain empty if it showed a film which could not be made fashionable. To my surprise this fate befell Preston Sturges's *The Great McGinty* (then oddly known in Britain as *Down Went McGinty*), the one hitherto inaccessible film of a man whose irrepressible wartime comedies (*The Lady Eve*, *The Miracle of Morgan's Creek*) had been the talk of the town. A disaster even more cataclysmic was *The Scoundrel*, a doleful but witty fantasy written by the authors of *The Front Page* for the 1935 starring début of Noël Coward. One could hardly call it a masterpiece, but I enjoyed myself despite the fact that only three other people came to the performance I attended. One line still stays with me: 'An Arabian queen, famous for her legs.'

Cambridge boasted no Odeon but had five ABC cinemas, of which the Central was third in box-office capacity though first in comfort. The huge Regal, next to Downing College and opposite the University Arms, called itself 'East Anglia's premier cinema', but although clean and efficient it was shapelessly designed and always seemed cold, even in summer. One had to endure it to see such new standards as *The Happiest Days of Your Life* and *The Third Man* (which I did, for one could not have moved in Cambridge society without an intimate knowledge of both and the ability to remember at least part of Orson Welles's cuckoo clock speech); but I was always secretly pleased if the Regal had a flop and did no business. Its second features were nearly always abominable; unlike the other ABCs, its flagship status seemed to prevent it from varying the official circuit release to suit the idiosyncrasies of a university town. It was here that I became aware of the atrocities still being perpetrated in the name of British

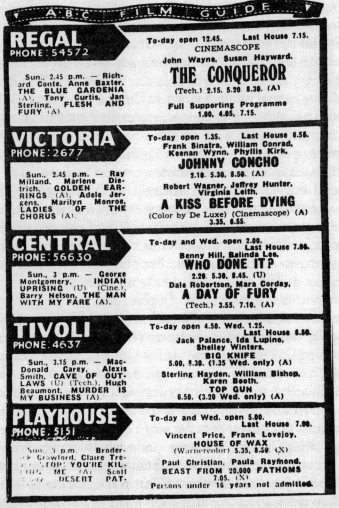

▼ A·B·C FILM GUIDE ▼

REGAL
PHONE:54572

Sun., 2.45 p.m. — Richard Conte, Anne Baxter, THE BLUE GARDENIA (A). Tony Curtis, Jan Sterling, FLESH AND FURY (A).

To-day open 12.45.   Last House 7.15.
CINEMASCOPE
John Wayne, Susan Hayward,
THE CONQUEROR
(Tech.) 2.15. 5.20. 8.30. (A)

Full Supporting Programme
1.00, 4.05, 7.15.

VICTORIA
PHONE:2677

Sun., 2.45 p.m. — Ray Milland, Marlene Dietrich, GOLDEN EARRINGS (A). Adele Jergens, Marilyn Monroe, LADIES OF THE CHORUS (A).

To-day open 1.35.   Last House 6.55.
Frank Sinatra, William Conrad, Keenan Wynn, Phyllis Kirk,
JOHNNY CONCHO
2.10. 5.30. 8.50. (A)

Robert Wagner, Jeffrey Hunter, Virginia Leith,
A KISS BEFORE DYING
(Color by De Luxe) (Cinemascope) (A)
3.35, 6.55.

CENTRAL
PHONE:56630

Sun., 3 p.m. — George Montgomery, INDIAN UPRISING (U) (Cine.). Barry Nelson, THE MAN WITH MY FARE (A).

To-day and Wed. open 2.00.
Last House 7.00.
Benny Hill, Belinda Lee,
WHO DONE IT?
2.20. 5.30. 8.45. (U)
Dale Robertson, Mara Corday,
A DAY OF FURY
(Tech.) 3.55. 7.10. (A)

TIVOLI
PHONE:4637

Sun., 3.15 p.m. — MacDonald Carey, Alexis Smith, CAVE OF OUTLAWS (U) (Tech.), Hugh Beaumont, MURDER IS MY BUSINESS (A).

To-day open 4.50. Wed. 1.25.
Last House 6.50.
Jack Palance, Ida Lupino, Shelley Winters,
BIG KNIFE
5.00. 8.30. (1.35 Wed. only) (A)
Sterling Hayden, William Bishop, Karen Booth,
TOP GUN
6.50. (3.20 Wed. only) (A)

PLAYHOUSE
PHONE:5151

Sun., 3 p.m. — Broderick Crawford, Claire Trevor, STOP! YOU'RE KILLING ME (A). Scott Brady, DESERT PAT-

To-day and Wed. open 5.00.
Last House 7.00.
Vincent Price, Frank Lovejoy,
HOUSE OF WAX
(Warnercolor) 5.35, 8.50. (X)
Paul Christian, Paula Raymond,
BEAST FROM 20,000 FATHOMS
7.05. (X)
Persons under 16 years not admitted.

The ABC Opposition, Cambridge A composite weekly advertising block from an edition of the Cambridge *Daily News* in 1956, the year I left Cambridge for good. It was clearly not an outstanding week. The Rex's offerings from the same issue (p. 306) are at least marginally more interesting.

quota: *The Man in Black*, *A Case for PC 49*, *The Case of Dr Morelle*, *Vengeance is Mine*, *Death in the Hand*, *But Not in Vain*, *The Six Men*. They were too bad even to laugh at; and their American equivalents (*Assigned to Danger*, *Pride of Kentucky*, *Killer Shark*) showed no improvement at all.

The Victoria, splendidly placed in the Market Square, was a physically objectionable picture house, old and creaky and smelling of wet lino, with a low, nicotine-stained ceiling. It was too wide for its length, its screen was so high that in the stalls you got a crick in the neck, and it provided a poor view from almost every seat. To add injury to insult, the space between the rows was so narrow that a tall man was bound to bark his shins. But its position and its capacity ensured fairly full houses even at matinées, when it was especially popular with shoppers anxious to take the weight off their feet. I queued for hours there to see Bob Hope in *Fancy Pants* ('No popcorn during my picture, peasants') and the almost unendurable but highly fashionable *The Tales of Hoffman*; even a revival of *The Hunchback of Notre Dame* drew evening queues, and the occasional exploitation piece, like *Intimate Relations*, the dreadful British version of *Les Parents Terribles*, seemed to do well without causing resentment in those who had been deceived. On the other hand, the Central Cinema, seating only eleven hundred, always drew what seemed in the circuit's eyes to be the poorest of the week's releases, often running it for three days and filling in the rest of the week with re-issues. The one attraction I had to queue for there was *Abbott and Costello Meet Frankenstein*, which turned out to be a much smarter spoof than anybody had given it credit for, and raised the roof with some of its lines, as when the unfortunate Lawrence Talbot tells Lou Costello, 'You don't understand, every night when the moon is full I turn into a wolf' and gets the reply: 'Yeah, you and fifty million other guys!'

The remaining ABC halls, the Tivoli and the Playhouse, were knobbly, antique little places in the suburbs, with gas radiators which always smelled dangerous without giving out much in the way of heat. The Tivoli also had the disadvantage of sloping down almost into the Cam, so that the front stalls flooded when the river rose, and the record high water level was shown by a stain across the lower half of the screen. Both usually took second runs, and seldom filled up, but every now and then there would be assigned to them, usually simultaneously, the première of some item which had been labelled box-office poison. Thus I had to suffer the Tivoli's shortcomings in order to see John Huston's *The Asphalt Jungle* and Max Ophuls's *Letter from an Unknown Woman* (which played as second feature to Burgess Meredith in *San Francisco Docks*). The Playhouse banged its loudest publicity drum for a weird but by no means wonderful British version of *The Fall of the House of Usher*, shot on a shoestring in Brighton and no doubt something which that delightful actress Gwen Watford would prefer not to remember.

It took me a long time even to locate the Kinema or the Rex, but it did not seem to matter, since they were independently-owned halls which had to snap at whatever minor product was left when the ABCs had taken their fill. It turned out that the Kinema stood on the far side of Parker's Piece and a few hundred yards down Mill Road, an insalubrious part of town in which undergraduates *in statu pupillari* were not encouraged to linger. It had once been a town hall of sorts, though it now had a lorry-drivers' café attached to it and was approached from the street through a narrow, arched pink corridor, the walls of which had that kind of stipple effect which attracts uncleanable layers of sticky dust. If it had not been for a few garish film posters one might have considered oneself, as one approached the makeshift pay box, to be entering a fairground Ghost Train or Dante's Inferno. Once inside the auditorium, however, one could quickly forget the surroundings, for here was a steep rake and a well-lit screen, while the few seats which were not broken seemed sufficiently receptive to one's body contours. Unfortunately the patrons were noisy – kids in the afternoon and yobboes in the evening – and the attractions were usually low-grade throwouts from Columbia, a very variable supplier which at the time seemed not to be on friendly terms with ABC. Since the Arts seldom touched its product either, it was to the Kinema that one had to go if one wanted one's movies introduced by the lady with the torch and accompanied by an episode of *Flash Gordon Conquers the Universe* or *Batman and Robin*. What the doctor ordered in Mill Road was Jon Hall in *Hurricane Island*, Randolph Scott in *Hangman's Knot*, Louis Hayward in *Dick Turpin's Ride* and Johnny Weissmuller as *Jungle Jim in the Forbidden Land*. If by an oversight some item as high-toned as, say, Welles's *The Lady from Shanghai* got slipped in as a second feature, the management could take steps to see that it did not happen often enough to upset the regular customers.

There was a poster in Market Square, changed weekly, which advertised a cinema called the Rex, but I made several random enquiries without coming across anybody who actually knew where it was. Some of them thought you had to go past the Magdalene traffic lights and up the hill, but after that both memory and inspiration faltered. One dull and overcast afternoon in November, however, lured by a double-bill of circuit rejects (*Chicken Every Sunday*, too American; *That Lady in Ermine*, Lubitsch's last film, too effete), I determined to investigate. By trial, error, and persistent questioning of passers-by, I learned the secret.

You turn *right* at the lights, walk along Chesterton Road until it comes down to the river on the right, then turn left up Hertford Street, the only real hill in Cambridge but otherwise undistinguished and packed with Victorian villas. Halfway up, an unnamed linking alley on the left lands you in a semi-cul-de-sac which is Magrath Avenue; and at its north end, facing the backyards and garages of the Hertford Street houses, I found a vast, ugly, jerry-built barn of a building with the letters R★E★X stripped down its stucco in red neon. The left-hand end of this architectural abomination had a tiny entrance with the word BALL-ROOM on a sign above it; the cinema, further along, was obviously quite spacious, although the fake marble steps were cracked and the still display cases were falling apart with rot. Lined up outside was a long row of bicycle blocks, but all were empty, and grass flourished through splits in the concrete. The signboard above the canopy bore only tattered strips of posters which had presumably advertised former attractions. There was no sign of life except for an elderly lady doing her knitting in the pay box. One would not have known what was playing had it not been for a category board which had been placed on a rickety easel at the top of the steps. (Shades of Bolton's Theatre Royal.) *Chicken* was spelled without its middle 'c' and *Ermine* without its final 'e'. Whistling softly to myself, I followed the wall past two crash doors to a sign which read *Car Park*, and found myself in a small muddy area facing the back end of a factory. The car park was as empty as the street.

I did not go in on that occasion. But there came a week in the following term when the Rex could no longer be resisted, for as support to a rather dismal symbolic fantasy called *The Boy with Green Hair* it was showing Fred Astaire and Ginger Rogers in *Top Hat*, which I had not seen since 1935. Choosing a wet afternoon, I cycled between the showers as far as Magrath Avenue, dumped my bike in a sheltered spot, paid my one and ninepence and hurried into the rear stalls, looking neither to right nor left, as though I were afraid of being spotted by the proctors. The auditorium showed unmistakable signs of having been loved by nobody for a great many years. Luxury had never entered into its construction: it was simply a roof and four walls, three of them directly exposed to the elements, which could rage fiercely on the top of that single Cambridge hill. The cinema's normal temperature, therefore, fluctuated between cold and very cold. The architectural plan, if there had ever been one, must have packed in as many seats as possible at the lowest conceivable cost. There were in fact twelve hundred seats, which is a great many for any suburban cinema, even a well-run and well-booked one, and the Rex had neither advantage. Owned by a tiny circuit which had clearly written it off as a tax loss, it was booked, I found, by a distraught manager who had long ago given up the unequal battle with the ABC circuit, and could often pay neither his staff nor his fuel bills.

The lights dimmed and the 'Coming Shortly' slides flashed on to the screen. *Death from a Distance*; *Hoppy Serves a Writ*; *Old Mother Riley Headmistress*; *Shadow of the Eagle*; and a handful of Poverty Row westerns which I had seen listed in the *Monthly Film Bulletin* but never dreamed anybody would book. There were six other people in the stalls area, two of them apparently asleep; there could not be anyone in the circle because the steps had been roped off and a sign said *Danger! Men at Work*, though there was no sign of structural restoration. To be fair, the screen was of a good size and the projection quite reasonable . . . but those seemed to be the only merits. The front stalls sloped up towards the screen, an arrangement I have never liked, and the mid-stalls area was very flat, so that, if a full house ever materialized, several hundred people would have trouble with sight lines. I was appalled by the torn and dangerous carpets; the smell of sweaty feet and worse; the broken seats, many of them swaying on one bracket; the cobwebs hanging quite openly from the less reachable corners. How the place had survived for so long was a complete mystery, and after that first dismal visit, which all but dampened my ardour for *Top Hat*, I decided to let it remain one. A couple of months later, however, I ventured once more, having noted a Sunday coupling of Hal Roach's *The Housekeeper's Daughter* with Laurel and Hardy in *The Bohemian Girl*. This time the Rex was nearly a third full and looked more cheerful: I realized that money and a few good films could make it a tolerable place for a filmgoer to be seen in. But since it seemed unlikely that either of these benefits would come about, I forgot about the Rex until a year or so later, when it returned to my thoughts with considerable impact.

FIFTEEN

Next Week's Films

Although English literature is generally regarded as the cushiest of all university subjects – the theory being that it is virtually impossible to fail providing one has a little taste, a lot of nerve, and a flair for putting sentences end to end – in my day it was equally impossible to get a first-class English degree without a great deal of hard work and a touch of genius. I still have most of my essays: they were written in a meticulous hand which tends to conceal their paucity of thought. I totally respected my supervisor, but he was difficult to like, taking literature so very seriously that every chance remark was considered at cabinet level. He must have sighed a lot over my tendency to be frivolous, but he usually gave me a beta plus minus, a mark which seems to indicate some degree of indecision in the person awarding it. He wrote at the foot of one essay:

Written with much verve and conviction, and a perfectly adequate statement of the case, but you will have to beware of appearing over-confident, and your wealth of references through to contemporary life continually arouses my misgivings about your sense of the character of medieval Christendom.

And on another:

Well argued, but ill demonstrated. Not far from a kind of critical journalese.

He had my number, all right. I was too busy to immerse myself wholly in remote literary epochs, and my work, hastily cribbed from the less obvious books and briskly cobbled together in a bold but unscholarly way, merely skated over the surface of other people's opinions. All the same, my examination marks at the end of the first three terms were surprisingly good and, as a result, my tutor, Tom Henn, drew me aside and murmured that next year, if I undertook to keep my nose to the grindstone, he would 'run me for a first'. I thought about this for a long time before deciding to be perfectly open with him. My other activities, I said, were on the whole more important to me than Piers Plowman and Alexander Pope, and if I were prevented by study from doing what I liked, then I would probably feel so miserable that I would fail to pull off a first anyway. He shrugged, and we came to a mutual understanding that I would get a good second (which I did) while continuing to devote about half my time to what Tom called 'extra-mural activities'.

Not that Cambridge was exactly agog for my acting talents. However, in a college revue called *The Cat's Whiskers* – 'Cats' being the nickname for my college, St Catharine's – I imitated Tom Henn in a spoof about his partiality for the works of W. B. Yeats and J. M. Synge; I wrote the lyrics for a song called 'The Lady in the House across the Street'; I played the drawling half of the Western Brothers, still popular radio commentators on life's follies and foibles; and I spent most of the show wandering in and out of the other numbers dressed as Groucho Marx in a cap and gown. This went over big, especially one night when our rather prissy college chaplain was in the front row. I announced at the final curtain that everybody could go home as I was off to bed with a hot toddy; I then looked accusingly at the chaplain and said: 'That's a drink.' He chortled so much that he nearly choked. Next morning when I read in chapel for the Bishop Browne Bible Reading Prize he looked at me rather oddly, and I was surprised when I heard later that I had won it.

I did some acting for the Mummers, a group founded in the twenties by John Clements and Alistair Cooke. In James Elroy Flecker's *Hassan* I provided comic relief as the Captain of the Imperial Guard ('Master of the world, I am but dung') and in *1066 and All That* I was several barons and a magistrate, the latter having to deal with the sketch about the cat that crept into the crypt. But perhaps my most celebrated performance was in an Old Time Music-Hall at the ADC when, fortified each night by two Audit Ales, I gave a fruity rendering of Harry Champion's 'Any Old Iron'. As an encore I offered 'I'm 'Enery the Eighth I Am', and was part of a trio which sang 'Dirty Work' ('Ere we are, ready and willin', to murder your mother-in-law for a shillin'). One of my companions here was Peter Hall, later Sir Peter of Stratford, Aldwych, and the National; his solo was 'Where Do Flies Go in the Wintertime?'*

To be in the annual production of the Marlowe Society was a mark of honour among undergraduate actors, even if one only propped up a pillar. Despite the society's name, the work performed was almost always by Shakespeare, and in my day the producer was always George 'Dady' Rylands of King's College, a senior fellow who also dab-

---

*It was indeed an all-star show. Donald Beves, vice-provost of King's, sang 'Daddy's on the Engine'; Daniel Massey portrayed 'The Galloping Major'; and the speciality of the Rev. Geoffrey Beaumont of Trinity was 'My Baby Has Gone Down the Plughole'. Other performers, since better known on the professional stage, included Peter Woodthorpe, David King and Tony Church. About the only undergraduate of contemporary note *not* to appear in this production was Julian Slade, then busy with a new musical comedy every year, two of them in my view at least the equal of his later *Salad Days*.

bled in producing for the professional stage. He was regarded as the ultimate Cambridge authority on verse-speaking, and brought down to rehearsals many of his West End friends, including Joyce Carey and Miles Malleson. In *Coriolanus* I had a range of small parts, including Second Citizen to Peter Hall's First and Mark Boxer's Third. I was also a member of the Guard, and Fourth Conspirator. But my big scene was at the beginning of Act Two, when Joe Bain and I had the stage to ourselves as Cushion-Laying Officers, our function being to prepare for the majestic entry of Coriolanus and generally bring the audience up to date with events. As the scene was in prose, and involved none of his leading actors, Dady had no interest in it at all, and at every rehearsal decided to cut to the grand entrance. Joe and I, who were word-perfect after privately rehearsing while feeding the ducks by the river, made a joke of it, but our astonishment can be imagined when the scene was again cut at the final dress rehearsal, because time was pressing; and so after the final tableau, during the on-stage party, we reminded Dady of the fact.

His mouth opened wide. 'What do you mean, never rehearsed it? Didn't we do it this very afternoon?'

'No, sir, you cut it.'

'Cut it, did I? Ah, well you're intelligent chaps. Can't do it now, can we? You'd better play it as you think fit. Not an important scene, anyway: it's the poetry they come for, you know.'

Joe and I walked away seething; but the challenge had been issued and must be accepted. Our scene should not go unnoticed. On the first night, after a dreary and humourless first act, we marched on with our armfuls of cushions to face a restive audience, and in my fruitiest Zummerzet accent I enunciated:

Cum, cum, they be almost 'ere. 'Ow many stands for consulships?

Joe's response was fully in kind, and the audience's mild titters built up as we left the stage to a smattering of applause. Dady was standing bemusedly in the wings. 'Er . . . who told you to play that scene in that particular manner?' he asked. We reminded him that he had instructed us to do as we thought best; that was it. 'Ah,' said Dady, and there was a pregnant pause. 'Ah well: they seemed to like it, didn't they? You'd better carry on.'

I believe *Coriolanus* was my last appearance in any stage play, though during the previous vacation in Bolton I had persuaded my beloved Little Theatre to let me produce and star in an under-thirties production of Thornton Wilder's play without scenery, *Our Town*, which tries to relate universal matters to the small details of life in a New Hampshire village at the turn of the century. For myself I grabbed the part of the Stage Manager, who not only narrates but takes over minor roles as required. I am sure I did not look the right age or shape, but rather magically I felt it as I leaned against the proscenium arch, spouting crackerbarrel philosophy and smoking a pipe. At any rate you could have heard a pin drop during the funeral scene, as the heroine joins her elders in the cemetery and the Stage Manager gets down to the basic feeling of the play:

Now, there's some things we all know, but we don't take 'em out and look at 'em very often. We all know that *somethin'* is eternal. And it ain't houses, and it ain't names, and it ain't earth, and it ain't even the stars . . . everybody knows in their bones that *somethin'* is eternal, and that somethin' has to do with human beings . . .

The final applause was thunderous, an emotional binge. I

had arranged what I hoped was a clever curtain call, starting and ending with an empty stage, but the audience simply would not let us go. I walked on air for days, especially when the reviews came out:

One of the best plays ever produced in Bolton . . .
Leslie Halliwell's success in a nearly constant narrative flow, without perceptibly raising his voice, and yet retaining a complete hold over the audience, could only have been achieved by means of the perfect, unhurried naturalness which comes from the sinking of personality in a part . . .

It was a perfect swan song. While in Cambridge, I had been reporting for *Varsity*, which was such absorbing fun that it made me determine, temporarily at least, to take up a journalistic career. At *Varsity* you met a variety of people, and learned things you did not previously know about a great range of subjects. You retired to the scruffy editorial suite above the Scotch Hoose restaurant and typed up your stories in the approved Fleet Street manner, with your hat on if you liked; then on Friday at eight, after dinner in Hall, you cycled down to the *Daily News* press behind the New Theatre and watched it all set by linotype, pressed into cardboard and thence into curved metal moulds. These were fixed into enormous printing machines, and soon after midnight the newspapers came flowing down to be collected into bundles, just as I had seen it happen in a hundred American movies starring Lee Tracy or Edward G. Robinson. On Saturday one watched the copies being sold, heard the articles being discussed; then on Sunday afternoon came our own critical meeting at which the staff tore the current issue to pieces and planned the next one. We sold 7000 copies a week and made a tidy profit, which we had to disperse in parties twice a term since we were not allowed to do anything else with it except make occasional donations to charity. The university authorities seldom interfered unless we overstepped the mark in some direction (we once made fun of the benzedrine habit); the dons in fact seemed to enjoy being interviewed. However it was sometimes a strain to fill twelve pages, and in certain issues the headlines were very big and the stories very short.

The editor and the department heads changed every term; I worked my way through news and features until I got what I wanted, the critics' page. This involved a frantic start when a freezing early January delayed some arrivals at the beginning of term and I was forced to fill the entire page myself under various aliases compounded from my own name: Robert James, James Leslie, Leslie Halliwell, H. Robert. I also assigned myself to a back-page column of my own invention, offering capsule reviews of every film to be seen in Cambridge during the seven days following publication. Under its stylish half-tone heading it quickly became an essential feature of university life, and of course it gave me the advantage of free admission to every cinema in town. I tried to be fair, but there were a great many bad films around, and some of the entries must have sounded malicious, for a correspondent one week suggested that I should sign the column *Deadly Ernest*. Typical entries from the early days included:

PANDORA AND THE FLYING DUTCHMAN. An arty phantasmagoria which wears Omar Khayyam's moving finger to the very bone. The effect is curiously comatose, and the whole can be recommended only for Jack Cardiff's colour photography.

ALONG THE GREAT DIVIDE. An eccentric psychological western which wastes Kirk Douglas but maintains a superior surface gloss. Plus MADAME LOUISE, a farce which was funny on the stage and should have stayed there.

MEET THE INVISIBLE MAN. A mechanical farce which misses most of its opportunities but isn't bad for Abbott and Costello. In support, CALAMITY JANE MEETS SAM BASS, with entirely predictable results.

HOME AT SEVEN. R. C. Sherriff's puzzle play is acted with distinction but has been encased in a cheap and uncinematic production emulating the present crude television techniques. Also REMEMBER THAT FACE, a well-directed chunk of waterfront knockabout.

CARBINE WILLIAMS. A Readers' Digest curiosity about a shady character who invented a gun while serving a manslaughter sentence. Hardly James Stewart's cup of tea, nor mine either.

Sunday revivals bring to the Victoria THE WOMAN IN WHITE, a fairly stylish version of Wilkie Collins's mystery romance; to the Central, a well-made psychological thriller called THE DARK PAST. Addicts may find TRADE WINDS, with Fredric March as a detective scouring the Far East (in back projection) for suspects, worth a trip to the Tivoli; and at the Arts, those who have not already done so are recommended to catch THE GHOST before he GOES WEST.

It was supposed to serve a purpose rather than to scintillate with wit; what I had not expected was that it could very easily make or break a programme at the box office, which made the managers cultivate me more assiduously than ever. The exception was the Rex Cinema, where no one, I imagine, ever read *Varsity*; it became increasingly difficult even to find out what had been booked there. The man on the other end of the phone, when there was an answer, usually sounded drunk, and the sparse information I obtained in this way often turned out to be wrong.

One day, however, a new voice answered my call, a bluff and jovial voice with the air of someone in authority. He gave his name as Webb and said he was the new owner, but could not find the booking book. This seemed a development worthy of investigation, so I dropped by after lunch, and discovered a man in a grey suit on his knees in the stalls, fixing a broken chair with a new giant-size ratchet screwdriver of which he told me he was particularly proud, since it was the only one in Cambridge and likely to remain so for some time. When he stood up I saw an enormously corpulent man with a toothbrush moustache, a rather small pointed head, and no hair. He looked a well-used fifty, but said he was thirty-three (and later insisted on proving the fact). It appeared that word had come to him that the previous owners were looking for a profitable get-out from a business to which they were plainly unsuited. Mr Webb, a successful local haulage contractor, had recently sold his business under a covenant not to set up shop in competition for five years. He was thus in search of a temporary business, and after a brief negotiation had found himself the owner of a large and derelict place of public entertainment, to wit one cinema and one ballroom with joining kitchen. With no idea whatever of how such venues should be run, but operating on the principle of in for a penny in for a pound, he had picked up the lease of the Kinema at the same time, and now hoped to give ABC a run for its money by operating both halls in the way he would have operated a haulage business, that is by native cunning and brute force.

George Webb was not a man to let ignorance deter him. A sporadic filmgoer at best (between shivering at *King Kong* in 1933 and sleeping through *Henry V* in 1945 his experience of the art form seemed to be nil), he was a self-made man who had terminated his secondary schooling at the age of thirteen and educated himself in the motor trade. A legacy enabled him to set up his own garage while still in his teens, and he carried it on throughout his army service, which by dint of some manipulation never took him further away than Newmarket. After the war he diversified his interests, gaining a reputation for working harder and longer than any of his employees; and his opponents bought him out from fear that he would soon corner the local market. George did not conceive failure for himself, and despised it in anyone else. His motto, as he frequently told me, was: 'If you see anybody in the gutter, kick him.'

Having never met anybody like George, I was fascinated to watch him operate. Even the original bull in the china shop can hardly have rubbed up so many people the wrong way in so short a time: ill-wishers on that first afternoon included an usherette, a doorman, two film salesmen and his wife. Clearly in the motor trade the best way to get things done had been to shower people with threats, abuse and four-letter words, mixed with the occasional quick smile to show the victim that there were no hard feelings. One of the salesmen left without being able to say the same: the mildest phrase he uttered was 'big bald-headed old bastard'. George would not have denied that this was a recognizable description; indeed he would have basked in the glory of it. But underneath his tough skin there was a very interesting and oddly likeable character. He barged blindly into every detail of his new business, and what he did not know he made it his business to find out. For him no job was too trivial or mean, from mopping out the ladies' loo to tiptoeing through the circle void in order to switch on the extract fan. He mended fuses, replenished the sales desk, sold tickets, led customers to seats: he had to, for he never employed enough staff to cover tea breaks. What he also needed was a quick course in film appreciation and booking tactics, and he saw in me his chance to get those commodities for nothing. Our phone conversation ran along these lines:

'Mr Webb, what's on next week?'

'Er, *Cairo Road* and *Tarzan and the Slave Girl*. Will we do any good?'

'I doubt it. *Cairo Road*'s not known – it died in London, and it's an 'A' so the kids can't get in in the evening. And why play *Tarzan* when the kids are at school in the afternoon?'

'Will you be coming up?'

'Shouldn't think so: not my line.'

'You're a bloody lot of comfort. What would you book in my place?'

'Something good that happened to run out of term, then you'll get the undergrads who missed it.'

'Like what?'

And so it started. Get some Bob Hope comedies, I said, and the older the better; and some early Marx Brothers, the ones which had delighted the Film Society but had not been shown publicly for seventeen years. Danny Kaye as Walter Mitty, and Walt Disney's *Fantasia*, and Gene Kelly in *On the Town*, and *Destry Rides Again*, and *Citizen Kane*. The first of my suggestions to pay off was Launder and Gilliat's recent chase adventure *State Secret*, shot in the Dolomites and possessed of a witty script; it had played twice at the ABCs, but not in term time. When *State Secret* came to the Rex the other halls were having a thin week – *Highly Dangerous*, *My Blue Heaven*, *September Affair* – and it was only right and proper that my column should say so and send readers to the Rex. On the other hand, I said they should avoid the abysmal second feature which George had allowed the traveller to foist upon him. The programme ran for three days, and on the following morning George tracked me down at *Varsity* to say that he had done nearly twice the best business in the recorded history of the Rex, and it had all come in during the twenty minutes before the last feature started, just as he was ready to shut up shop. Henceforth he regarded me as a kind of witch doctor, and insisted on taking me out to a curry supper that evening, since he urgently needed my further predictions. It was easy to work out a few likely double-bills, and before the end of that term George had done astonishingly well with *Duck Soup* and *Double Indemnity*; *Monkey Business* and *It's a Gift*; and *Things to Come* and *Occupe-toi d'Amélie*.

As a frequent non-paying patron, I was surprised to find how easily the whole ambience of the Rex could be improved by a full house, despite George's antipathetic attitude to public relations. He had promptly sold off the car park, so Magrath Avenue became jammed with vehicles, to the anger of householders who had been accustomed for years to a quiet life. Even though he had paid a few bills and now had an ample supply of coke, he was more than reluctant to use it. Should the sun shine fitfully on a January afternoon, he would order the boiler damped down in anticipation of the evening rush. 'You can never warm a place up with heating,' he said illogically, 'only with bottoms in the seats.' Should a patron complain of the cold, he would be practically frogmarched by George to the battered thermometer which hung at the back of the stalls (the warmest spot anyway) and which against the 56 degree mark had in clear printing the word *temperate*. The temperature in the cinema usually *was* 56 or very slightly below, and George wanted to know what was the matter with that, adding pleasantly that he personally never had it nearly so warm at home, and perhaps the patron was sickening for something. But even when he did try, the Rex was impossible to heat properly, because of its exposed position, its paper-thin walls, and its two draught-inducing mid-stalls emergency doors which the fire authorities would never allow him to label except simply as EXIT.

It became an unwritten rule at the Rex that the patron was always wrong. Even though a dignified lady might have been given a broken seat with a sharp spring sticking up out of it, she would go away apologizing for having chosen that particular resting-place. The toilets were a disgrace, and a daily subject for complaint, but George's regretful answer was that if he had them refitted, they would immediately be wrecked by louts who had it in for him. He rejigged the price plan so that more than half the stalls were 2s 7d, with six rows of broken front seats at one shilling and the next six rows at 1s 9d, the most popular price. However, as soon as the undergraduates began to pour in at seven o'clock, George would hurry out into the foyer, looking harassed, with torch in hand, and shout apologetically: 'Stop the one and nines.' His theory was that undergraduates, having come all this way, would not be seen in the 'bobs' so that the two-and-sevens would be full in no time; it did not worry him that once inside they would discover that the one-and-nines they originally wanted were still empty. He never listened to my remonstrances about keeping faith, asserting that it was his right to charge what the hell he liked, and that anyone he annoyed would still come back next time there was a film he wanted to see, which with my help would be frequently. His Parthian shot was unanswerable: 'They'll sit on orange boxes with lavatory seats round their necks and pay ten quid a head for the privilege, if they want something badly enough.'

Despite its deficiencies the Rex became fashionable. Or perhaps it was *because* of them. The audiences developed a love-hate relationship with it, but there was no denying that in terms of its programmes at least it gave excellent value. The last double feature would begin as soon after seven as possible, allowing undergraduates to get there after a gobbled 6.30 dinner in the Hall but ensuring closedown in time for the last buses. It was almost eerie to stand at 6.55 outside a near-empty cinema, imagining hundreds of bicycles being ridden furiously in our direction. Soon they would begin to swerve around that quiet corner, followed by the fastest and hardiest of the walkers. By ten past there would sometimes be a moving queue fifty yards long, and the whole district reverberated to the clank of cycles being laid five deep against any convenient wall. The residents stood at their doors in amazement; one told me that in his recollection the last queue at the Rex had been in 1930, when Eddie Cantor played there in *Whoopee*.

'The Best Value in Show Business' was a slogan I suggested to George; he used it henceforth in all his advertising. On Saturdays he brought next week's copy down to my college in his Rolls Bentley so that I could correct it over a lunchtime drink; spelling, he said, had never been his strong point. The slogan seemed a fair enough description of those massive programmes which packed the place for three days and the constituents of which were hurriedly reallocated in other combinations three terms hence:

French without Tears *and* Trouble in Paradise
The Pirate *and* The Big Store
The Lavender Hill Mob *and* Green for Danger
The Happiest Days of Your Life *and* Night Train to Munich
The Lady Vanishes *and* Brief Encounter
Blithe Spirit *and* Destry Rides Again
The Philadelphia Story *and* The Marx Brothers Go West

The Marx Brothers quickly became our mascots, and we were certainly instrumental in the great Marx revival of the early fifties which spread like wildfire through London and the key cities. We persuaded Paramount to strike one new print of each of the early films. The cost was soon covered, and the prints slowly fell into ribbons, but our whacking takes caused the renter's percentage to rise, for Wardour Street was never slow to make money out of someone else's ideas. Meanwhile, across college dinner tables those familiar lines would echo:

- Do you suppose I could buy back my introduction to you?
- I don't normally mind being insulted, but I resent it from a character whose head comes to a point.
- I could dance with you till the cows come home. Come to think of it, I'll dance with the cows, and you come home.

Two incidents stand out from my last term as an undergraduate, in the spring of 1952. George had been offered, by a small and not too reliable company, the Cambridge première of what turned out to be Laurel and Hardy's last feature, *Robinson Crusoeland*. He consulted me: I demurred at first, because all reports said it was dreadful, but eventually we coupled it with René Clair's *I Married a Witch* and gave it seven days in Whit week, when the kids would be home and the undergraduates would probably be busy with exams. To George's surprise the renter proved willing to go fifty-fifty on extra publicity, and throughout the previous week a pair of Laurel and Hardy impersonators paraded the streets of Cambridge in sandwich boards advertising the show. The result was astonishing: a full house on the opening Sunday afternoon before the lights went down, and that despite strong sunshine outside. It was a thoroughly mixed audience, and even before the house lights dimmed George was busy flashing his torch at some noisy yobboes in the front rows. Unfortunately the show began with a short, added as an extra incentive to the university section of the audience; it was Norman McLaren's abstract jazz doodle *Begone Dull Care*, already cherished by Film Society *aficionados*. Within three minutes the yobboes were cat-calling to a man, and two of them erected multi-coloured golfing umbrellas which they seemed to have brought for the express purpose of impeding the view of the people behind. Suddenly six undergraduates in the front row of the circle stood in unison and yelled: 'Shut up!' The reply, somewhat less unified, was:

'Shut up yourself!' All over the auditorium dark figures rose and began to leave their seats; even George had panic in his eyes, as a riot seemed inevitable, and our ears were assailed by the waves of picturesque abuse. Then suddenly the pace of the film accelerated, and all eyes turned to the screen to be hypnotized by a dazzle of coloured dots accompanying a rousing finale by the Oscar Petersen Trio. Once off guard, the would-be belligerents were transfixed, and *Begone Dull Care* rattled on to a triumphant conclusion, amid cheers and sustained applause. When the programme ended and *Begone Dull Care* came on again, I noticed that most of the yobboes stayed to watch it, this time with obvious delight. Meanwhile *Robinson Crusoeland*, as I feared, had been embarrassingly bad: made in France, by a company which went bankrupt halfway through production, it forced poor Stan and Ollie to make bricks with no straw at all. Distressingly, Stan looked deathly ill and Ollie was the size of a small warehouse. By Wednesday the Rex was playing to half-empty houses.

While exams were still in progress there was a four-day run (Sunday to Wednesday) of *The Blue Angel*, one of my more hesitant suggestions in the cause of art. George thought he remembered that it was saucy, which is probably why he agreed to book it, though he insisted on the English version rather than the German. Because of my own exams I did not get up to the Rex until the Wednesday, and as I put my bike into a totally empty rack at 6.50 pm, George came out on to the step to tell me that business had been terrible. He said it with some malice, presumably to prove that I was not infallible and that therefore he did not owe me anything. I shrugged and mentioned the sublime weather, but I was puzzled all the same, since the foyer poster of the Dietrich character had caused many ripples of interest, and George had been looking forward to an overflowing till, especially since he had booked the film for a flat rate of five pounds, which meant lots of profit if the picture did well. As I stood with him briefly in the empty foyer, I suggested that he should have put something stronger with it than *The Saxon Charm*, which was the cheapest English-language film he could buy for £2 10s 0d, and totally unknown; but all the same I felt I had let him down, and went upstairs in some disquiet. George called after me that since there was nothing doing he would be off to the New Spring to drown his sorrows; he did not invite me to join him.

A Broadway comedy-drama, allegedly based on the career of theatrical producer Jed Harris, *The Saxon Charm* was heavier and duller than I could have imagined. I should never have let George book the film. But about halfway through I was disturbed by noise from the stalls, and on peering over the rail I was surprised to see the one-and-nines filling up. As I glanced behind me, half a dozen customers also arrived in the circle, to find as usual that no usherette was present to guide them over the dangerously worn stair nosings. I hurried to the circle steps in search of assistance, and found to my astonishment an enthusiastic and voluble queue of gowned figures, growing longer by the minute, stretching through the main doors and down the street. Somebody had rung the New Spring for George, and he arrived at that moment, his piggy eyes glinting in astonishment and greed at this unexpected turn of fortune. It was rather like one of Hollywood's putting-on-a-show musicals in which disaster is averted by the magical last-minute appearance of a society crowd including all the most influential Broadway critics and backers. Clearly my fellow-students, though really too busy for movies that week, had been unable to resist the last chance of seeing what was reputed to be a sexy classic. When *The Blue Angel* began, ten minutes late in order to get everybody in, all usable seats were filled, and George was wishing he had mended the broken ones properly. There were even forty people standing behind the stalls, in direct contravention of the fire regulations.

I stood in the circle gangway myself, deputizing for an usherette who had been co-opted for extra ice-cream sales. My consuming worry now was whether *The Blue Angel* would live up to the expectations of twelve hundred excited undergraduates. The story, of a stodgy old professor who goes to a night club in order to clear his students out, and then himself falls for the tawdry singer, has a very slow start, and for a while I thought the packed audience might vent its exasperation by loudly mocking the Teutonic gloom of the sets, the heavy emotionalism of Emil Jannings's acting, and the amazingly heavy-limbed chorus girls who strutted on the stage of the club. But there was never more than a warm buzz of murmured comment, and not even that once the pathetic central situation was established. Von Sternberg's direction tightens the grip like a tourniquet, and by the time Dietrich as Lola-Lola had with overpowering emphasis sung the final choruses of 'Falling in Love Again', while the old professor staggered back through the snow to die in his classroom, that crowded cinema was as silent as the grave. When the lights came on at the end I hurried to help open the exit doors, but for five or ten seconds nobody moved. Nobody spoke, either: it was as though they had been frozen solid by some mysterious ray from a Saturday morning serial. Gradually they began to reach for their belongings and move towards the exits but, whereas normally there would have been a mad noisy scramble for bikes and a twenty-mile-an-hour dash down the slumbering streets, tonight everybody filed out sombrely, more than a thousand of them, like monks in a processional. Once on the street each man stood by politely until his bike came to the top of the heap, then pedalled away so slowly that his gown did not even flap in the moonlight. The pedestrians followed suit after their fashion; just a few could be seen indulging in earnest quiet discussion.

George came out and stood beside me on the step until the last figure had rounded the distant corner. Then he said: 'That stunned 'em, boy. I told you it would.'

Sixteen

The Front Page

My three years as an undergraduate, like all pleasant things, came to an end. I had made a lot of friends, assimilated a variety of useful experience, and gained a fairly good degree in English literature. I was on the market. During that last term I sat for all kinds of boards, and even journeyed to Gosforth-on-Tyne for an interview with a manufacturer of detergents, who required me to demonstrate my intelligence by fitting eccentrically-shaped wooden blocks into equally eccentrically-shaped holes. But Cambridge had mollycoddled me, and every glimpse of the business world made me shudder. I had rejected a thought of the Church, telling myself that I simply was not 'good enough'; publishers did not seem to want me; I had no idea how to make use of my cinema knowledge. In some desperation I signed up for the teacher training college, which at least would keep me in Cambridge for another year. But then one of my least likely hopes came through. I was offered a job on *Picturegoer*.

In 1952 the circulation of the weekly magazine which had so influenced me was at its peak, getting on for half a million; Odhams Press was proud of it. The recently appointed editor, Connery Chappell, had achieved this by jazzing up the layout so that it was all brown blobs and squiggles, unreadable to anyone with a mental age higher than seven and a half. Distressed by its increasingly gossipy content, its short paragraphs and shorter sentences, its lack of critical values and its pin-up pictures, I had not for the last year or two been a constant reader. Yet it was still the most professional fan magazine on the market, and now that I no longer had the film trade papers which George passed on to me, I needed it again for the credits of the new releases. Surely, I thought, I could steer it back towards its previous eminence as the journal which had taught me so much about the movies? Connery Chappell himself proved reassuring, a shrewd and genial fellow who, like Baron Frankenstein, despised the monster he had produced while revelling in the skills which had enabled him to create it. I had managed to get the job by sending him clippings from 'Next Week's Films': I suppose he liked their conciseness. Anyway, though he could not offer me a NUJ ticket there and then he suggested I might work on a retainer while this was arranged.

The *Picturegoer* offices were on the fourth floor of the Odhams building at the north-east end of Shaftesbury Avenue, near the top of Drury Lane. The paper was written by a surprisingly small group of people, fewer indeed than one would gather from reading it, for we all contributed to each issue several pieces under a variety of by-lines. ('Martin Hands' was a popular favourite, and in one issue seemed to write more than anybody.) There was Margaret Hinxman, gracious, intelligent and enthusiastic; Derek Walker, a lithe and engaging young journalist from a Sheffield daily; Donald Hunt, a glum-faced but quick-thinking old pro; Harry White the sub-editor, who felt he had failed unless every story we submitted was re-written in his own style; and dear old Lionel Collier, emaciated but sartorially elegant, always with a carnation in his button-hole. Now nearing retirement, he continued to battle away in charge of the review page, and films, in his pontifical paragraphs, still 'failed entirely to jell', provided 'a full measure of entertainment value', or were deficient in 'technicalities'. He must have realized that he stood in the shadow of the axe, since his was not the language of the new *Picturegoer*, but he showed no sign of caring.

My appointment clearly arose from the fact that Lionel Collier was both too bored and too important to review the second features which at that time poured forth in profusion from the vaults of Columbia, Republic and Monogram. One solution was to call in Josh Billings, the burly *Kine Weekly* reviewer, who had already seen every film for trade purposes and was happy to earn a couple of guineas by rewriting his reverberant clichés for a lay audience. The other solution was to send the most junior member of staff. I saw in my first month, usually in underground Wardour Street mini-theatres at ten o'clock in the morning, Sterling Hayden in *The Golden Hawk*, Louis Hayward in *Captain Blood Fugitive*, Glenn Ford in *Torpedo Run*, John Carradine in *Captive Wild Woman*, Johnny Weissmuller in *Jungle Moon Men*, Jerry Desmonde in *Alf's Baby*, Diana Napier in *I Was a Dancer*, Diana Dors in *The Last Page*, George Montgomery in *Indian Uprising*, George Raft in *Loan Shark*, Donald Houston in *My Death is a Mockery*, Mickey Rooney in *Sound Off*, and Johnny Mack Brown in *Law of the Panhandle*, not to mention *Mother Riley Meets the Vampire* and *The Bowery Boys Meet the Monsters*. Enough, no doubt, to put most people off movies for life, but somehow I retained my enthusiasm. Indeed, I rather enjoyed setting my increasingly stern professional standards against such rubbish. The first decent film I was sent to was Stanley Kramer's *The Happy Time*, about the sexual awakening of a French-Canadian teenager. What I liked was the cheerful family atmosphere (the father was Charles Boyer) and the fact that the characters went to the local cinema to see a Rudolph Valentino silent; indeed I enjoyed it so much, perhaps by contrast with what had gone before, that I put it in for a Seal of Merit, *Picturegoer*'s newly invented equivalent to the Hollywood Oscar. Connery Chappell thought I must be mad and went to see for himself; then he returned and sent Donald and Margaret, who thought *The Happy Time* splendid. But after much editorial discussion, and a pat on the back for me, it was only given the maximum four stars for trying.

Since the paper had such a complicated layout, with photogravure on every page, we had to go to press nearly five weeks ahead of publication, which meant seeing the new films at the first possible opportunity. This was usually, for a big attraction, at an evening screening in a luxury venue, but since such occasions involved free liquor they were invariably attended by the editor or a senior staff member, who had to judge on the amount of space in the paper which should be given over to each 'blockbuster'. For programme-fillers Josh Billings and I, with a few other diehards, had to drag ourselves along to the morning screenings; even these might never have been held had it not been necessary to project the film for trade registration purposes. One Monday I turned up dutifully at Columbia's non-air-conditioned cellar to see an unknown item called *Hidden Secret*. Josh Billings was already reading the synopsis, and groaned as I came in. 'Charles Starrett again,' he said. 'I really don't know why I stay past the first reel.' But it was just as well he did, for the film, though entitled *Hidden Secret*, did not star Starrett, nor was it a western; it was a piece of Far Eastern thick-ear in which tough Yanks routed a gang of communists. Nobody at Columbia could even understand what had happened. Investigation revealed that what we saw had originally been called *A Yank in Indo-China*, and that an executive given to personal brainwaves had ordered the title changed to something more enticing, not realizing that this would give him two films called *Hidden Secret*. The solution which emerged was to change the title of the Starrett piece: it became *Range War*.

Apart from reviews, I wrote some features: about the history of the Dead End Kids ('Waterfront Winners!'), about Joan Bennett's new beauty book ('Joan Tells Her Secrets'), about new trends in horror films ('This THING's started something'). And I went to interview stars and directors of minor importance. I felt I had truly 'arrived' when one day the editor sent me to Ealing Studios to assess the rough cut of Michael Balcon's latest controversial drama and discuss it with the director, Sandy Mackendrick. 'The scuttlebut says it's good,' he told me, 'but it can't be up to much because there's nobody in it. Jack Hawkins, Phyllis Calvert . . . not even Alec Guinness.' So there I found myself that afternoon, watching *Mandy* in an Ealing viewing-room, surrounded by executives and technicians all watching my lip for the slightest quiver of adverse reaction. I made what seemed to be appropriately approving noises, but even though I quite liked *Mandy* I am sure I did not realize its significance as a milepost in the history of the serious British film about the problems of ordinary people, a genre which served the cinema well for the next ten years and was then absorbed by television. The discussion with Michael Balcon was especially embarrassing since I was unsure how far to commit myself; but as it happened all turned out well, for Connery was so intrigued by my report that he went to see *Mandy* himself and gave it the page one treatment.

Finally I contributed to the gossip page. Composed

mainly from press handouts, or at least using them as a
starting point, it was reasonably intelligent and well
informed, dealing with such topics as:

IS HOLLYWOOD GROWING UP AT LAST?

RUNNING THE GAUNTLET OF EQUITY'S SNIPING

IT'S TIME FOR SOME STRAIGHT TALK ABOUT 'THE GIFT HORSE' —
HASN'T IT ARRIVED TEN YEARS TOO LATE?

THERE'S SENSE AT LAST IN THE RE-ISSUE POLICY

DO YOU WANT CONTINENTALS AT YOUR LOCAL?

On the other hand, I was kept out of the reader service
section, though I did discover that the current 'George' was
a pale and bespectacled young man who, day in and day
out, sat in a large alcove surrounded by filing cabinets and
five moderately nubile girls. To such readers as cared to
send a stamped addressed envelope he would still forward
details of the colour of Betty Grable's hair and the number
of Robert Taylor's marriages. The service was both accurate and speedy, and each week many readers turned first
to George's selection of his most interesting replies.

That summer was in many ways a happy time for a lad
from the provinces who could still be thrilled by free passes
to West End cinemas and by the sight of buskers entertaining theatre queues, and who felt it the height of sophistication to end the evening with coffee in some outlandishly
decorated Soho clip joint serving a tasteless London version of the new-fangled Italian espresso. There was a
prevailing atmosphere during these months of rather

desperate gaiety, a hangover from the previous year's Festival of Britain. You could still feel that London was the centre of the world, especially if you went to Hyde Park every Sunday afternoon and listened to the eccentrics at Speaker's Corner. For me, simply to wander through the famous but unfamiliar London streets was fun enough, though care was necessary in the evening when running the gauntlet of Soho tarts, who in those days were so thick on the ground that they had to share doorways. It was a thrill indeed to make my first acquaintance with the Tower of London and the British Museum, and to follow up such excursions with tea in a novelty restaurant such as the Salad Bowl in Lyons' multi-storey Coventry Street emporium. Here in 1952 you got carpets and waiter service and tablecloths for your 2s 11d, as well as more food than you could eat, including a selection of the most succulent desserts in London. To complete such a day, which had probably begun with a press preview, I required no better nightcap than a visit to a news cinema, at which the newsreel was always the least important item. The programme might well include a revived Laurel and Hardy, a Leon Errol, or an Edgar Kennedy; there could also be on offer a Pete Smith Specialty or a James A. Fitzpatrick Traveltalk. But the bulk of the hour would be filled with the wild animated adventures of Tom and Jerry, Bugs Bunny, or Tweetie Pie and Sylvester, all of whom were then at the peak of their form. Strictly speaking, Sylvester was never billed, but in my circle he had a fan club all his own. He was the villainous lisping cat who in Warner cartoons stalked the canary with friendly cries of 'Hello, breakfatht', only to be promptly flattened by a steamroller or squeezed out through a mincer or exploded by an inadvertently swallowed bomb. He was such an incompetent menace that you couldn't help feeling sorry for him as he stumbled around muttering: 'There mutht be thome eathier way for a puthy cat to get thome thuthtenanth.' Once he found himself in Dr Jekyll's laboratory and made a grab at the nearest foaming beaker, not knowing the devastating effect it might have on his personality. 'Ah,' he cried greedily, 'thoda-pop!'

As the airless, dirty summer progressed, however, I became notably less contented with my lot. The dingy theatrical digs in Maida Vale, where I had temporarily moved in with my old school friend Jimmie Beattie, seemed a let-down after the clean and cosy college rooms which I had occupied for the last two years, and I felt the effects of Jimmie's disappointment when, having elected to pursue a career in the professional theatre, he could manage nothing better than a walk-on in Picasso's *Desire Caught by the Tail* at the Watergate, and a short run of saying 'Right, chief' as Paul Temple's assistant on the radio. London at close quarters was a drab place, still disfigured by bomb sites, and I knew I would never be really happy in it without an intense devotion to my work, which *Picturegoer* did not inspire. The fact was inescapable: the magazine had changed, and I had changed, and there was little left in common between us. I felt I should now be writing for *Sequence* or the *Monthly Film Bulletin* rather than straining to produce the jargon which Harry White demanded. The last straw was when I picked up the issue containing my feature on Ginger Rogers's future (dancer or actress?) linked to the première of *We're Not Married*. After arguments about the style, I had gritted my teeth and twice rewritten it to order. 'Shall She Dance?' had been my title. 'Box-Office Ginger' was what I now saw. And every second sentence had been rewritten yet again, culminating in a summing-up which made no sense whatever:

Her eyes are still mischievous – yet they're still on Ginger and that new line in box-office Ginger she's trying to put into her Hollywood contract.

I shuddered at the thought that somebody might notice my by-line above it.

SEVENTEEN

There's No Business Like the Picture Business

While I thought about the future I took a month off, starting with two weeks in Paris: my first trip abroad, my first journey by air, certainly the first time I had lived even temporarily in a room up 128 stairs in a building with no lift. Paris provided dazzling new sights and sounds, but the films were familiar old friends, thanks to the city's plethora of re-issue theatres: the Marx Brothers in *Horse Feathers*, James Stewart in *Mr Smith Goes to Washington* and Bette Davis in *The Little Foxes* all enjoyed my patronage in cinemas near the Etoile, and my only confusion was in not understanding, when the usherette stood flashing her light after showing me to a seat, that she expected a tip.

In the restaurant at the top of the Eiffel Tower I reached a decision. For months now George Webb had been tempting me with offers to make me rich if I would only come back to Cambridge and run the Rex and the Kinema for him. When pressed, he admitted that the starting salary would be £7 10s per week; but that was ten shillings more than I had been offered three months earlier to run the Arts Cinema. The money did not seem to matter. Cambridge was my Land of Oz, a fairytale world which I had loved and lost, and here was a chance to get it back, while into the bargain doing something I would enjoy. When George also promised me a share in the profits (which I never got) I agreed that I would do what he wanted for a maximum period of two years while thinking about my ultimate destiny. We shook hands. It was going to be marvellous, he said; look, there were men laying ruboleum in the foyer at that very minute, and my word was George's command, and by the way, here was an open date book just waiting to be filled with my brilliant ideas. I knew from the glint in George's eyes that there must be a snag or two; but I suffered him to buy me an expensive dinner while I worked out the programmes he was to order. I parted from *Picture-goer* on friendly terms, and at the beginning of October 1952 I reported at the Rex for full-time duty.

It was more than a tiny bit daunting. As a patron, with a free pass and some influence at court, I had been prepared for a few hours each week to tolerate the building's inadequacies. As a venue in which I was to spend long working hours on seven days of most future weeks (for George expected no less, and I was a willing horse) it was undeniably hard to bear. I felt sure from the start that it offended against the Factory Acts. It was so very dirty. There had been no renovations in living memory, and the current wave predictably stopped with the ruboleum floor in the foyer, on which George could scarcely renege since an angry patron had threatened to sue him after tripping on the ancient matting which had preceded it. After a week of my persuasion he finally agreed to a cheap spray-painting job on the foyer walls, but that was as far as he would go. You go to the pictures to see the pictures, he said. There was absolutely no point in spending money on the auditorium, since it was dark nearly all the time, and if the out-of-reach cobwebs offended me he would gladly issue instructions to keep the place dim even during the ice-cream interval. Not then having his gift of the gab, I was temporarily stymied, but on my first spare morning when

George was busy elsewhere I turned up all the lights and made an inspection report as follows:

SCREEN. Sound but needs metallic painting. Damp patch in lower right hand corner near defective exit door.

BACKSTAGE AREA. Disgustingly filthy and derelict. Enough dirt on the stage to grow mushrooms.

MAIN CURTAINS. In desperate need of dry-cleaning: their smell fills the front half of the stalls. Must be left open because the cable is likely to stick without warning.*

AUDITORIUM WALLS. Caked with nicotine grime and cobwebs.

FRONT SEATS. Those which remain are in an extremely dangerous condition: whole rows could collapse.

REAR AND CIRCLE SEATS. Tolerably sound but lumpy. Many are moth-eaten.

CARPETS. Badly worn, with some dangerous holes.

NOSINGS. Dog-eared, unpainted, only occasionally attached to carpets. Many missing altogether, not a good idea on the circle stairs.

ATMOSPHERE WHEN EMPTY. Foul, and not helped by spraying with cheap scent.

TEMPERATURE. Freezing in winter, stifling in summer unless someone makes the inconvenient, dirty and dangerous journey through the circle void to the extract switch.†

DOORS. Sound, but draught-inducing. Protective curtains untouchable.

PROJECTION BOX. A tin hut apparently attached to the roof as an afterthought, and reached by a vertiginous outside staircase. Machinery by Heath Robinson.

STAFF ROOM. The broom cupboard under the circle stairs.

---

*The cable once snapped. I was standing in the back stalls enjoying *Kind Hearts and Coronets*, and the main curtains suddenly closed on the scene in which the hearse arrives for the funeral service. It took four of us half an hour to do anything about it, and when we emerged, covered with filthy oil, the patient audience gave us a rousing cheer.

†The journey through the circle void (i.e. the space below the circle and above the rear stalls ceiling) could have had the direst of results because, once toppled from the narrow gangplank, one would have fallen right through the asbestos ceiling of the stalls on to the audience beneath. I was never clear why we didn't simply extend the flex down to a switch in the manager's office, unless it was that George did not like life to be too easy.

TOILETS. Beyond comment, and offensive to non-users if the wind is from the east. A new start is indicated.

MANAGER'S OFFICE. A long cupboard about twelve feet by five. Being the only private chamber in the building apart from the toilets and the ballroom kitchen, it must house the entire executive, clerical and administrative staff, comprising owner, manager, accountant, and at certain times the ballroom manager, who must also invite his visiting performers to use it as a dressing room. Walls originally painted bottle green; this shade now obscured by earth-coloured deposit of dirt and nicotine. Concrete floor covered by odd scraps of disgusting carpet. Door kept locked; cleaner never allowed inside.

STOCK CUPBOARD FOR CHOCOLATES AND CIGARETTES. High shelving in manager's office.

OUTDOOR STILL CASES. Rotting and unlockable. Never used.

FACADE AND EXTERIOR GENERALLY. Scruffy in the extreme, though unlikely to be noticed by most patrons, who come along the street and not across it. The shock comes after they have paid.

I typed this out at the old machine which, by a flip of the wrist, could be made to disappear into the innards of the manager's desk. I left copies at strategic points. George gave no sign of ever having noticed them, but one by one they all disappeared.

Although in theory I was the manager of this crumbling edifice, I seldom did anything even remotely managerial. Old Harry Habbin, our white-haired and shaky but most amiable accounts clerk, looked after all George's money matters in between keeping a pub on the Newmarket Road. If a staff problem arose, George would quash it with a few well-aimed shafts of invective. He had no truck with unions, even less with human considerations, and would frequently award the sack at a moment's notice without flinching or considering the possible consequences. (To give him his due, he would very likely take it back half an hour later and on the same evening buy the bewildered victim several drinks.) The only employees safe from his wrath were a couple of hardy specimens who had stood up to him and thereby earned his respect. In such conditions of employment we were unlikely to acquire, much less retain, any models of beauty, efficiency, or tact; and indeed the staff of the Rex, at any time during my tenure, might have served more than adequately as inspiration for a Charles Addams cartoon. I was particularly awed by a blank-faced rural girl who was forced by severe menstrual trouble to absent herself on several days a month; by a limp-wristed ex-ballet dancer who when he should have been shining his torch was usually to be found giggling with his boyfriends in the back row; and by a gaunt ex-army doorman with a twisted leg and a curiously distorted face. (It took little in the way of make-up to dress him up as the Frankenstein monster for a publicity stunt.) Meanwhile from her pay box grey-haired Miss Cleaver surveyed all the goings-on without leaving off her knitting, like Madame Desfarges at the guillotine.

George had an awe-inspiring relish for the physical pleasures of life. When his figure was trimmer, sex had no doubt been among them, but the indulgences most apparent now were beer, spirits, very expensive cars, late hours, rich food and cigars, and I often feared that from their cumulative effect he would explode all over me, or squash me while expiring from a heart attack. What he loved most, however, was an argument, and he had no objection to being in the wrong if he could bellow his way out of the situation at the person who told him so. When he had shouted at everybody on the cinema side, he would transfer his interest to the staff of the so-called ballroom, which in fact was unworthy even of the description dance hall. Like the cinema, it was staggeringly short on facilities. The kitchen was Dickensian. The toilets were minimal. The main area, a drab rectangular place full of tables which sometimes refused the weight of drinks and basket chairs which tore at the girls' dresses, had at one end a balcony, part of which had long been declared unsafe and was roped off. A liquor licence had been granted for only two nights a week, and on these gala occasions drinks would be dispensed from the small bar under the balcony by a local publican called Jock Freestone who, as a result of over-consumption of his own provisions, suffered badly from the gout and informed patrons at frequent intervals of his constant excruciating pain. A couple of hundred people usually turned up on a Saturday, half as many on Friday and a handful of Old Tymers on Tuesday; on other nights there was roller skating, but this failed to cover the wages of the man who stood at the door. The band, composed of local talent, had to arrive fully attired for performance because there was no changing room; it never looked up to much, but the sound it made was surprisingly adequate.

Around Cambridge the Rex Ballroom had always had the worst kind of reputation, largely engendered by local residents who objected to its patrons being sick in their gardens. Undergraduates steered clear of it until George engineered a meeting with the Secretary of the University Jazz Club and persuaded him by the offer of cheap rentals to hold the club's weekly and termly festivities there. The resultant cacophony travelled through paper-thin walls into local houses as well as the cinema next door, but George waved away complaints with muttered comments about the noise being an Act of God, like the patter of rain on the roof. The Jazz Ball held in the last week of each term had to be seen to be believed, if you could get close enough to see it. Oversold three weeks in advance, its seven shilling tickets changed hands in the street outside for three quid, and for those unlucky enough to enter, the easiest way to make progress through the sweaty throng of addicts would have been to walk on their close-crowded heads. It was impossible to sit down because George had craftily removed all the chairs so as to get more people in, while in order to encourage business with Mr Freestone the temperature was kept at more than eighty degrees. Such occasions were, mercifully, exceptional. On non-jazz evenings the Rex remained the jaded province of American airmen from Mildenhall and the easier kind of local girl, augmented by a few notorious Newmarket tarts (each of whom, I was amused to find, George knew instantly). It was only by sheer persistence and some lying that George was able to raise the tone a bit by persuading agents to send him a few well-known touring bands who would help to bring back the Rex from beyond the pale. Roy Fox, Stanley Black, Ted Heath, Mick Mulligan (with George Melly), and Chris Barber were among those who made popular appearances, and to each leader at least I had to offer my office as a dressing-room.

After the cinema's first term under my so-called command, George did agree to a few improvements, but they were aimed at getting the queues in more quickly, encouraging after-sales, and publicizing the programmes. He installed in Miss Cleaver's pay box a new Automaticket machine. He bought a new glass-and-chrome chocolate cabinet, stocked it solely with cheap brands on which through trade arrangements he could make an excessive profit, and hired a personable ex-circus bareback rider named Rita to stand behind it in the evenings. He increased our advertising space in the *Daily News*. And he increased admission prices so that he should not be the loser by all these improvements. I did eventually persuade him to pay for some new still cases, and to keep them filled, but that was as far as he would go. On the other hand he would agree to anything that cost only his own labour, for having nothing else to do he was with us every day from mid-morning and usually worked longer hours than anybody, apparently always in the same grey suit which he treated abominably, hoisting himself up on fire ladders to fix flickering gas jets, or scrabbling on his knees among decrepit seats in search of a missing screw. When he had had enough of that, he might ask me which renter he could ring up and abuse in the hope of getting a juicy booking away from the ABCs. Then there was the sales stock to replenish, last night's takings to be driven to the bank, the pay box to be checked, the fire inspector to be fobbed off. The only thing with which he did not help or interfere was the clerical work, for George knew his limitations, and reading and writing were certainly among them: so I gladly got on with the advertisement copy, the advance write-up for the *Daily News* show page, the still and poster and trailer orders, and the layout for our weekly cards which were screen-printed in Walthamstow and exhibited in local pubs and shops in exchange for free passes.

The daily routine was simple enough. We opened for business soon after one o'clock, and ran continuously until a quarter to eleven. I lived down by the river, renting a bed-sitter from a Mrs Lavis, who owned one of a splendid row of 300-year-old cottages and had had hers rather resplendently refurbished. It was all I needed as a contrast with the squalid ambience of the Rex: a quiet, clean, charming place to read and sleep and have breakfast, and do *The Times* crossword at night as I sipped my cocoa. I also found time there to write a novel called *Portion for Foxes*, which never saw the light of day although the title was subsequently used by another author. Ninety per cent of my life was lived and enjoyed at the Rex, and if enjoyed seems the wrong word I was still, despite all the drawbacks, experiencing a dream come true, devising my own programmes from a choice of the best films in the world, and showing them to audiences which for seven months of the year at least were among the most appreciative one could find.

The method of booking films was a complicated business for the uninitiated. The exhibitor, whether circuit or independent, hired them from a distributor, who was usually also a producer: Rank, Paramount, British Lion, Warner, Fox, Columbia, MGM. On a lower level there were a score of selling agents who picked up the rights to whatever re-issues, independent releases and exploitation items they could find. All were of interest, for our range was nothing if not catholic, and many interesting but uncommercial productions had to fight their way for recognition through the unlikeliest channels. Companies both big and small announced their wares in the *Kine Weekly* or *Today's Cinema*, and every new release could be seen at a London 'trade show'. If anything enticing came along, and there seemed for whatever reason to be a chance of wresting it away from the ABCs, George and I were on the phone or in the car like bullets from a gun; but most of our programmes were composed of re-issues or of good new films rejected by ABC's shortsightedness. To get these (since the more anxious we seemed, the higher the price would rise) we could well afford to wait for the regular visits of the travelling salesmen.

These mainly welcome visitors, each of whom had the whole of East Anglia for his pasture, came our way every three or four weeks unless George had banned them from the premises, which was not at all unlikely. I was even glad to see the ones I did not much like, for there was no pastime I enjoyed better than running my eye over their glossy brochures and re-issue lists. Even though we might need recourse to head office before a deal was settled, these were the boys who made out the contracts and got the commission. I think they enjoyed the bad language and the whisky sessions as much as George and I did, for the Rex call cannot have been anything but a welcome relief from the dim hotels and the long East Anglian weeks spent away from their wives, selling routine films to exhibitors who, by and large, could not distinguish between Charles Boyer and Charlie McCarthy. George Doubleday of Fox, Bert Morris of United Artists, Ken Webster of Warners, Johnny Knell of Rank were among those who spent many animated hours at the Rex, with frequent adjournments for refreshment to the New Spring. Most spectacular of them was Dudley Pritchard of Columbia, a dapper, moustachioed man who came and went like a freshly lit firework. He looked like a superannuated major, and had perhaps too keen a liking for the good life. Pretty usherettes and even patrons needed protection from him: 'Never let him in the back stalls on his own,' said George. But Dudley could laugh at his own weaknesses. Every call finished up as a late-night drinking session over which Dudley would preside like a one-man floor show, doing his Jolson impressions or telling the latest smoking-room story. ('Frenchman doing press-ups in the park. Gendarme comes over and says: "But monsieur – ze lady 'as gone!" ') They were full days. But neither Dudley nor his rivals could ever quite understand what we saw in their oldest, and to them poorest, films, which they found unsaleable at any other hall. After a few drinks they would sometimes try to protect us from them; but for the most part they behaved like good salesmen and cheerfully sold them to us at the highest prices they could get.

Programmes were usually sold on a percentage of the net takings, i.e. after the deduction of entertainments tax. If on a three-day booking we sold a hundred pounds worth of tickets, about £37 would go straight to the Customs and

Excise and another £3 to the Eady levy which was supposed to assist British production. (On Sundays there was an additional charity tax.) The remaining £60 was the net from which the distributor took his percentage. This could range from fifty per cent for a big new film plus shorts, down to twenty-five per cent for a re-issue programme or a programme of previously-proven low money-making potential. The percentage always covered the entire programme, but if the distributor had no suitable second feature he might reluctantly give an allowance of five pounds or so, enabling one to be bought elsewhere at 'flat rate'. Most cinemas paid on a sliding scale by which both parties were safeguarded, for the more money you took, the higher the percentage you paid. The Rex, however, had no established scale, and no renter could be persuaded to adopt one at the figures George suggested, by which we would have had to break a house record to pay as much as forty per cent. We usually compromised by paying about a third, providing the programme consisted of two features which by our standards were attractive. This policy of selected double-bills caused blind resentment in Wardour Street (known as the only street in the world which is shady on both sides) until it dawned on the reactionaries that this was our only way of delivering good returns. I remember once asking Paramount to couple a Bob Hope re-issue with one of the antique Marx Brothers films which had previously done well for us as a top feature but which in ninety per cent of the country Paramount could not have given away. We were hoist by our own petard of success, and I received the following stern intimation from Paramount's head office:

We cannot depart from our definite rule not to couple important pictures. It is not in your interest or ours. If you start doing this sort of thing you will make your public always want it and then they will never be satisfied with whatever you give them.

We eventually broke this man down by booking nothing at all from his company until we got our way; and even Paramount finally conceded that we might possibly have the best ideas on how to run our own cinema.

As percentage programmes clearly left George with only a fraction of his original take with which to run the cinema and make a profit, he soon got the idea of buying more 'allowance' pictures than he needed and combining two of them in a programme which, even though the returns might be modest, would leave him with more profit than did a block-buster. Thus for a total of ten pounds per programme, for three days, we played *Rope* with *My Darling Clementine*, and *Extase* with *All that Money Can Buy*, and did very nicely, thank you. But in the film business you can't keep secrets. Two travellers happened to drop in one evening when we were playing allowance pictures contributed by them, and found us too busy controlling the queues to talk. It did not take them long to calculate the commission they were losing, and 'flat rate' programmes became very few and far between after that.

Wardour Street had an insane logic of its own. I was refused a booking of *The Lady from Shanghai* on the grounds that it might damage the chances of the new Rita Hayworth film being readied for release. I was given incredulous looks and fatherly advice when I tried to book *The Grapes of Wrath*: it seemed that old men still told their sons sad stories of the loneliness they endured on its first runs. If I made it too obvious that I must have a certain film, I was forced to take two duds with it or no deal. All kinds of sleazy rubbish with sub-titles were foisted upon me with the reasoning that you can't tell one French film from another. One who no doubt could not was the old stager who tried to sell me as a programme *Dieu a besoin des hommes* with a primitive exploitation piece called *Amok*, about abortion in the Far East. 'Just the ticket for Cambridge, this long-haired stuff,' he said. But he did know when he was beaten. One of our conversations went like this:

'Now here's a smashing little British quota picture you should pick up if you want to do yourself a favour. The circuits are crying out for it, but the producer used to be an exhibitor himself and he wants the independents to have first crack. It's fast and it's very funny, and I tell you there's one girl in it who – '
'I saw the trade show.'
'Ah. Then say no more. I agree with you. It stinks. So what about this next one? . . .'

The British quota regulations took a long time to die. Most of the time they simply encouraged incompetence. In the fifties, roughly speaking, exhibitors were obliged to show one British film in every three, and as a result any rubbishy film could get bookings if it gave work to British technicians. One fly-by-night company called Adelphi had a catalogue consisting exclusively of candidates for the title of worst film ever made. I have mentioned *I Was a Dancer* and *Alf's Baby*, but they added insult to injury with *Who Killed Van Loon?*, *You Lucky People*, *The Crowded Day*, *Don't Blame the Stork*, *The Happiness of Three Women*, *What Every Woman Wants* and *Is Your Honeymoon Really Necessary?*. What seemed especially galling was that the Eady levy was extracted from the likes of us to finance the good British productions which all went to the ABCs. But our frequent pleas were eventually successful: the levy was abolished in our case, and we even got a quota reduction. In fact we played more British films than most halls, but our choices were 'classics' and a film lost its quota 'life' after four years.

My first few months at the Rex were singularly depressing in terms of results. Though not physically present, I had booked September, a non-university month, by persuading the renters to give us some of the co-feature first runs of which there was then a glut. Ann Sheridan in *Just Across the Street* doubled with John Lund in *Bronco Buster*, Audie Murphy in *Sierra* with Boris Karloff in *The Strange Door*. The takings were worse than disastrous, audiences having clearly decided that if it played first run at the Rex it couldn't be any good. We did slightly better with high-class re-issues of middlebrow appeal: *London Belongs to Me* with Carol Reed's *Bank Holiday*, *Black Narcissus* with the Crazy Gang in my old favourite *Alf's Button Afloat*. But the best takings of the month were collected by an exploitation quickie called *Korea Patrol*, sharing a bill with a pro-Indian western, *The Battle of Powder River*.

George was obviously dejected, having regarded me as a kind of magic pixie who had but to wave his wand in order for crowds to besiege the doors. Nor did Full Term begin with much of a bang. We had goodish houses for *Quartet* and a Stanley Holloway farce called *The Perfect Woman*, but at the end of the week *The Brothers* (a moody piece about life on the Isle of Skye) and a lovely ghost farce called *Topper Returns* made no headway at all. It was clear that our gowned patrons no longer trusted my judgement because it was no longer impartial: the power of 'Next Week's Films' was in other hands. What we needed, I decided, was the backing of the national critics, and so henceforth every piece of Rex publicity was spattered with their reviews. Nor did I despise the sillier forms of showmanship. René Clair's *Belles de Nuit* would scarcely have broken the house record had it not been rechristened *Night Beauties* and exploited with stills of Gina Lollobrigida getting out of her bath. One of our most effective gimmicks was a tie-up with the local taxi service, whose front bumpers bore for a week the legend: 'One of Camtax's *Night Beauties*'. And at the rear: '*Night Beauties* at the Rex is a real bumper film.'

At the beginning of each term George authorized the printing of eight thousand copies of a booklet which assumed various forms, usually folded, but was always chatty and informative about the irresistible programmes shortly to be seen at the Rex. The copy for the second term began with confidence:

We feel that the Rex is now established as the University's favourite cinema. We further claim that the programmes detailed below, consisting of classics new and old, are the finest ever offered by any cinema in the world during a period as short as an eight-week term. It remains only for us to urge you to make more use of the matinées and to come at least ten minutes early for the last complete show, thus avoiding the tiresome queues which were so prevalent last term.

The brochures were eagerly awaited, and many could be seen standing on undergraduate mantelpieces right through to the end of term; we printed them on heavy card for this precise purpose. George and I were well rewarded for the trouble we took to get them into college pigeonholes under the forbidding eyes of the bowler-hatted porters, only some of whom were susceptible to the offer of rolls of free tickets. One or two even sniffed dubiously at the sight on the street outside of George's black Bentley. If rebuffed, however, I usually managed to wander back into the college on some later pretext and leave a stack of the brochures on the main table of the Junior Combination Room.

That first term was a mixture of triumph and tragedy. To my personal and professional chagrin some marvellous doubles failed rather badly, including the soul-stirring *Wuthering Heights* with the cynical *Nothing Sacred*; and

A Letter from the

REX CINEMA   Phone 3969

MAGRATH AVENUE

to all who value the Best
in Cinema Entertainment

* * * * * * * * *

Only freshmen will need to be told that the Rex is the Mecca of all those who like the cinema to be an art, or at least a craft, as well as an entertainment. We show only the very best, and our double-feature programmes of films new and old are renowned. This term, with our usual emphasis on civilised comedy, we believe we have broken our own past record. We guarantee every film a chosen winner; not one falls below the standard which our patrons have helped us to set. On Sunday mornings, too, the Film Society holds its meetings here, and its programme this term features Buster Keaton, Von Stroheim, Dietrich and Michèle Morgan. In fact, the film enthusiast could not do better than secure rooms as close to our paybox as possible! We hope that the notes which follow will make you a VERY regular patron.

Incidentally, like some other fashionable centres, we are a little hard to find at first. Turn right at the Magdalene traffic lights, then left up Hertford Street and left again into Magrath Avenue. The Rex stands on the highest point in the city.

We are entirely independent of circuit control. Our performances are continuous, usually on weekdays from 1.30 or 2 p.m. Sundays from 3 p.m. Last complete performance on weekdays between 7 and 7.15, Sundays at about 6.30. Our programmes are advertised in 'VARSITY' and the 'CAMBRIDGE DAILY NEWS.' And we do not distort our pictures on wide screens.

Monday, 18th October, 3 days.

DANNY KAYE   VERA ELLEN

WONDER MAN (u) (Tech.)

Mr. Kaye's most ingenious extravaganza, an amusing variation on the "Topper" theme. It features the comedian's celebrated impression of a Russian baritone with hay fever, as well as the opera sequence.   2.20, 5.35, 8.45.

Also

SIMONE SIMON   KENT SMITH

THE CAT PEOPLE (a)

A thriller with credentials, the first of a famous series produced by Val Lewton for RKO in 1943. Intelligently written and brilliantly directed, they are no mere pot-boilers. This one a Jugoslavian curse which works itself out in New York.   4.05, 7.15.

Thursday, 21st October, 3 days.

DAN O'HERLIHY   JAMES FERNANDEZ

THE ADVENTURES OF ROBINSON CRUSOE (u) (Colour)

Dilys Powell called it "one of the best films of the year," and it was Critics Choice when Luis Buñuel's film was shown. Luis Buñuel, famed for his classic demonstrations of surrealism and sadism, how could it fail to be interesting? Definitely a film for adults, and definitely a little masterpiece. O'Herlihy will be a strong contender for this year's acting awards.

Also MONTGOMERY CLIFT   JENNIFER JONES

in Vittorio de Sica's

TERMINAL STATION (a) ("INDISCRETION")

STAZIONE TERMINI has suffered many vicissitudes since de Sica began work on it three years ago. This version has been severely cut by Selznick but remains a polished, superior piece of film making, with the master hand of de Sica always in evidence. The film is entirely photographed in the actual setting of Rome's magnificent railway station.

See press for times.

Sunday, 24th October, 1 day only.

JIMMY DURANTE   JUNE ALLYSON

TWO GIRLS AND A SAILOR (u)

Two hours of top musical-comedy talent, with contributions from Harry James trumpet, notably in "Young Man with a Horn." And Durante sings his famous "Ink-a-dink-a-doo."

Also

A RED SKELTON COMEDY to be announced.

Monday, 25th October, 3 days.

ORSON WELLES   JOSEPH COTTEN

CITIZEN KANE (a)

Orson Welles' first, best and most famous film, which has gained more critical awards and featured in more "best ten" lists than any other film in the world. Sensational in technique, high-powered but ... as entertainment, it deserves all the superlatives you can think of.   1.10, 5.0, 8.55.

Also

ROBERT NEWTON   JEAN SIMMONS

ANDROCLES AND THE LION (u)

First Cambridge presentation of Pascal's version of the witty Shavian comedy, which can almost be taken as a skit on "Quo Vadis." Very funny, with an excellent cast.   3.10, 7.05.

Thursday, 28th October, 3 days.

GENE KELLY   FRANK SINATRA

ON THE TOWN (u) (Tech.)

Completing the great Gene Kelly musical trio, this brash, noisy, uninhibited carry-full of ... The ... "Prehistoric Man" number alone is worth the price of admission.   2.0, 5.25, 8.50.

Author as Publicist

One of the Rex's somewhat boastful programme cards. Thousands were personally delivered at the beginning of each term

King Kong drew surprisingly few punters, even though in the name of publicity I personally donned an extremely tatty gorilla skin and was driven around the Cambridge streets in a cage on the back of a lorry. Oversell? Or perhaps the wrong second feature. Lubitsch's *Cluny Brown*, though in its own right full of delicious moments, has little in common with a fifty-foot ape; but it was another of George's flat bookings, and he was a mite too anxious to use it up and make a killing. (A picture of me in the ape suit appeared in *Varsity* under the heading 'What Becomes of our Discarded Editors'!) We decided later that Lubitsch must be our Jonah, since we also failed to do business with his mordant anti-Nazi farce *To Be or Not to Be*; but then *Trouble in Paradise* played for three days and became a cult. Our biggest successes were *Blithe Spirit* and *Destry Rides Again*, sheer enjoyment all the way; *An American in Paris* with a Tom and Jerry Show; the Archers' wise and witty *A Matter of Life and Death* with their semi-documentary *The Edge of the World*, shot on Foula; and, biggest of all, a programme in which the support didn't help a lot, being that dour study of a western lynching, *The Ox-Bow Incident*. Most patrons spoke respectfully of it but did not bother to arrive until it was nearly over; for what they, and I, really wanted to see was *Citizen Kane*.

This was my first sight of the film which later became my all-time favourite. My abortive attempt at the Bolton Lido had been followed by ten years of fruitless search during which the mere mention of it to such cinema trade people as I met was greeted by shudders of dismay as they recalled the complaints it had brought from audiences who found it totally baffling. This is hard to credit today, but in 1941 audiences were not really used to bringing their brains to the cinema with them, and resented the suggestion that they should. Officially the film had been long withdrawn by

RKO as unsaleable, but over the years Welles had carved himself a secondary niche as actor, while Joseph Cotten had become a romantic star draw; and so, late in 1951, a single print was struck from the British negative as part of a batch of re-issues intended to make up for a temporary shortage of new RKO product. I booked it, flat rate, on the same morning as I first saw the announcement in the *Kine Weekly*, and it played for three days at the end of the week. On the opening Thursday, because of the length of the programme, *Kane* had to start at 1.30 pm, and after lunch with a traveller I had to race to get back by 1.25 pm. I was greeted by the pleasant sight of more than twenty bicycles in the racks, which probably meant an audience of at least fifty already seated; and more were arriving just as fast as they could pedal. I stood excitedly at the back of the stalls as the house lights dimmed and the green glow faded from the screen; and within the first half-dozen shots I knew I was in the presence of a master showman, or at least a master controller of RKO's studio facilities, which Welles once called 'the biggest toy train any boy ever had to play with'.

Kane is a young man's film about ambition and power and death, and perhaps in the long run it lacks both the compassion and the intellectual strength to come to grips with all its themes. But its real brilliance is in its sharp script, with scarcely a second wasted without some point being made, and in its pyrotechnic use of the film medium, which must have absorbed every specialist in the studio from plasterer to animator. Despite its flip attitudes, it is always thoroughly professional, and it takes the trouble to get things right. Its attitude is 'Let's point a moral but have a lot of fun doing it', and nowhere is this better demonstrated than in the stark final shot of Kane's treasures going up the chimney in smoke, a visual ended by the pan down over the electric fence to the sign *No Trespassing*, which is itself rather impudently replaced by fast-moving end credits accompanied by the tub-thumping vaudeville-style theme tune, a most effective use of *lèse-majesté*. And there, at the very end of the smallest credits, is the information that Kane has been played by Orson Welles. Box-office-wise, Thursday was excellent, Friday showed a fall-off, and on Saturday we broke the house record.

A lesser film which drew at least one full house was *A Yank at Oxford*. This sentimental romantic piece, luckily set in the Other Place, provoked howls of glee at every performance, with wolf whistles for Vivien Leigh and exaggerated sighs for Maureen O'Sullivan. The vivid reception came to an early crescendo during the scene in the train, when the ancient blimp played by Morton Selten, exasperated by the young American's naïve questions about Oxford, shuts him up with: 'I, sir, thank God, went to Cambridge.' A simple line, but the staff all put their fingers in their ears when it was due. *A Yank at Oxford* provided a further example of Wardour Street's insane logic. With the right co-feature we could easily have played it for a week, and wanted to, but it had been relegated years previously to MGM's Sunday list, and the London branch manager would therefore allow us to play it on Sundays only. So we did, once every couple of terms. MGM often behaved like that, throwing their weight around in the belief that they could do no wrong.

Out of term, we never had a hope of filling the house. The locals suspected us even more than before, and concluded that anything we showed must in some way be contaminated by the university. In our search for less prejudiced audiences we arrived at a fairly workable solution: 'U' certificate action adventures while the kids were

on holiday, sexy continentals (which would draw representation from a wide area) when they were not. By 'sexy' I
mean no more than the heavily censored British versions of
Manèges, *Quai de Grenelle* and *L'Ingénue Libertine*, which
seemed saucy enough at the time. To my surprise George
developed a passion for such items, and urged me to sit next
to him, and to whisper the sub-titles in his ear; he became
quite a critic over the subsequent curry suppers, a kind of
regular tip for me on which he never stinted. Nor was there
anything he enjoyed better than listening to me parrying
questions from patrons, such as whether the musical
sequences had been cut from *Duck Soup*, and why *Wuthering Heights* was not in colour. (It never had been, but the
patron insisted he had seen it that way in Great Yarmouth
just before the war.)

One spring evening a tap at the office door heralded a
gowned undergraduate wearing (I never discovered why) a
false beard and outsize glasses with revolving multi-coloured eyeballs. He wanted to tell us, he said, that *Monsieur
Beaucaire* had just gone up in smoke. (It had, too, while
our projectionists were both having a quick draw and a
cough on their outside staircase. Hooray for safety film, we
thought.) Then there was the famous *contretemps* during
the first performance of *Mr Deeds Goes to Town*, which
nobody had troubled to rehearse. When reel eight came
on, it proved to be reel eight of *Lost Horizon*, another
Columbia picture. Free tickets were handed out all round,
George refused to pay the film hire, and *Varsity* wrote the
story up under the headline 'Mr Deeds Goes to China'. (It
was Tibet, of course.)

Getting the old films we wanted out of the renters'
vaults, or the new ones away from ABC, often involved us
in struggles which nearly led to bloodshed. When the
travellers could not give us what we wanted, or alter-

natively when George felt the sap rise, he would decide to visit head office and jump on somebody in his heaviest hobnailed boots. After a few such visits we knew that any London branch manager if warned of our arrival would arrange to take the day off, so we began to take Wardour Street by surprise if we could. George might say suddenly, as we were cashing up one evening: 'Let's go to town tomorrow. I'll call for you at six o'clock.' On the first few occasions I thought he *meant* six o'clock, and set my alarm for 5.15 am; but with experience came the knowledge that he really meant 6.45 am. It was never a minute later than that, however, when his Bentley honked outside my window, for George wanted to beat the commuters' rush around Hendon, which could make an hour's difference if one was trapped in it. By travelling most of the way at 70 mph we usually managed to park in Soho by half-past eight, giving us time for a cup of tea and a bun in some sleazy café before we established ourselves in the lobby of Fox or Rank or Columbia, to watch the reaction of the incoming executives. At Paramount Mr Douglas Abbey's lips would set in a firm line when he saw us impassively waiting, and his bare nod to us was followed by a slamming of the office door behind him; at Columbia we had the satisfaction of knowing that we had aggravated the ulcers of Mr Mark Gordon, né Max Grodsky; but our favourite sporting turf was Rank, for the expression of unbridled dismay on the face of Monte Oslof as he caught sight of us and knew for certain that his day was ruined. As a combination, at that time of the morning, we must have been mighty unnerving, for I knew what I wanted and George made sure that I got it. It might take most of the morning, and voices would certainly be raised in anger, but the first glimmerings of a solution invariably coincided with opening time, after which all was amicably resolved in an appropriate hostelry: the George for Paramount, the Ship for Rank, the Crown and Two Chairmen for Fox. We never asked for the impossible, only for the improbable; they never gave us either if they could help it. All the same, I can't remember a London day when we drove back without a desirable first run contract on the back seat. We got *Animal Farm* in that way, and *Le Plaisir*, and *Conflict of Wings*, and *The Runaway Bus*, and *Magnificent Obsession*; all because the renter finally decided that the wrath of ABC would be mild compared to George's. Not that our trophies always did the business we expected, but at least they established us as a force to be reckoned with, and in business that is often half the battle. Besides, while in the renter's office I could sometimes prise out of an underling a copy of the current vault list, which might include single museum prints undeclared to the travellers. Thus the Marx Brothers' *Animal Crackers* came our way, a couple of rare Will Hays, and *Frankenstein* and *Dracula*.

I had no idea whether our cranky audience would take to these two horror classics or not, but it was surely worth a try; besides, I still had to see them myself! The existence of the prints having been discovered, Rank (who then distributed for Universal) reluctantly agreed to let us have them as a programme for twenty-five per cent, but disclaimed all responsibility for their technical standards. As the due date approached, I began to worry. Suppose the prints had dissolved into dust, as old prints are wont to do? Had anybody opened the cans to find out? Why had Rank been so reluctant? Perhaps the legal rights were no longer clear, in which case we might be sent a last-minute replacement programme, with an apology that the reels we expected had been accidentally dropped in the Thames or burned in a fire. But one morning, as I walked up Magrath Avenue in the morning mist, there they stood on the front step, having been deposited less than an hour before by Film Transport Services. As they were heaved on to the projectionists' shoulders and carried off to the operating room, the battered metal cases looked sufficiently warped and rusty to contain (in sections) the monsters themselves rather than their celluloid images. I made sure of being present at the exhumation, and warned our 'chief' to handle the prints with loving respect. He did so, removing a hardened gob of chewing gum from one of the reel ends, and carefully excising a splice casually made with a metal staple. I watched the rewinding procedure with all the anxiety of an expectant father. At last came the reassuring words: 'Yes, they should go.' *Frankenstein*'s reel-ends were very frayed, but not many frames were missing; *Dracula* suffered from a few strained sprocket-holes. Otherwise, the monsters were intact.

My announcements of the impending resurrection had met with a mixed reception. 'What, them 'orrible things again?' asked one of the local faithful. But there had been considerable university interest in our hurriedly-printed posters (the professional ones having long ago yellowed and withered) and the display of creased and faded stills which our agents had been able to dig up was surrounded throughout opening hours by a bemused crowd. In reply to my urgent letter National Screen Service wrote to regret that they had no regular trailers left in stock, but they had unearthed something which they hoped I might like even better. It was the very same combined trailer which I had seen at the Embassy all those years previously: no pictures, just shaky lettering falling into focus and daring its audience to sit through 'the two uncanniest films of all time'. Publicity was certainly not lacking: even the *Daily*

News was moved to print a 500-word eulogy written by me, for which the editor insisted on paying me three guineas.

To add further spice to the show I spent fifteen shillings on a Sylvester cartoon set in Hell and called *Satan's Waitin'*. It seemed to fit the general theme fairly well, and looked good in the advertising.

Came the fateful Sunday. (I had extended the booking to four days.) Forty minutes before starting time, a hundred addicts queued patiently for their mammoth fix, and when the box office opened, the Automaticket machine clicked with gratifying regularity. The two-and-sevens were genuinely full when the lights dimmed to reveal on the screen an antique 'A' certificate signed by Lord Tyrone of Avon, bearing the legend

Frankenstein (synchronized)

There was even a pre-credits sequence, a delightfully intense warning from a sinister gentleman in evening dress, easily recognizable as the actor Edward van Sloan, who was to play the old professor in the picture. He told us, on behalf of executive producer Carl Laemmle Jnr, that the story to come might shock us unless we steeled ourselves against its impact. Then, after brief credits bathed in a pale green light (my touch, this, but at least it lasted only thirty seconds) we were in a studio graveyard under wuthering skies, and soil was falling from a spade on to a coffin lid, with a surfeit of synchronized sound and a good deal of background crackle.

The old copies served us well, although their dried emulsion coating began to crack in the unaccustomed heat of the projectors. In the four days we suffered only one small breakdown, when an aged splice came apart: otherwise what we saw on the screen looked pretty good.

Business boomed: we averaged a house and a half a day, at which no exhibitor can complain. (A second local run of the award-winning *Marty* at the end of the week did less than half as well.) As entertainment the two films were a success only slightly qualified. Even those prepared to jeer at the stately acting prevalent in early talkies found themselves silenced by the overpowering gothic sensibility of the director, James Whale, by the brilliant mute acting of Boris Karloff, and, in Dracula, by the bravura personality of Bela Lugosi. Of course both films had dated. The love interest, mercifully brief, is not quite brief enough; most of *Dracula* is a play rather than a film; and some of the supporting performances, notably that of Dwight Frye (who plays a mad hunchback in one film and a mad insect-eater in the other) are simply over-emphatic. But the first two reels of *Dracula* and almost the whole of *Frankenstein* are put across with ghoulish good humour and a professional enthusiasm for something rich and strange.

On the Sunday we had one genuine faint (at Lugosi's rather gentlemanly blood-sucking) and one very penetrating scream from a lady near the front (who may merely have shifted position too rapidly on a seat with a loose spring). Otherwise the reception was polite, appreciative, and awed. A university paper featured a pretentious review lauding *Frankenstein* as a portmanteau of sexual symbolism and *Dracula* as a prolonged joke for necrophiliacs; I thought it was the other way round. And the Rank Organisation was so impressed by our astonishing success that they ordered new prints from Hollywood and sent them out on a widespread independent release. We offered to book the show again if they could find the missing scene from *Frankenstein*, showing the monster tossing a little girl into the lake to see if she will float like the flowers; but it never did turn up.*

As for George and myself, we enjoyed not only the excitement and the box-office figures but the publicity the programme gave us; and towards the end of the following term we took even more money with *Bride of Frankenstein* and *Dracula's Daughter*.

*Nor, ever again, did the epilogue to *Dracula*, which was tacked on to the end of the print we ran at the Rex. In this Mr Edward van Sloan again appeared in evening dress, this time to assure us that what we had been watching was only a film, which we were not to take too much to heart. However, he added, as we walked along dark lanes to our lonely houses, we were to remember that 'there *are* such things as vampires!'

As this book went to press in 1985, a print of *Frankenstein* containing the missing minute seen nowhere in the world since 1933, did turn up in the National Film Archive, and will be shown by Channel 4.

EIGHTEEN

Stupendous, Tremendous, Colossal!

Hardly did a month go by at the Rex without some extraordinary occurrence, which was just as well since George easily grew bored if I failed to present him with a queue every night. House records were constantly broken, but the figures became meaningless after the strange affair of the Coronation film.

For months we had known that there would be two major colour films of this eagerly anticipated spectacle, which in 1953 could be seen on television only in black-and-white. The Pathé version, *Elizabeth is Queen*, was to run forty minutes or so and would be shown at every ABC hall in the country, which ruled it out for us since every filmgoer in Cambridge was bound to see it. Rank's film was to be twice as long and narrated by Laurence Olivier, and since Rank had no direct circuit outlet in Cambridge they offered *A Queen is Crowned* to us. We rejected it on the grounds that fifty per cent for an elongated newsreel was ridiculous. In May Rank announced, having obviously seen the bill for the hundreds of Technicolor prints they had been forced to order, that in the second week of availability the percentage would be reduced to forty and in the third week to thirty; if anybody still wanted it in the fourth week they could have it for twenty-five. We gave this our serious consideration, and decided that since the fourth week fell in early July, when the undergraduates were gone and the kids were still at school, it would help our quota position and do us no great harm if we put *A Queen is Crowned* in for seven days as second feature to some perennial favourite such as *The Lavender Hill Mob*.* We could in fact imagine quite a throng of maiden ladies to whom this combination of HM and Alec Guinness might appeal very strongly, enough at least to give us passable matinées. So we booked it on the firm understanding that should it flop, an alternative programme of more certain entertainment value should be available to go in on the Thursday. I had already booked a holiday in Norway for that week, but George said not to worry, in the summer he could handle the Rex with his eyes shut, and it was not as though there was going to be much doing.

The royal event took place in the rain and cold of an early June day, when we were doing rather well with *The Life and Death of Colonel Blimp* and *It's That Man Again*. The Coronation films were released on the following Sunday, and it quickly became clear to press and public alike that *A Queen is Crowned* was the one to see, mainly because it was longer. However, all five ABC halls played *Elizabeth is Queen* over two weeks and did good business with it, after

---

*The Ealing comedies were among our mainstays, and the Rex audiences came to know almost every line by heart. In *Passport to Pimlico* they relished the badinage between Basil Radford and Naunton Wayne as the men from the ministry. In *Whisky Galore* they waited for the line of commentary over the shot of a score of children running from the door of a Scottish croft: 'The islanders are a people of few and simple pleasures . . .' *The Man with the White Suit* had the splendid bubbling noises which emerged from Alec Guinness's chemical apparatus. And in *The Titfield Thunderbolt* it was the gin-drinker's toast uttered by Stanley Holloway: 'Here's to our two magnificent generals, General Gordon and General Booth!' *The Lavender Hill Mob* had a splendour all its own, marred only by the fact that the bank robber played by Guinness had to be caught in the end. In those days the censor was firm on such things.

which public interest appeared to be almost exhausted; except that the press plaudits continued for the Rank version, and we were surprised at the number of people who heard we would be playing it and rang up to find out when. By the time I left for my holiday, headmasters were calling to enquire about school parties, and it was clear that George was going to have a busy week. He thereupon decided that a shorter programme would help him get more people in, and replaced *The Lavender Hill Mob* with a 55-minute Russian circus film called *The Big Top*. I demurred, but did not feel strongly about it.

I returned two weeks later, after a holiday which included in Stockholm *Titta del Spokar* (Martin and Lewis in *Scared Stiff*); in Oslo, Clifton Webb in *Elopement* and Cary Grant in *Ape-Streken* (*Monkey Business*); *The Great Lie* in a tin hut near the Arctic Circle; and *The Hunchback of Notre Dame* in Bergen on a rainy afternoon. George did not seem overjoyed at my return. I could not understand what I had done until he sulkily accused me of having deserted him in his hour of desperate need. What he meant was that he had had to work very hard indeed; but his bank balance had not suffered. The Rex's net takings at that time could vary from £200 in a bad week to £900 in a very good one. *A Queen is Crowned*, in seven days, had taken £3,000. At first I did not believe him; he showed me the books. It still seemed physically impossible; in those seven days nearly half the population of Cambridge must have visited the Rex. I sat there blankly, staring at the figures and wondering what I could ever do to top them. He had even contrived to keep the print for a second week, and taken a further £1,200. It must have been an exhausting fortnight. George had alternated as usherette, commissionaire and cashier. Mrs Webb had been brought along under duress for the sole purpose of answering the telephone. The problems of getting the crowds in and out had been such that twenty-minute intervals had to be the norm, and the last performance had not ended on any evening before 11.30 pm, even by cutting a reel out of the circus film. With only three complete shows a day, but four showings of the feature, George had averaged more than three full houses, which had to mean continuous queues from opening onwards, and standing room all the time. Cross at missing the fun, I vowed never again to predict the success or otherwise of any film; and the wisdom of this was reinforced in September, when we brought back *A Queen is Crowned* together with a new but undistinguished Dirk Bogarde thriller called *Desperate Moment*, and took £58 in three days.

Long before I took up my job at the Rex there had been trade reports of renewed international experiments with three-dimensional films, which had surfaced briefly in the mid-thirties and then descended to the level of giveaways in children's comics, the stereoscopic effect, gained by looking at very messy pictures through cardboard glasses with one red and one green eyepiece, which gave one of the overlaid images to each eye. During the Festival of Britain, however, the Telekinema on the South Bank had shown a programme of Norman MacLaren's abstract fantasies in this genre, using polaroid spectacles which allowed the full spectrum of colours: I remember one which consisted only of yellow clouds setting into place against a blue sky, one near, one distant, and so on. It shortly became clear that Hollywood had in production a few features in the process, for in those days anything which might knock television was worth trying. There was also some loose talk about 3-D *without glasses*, and it was whispered authoritatively that the Russians had developed such a system which was fine – until you moved your head! But towards the end of 1952 there was sudden publicity for an invention which claimed to give the effect of three dimensions simply by the shape of the screen. The Synchro-Screen, it was called, and Charles Chaplin was said to have been delighted when he saw *Limelight* on it in Paris. A week or so later I saw in the *Kine Weekly* a gossip item to the effect that the Synchro-Screen was being tried out at the ABC Bayswater, with good results. 'This is for us, boy,' said George, rubbing his hands. '3-D without glasses: I can see it on the canopy. Come on, we'll beat 'em to it.'

Next day before noon we were first past the Bayswater box office to sit in an otherwise empty circle watching Lana Turner move her lips to somebody else's voice in a stolid MGM version of the old operetta *The Merry Widow*. The film was projected on to a large plastic screen, from all four ends of which white wings jutted half-forwards, the result looking like a waxed cardboard trifle case on its side. For the proper effect the image had to fit exactly into the 'base': any overlap was extremely distracting. What precisely the effect was seemed hard to describe, even after one had experienced it. The dim reflection of the picture on the wings was certainly more restful to the eyes than the conventional sharp black edge. If one was told that the device added *depth* to the image, well, one would very probably believe it, though only if the print under review already had good contrast and clarity. The Western Electric man who took the opportunity of coming with us whispered in George's ear that in his view it was only a gimmick, and that ABC had decided not to proceed with it on a nationwide basis, especially since other technical developments were known to be in the offing. But George was already drunk on the publicity possibilities of owning the first Synchro-Screen in East Anglia. 'How much?' was all he said. He signed a cheque there and then, and there

was no point in arguing. Indeed, I was almost as excited as
he was, for the cost was only four hundred pounds, and that
should be easily recouped by the screen's curiosity value;
while its installation would at least ensure that the Rex's
filthy backstage area was cleaned up. The changeover took
place one Saturday night, just a week before Christmas,
after we had suffered a dismal three days with Errol Flynn
in *Captain Blood* and Eddie Albert in *An Angel from
Texas*. An army of men with poles and pipes descended
upon us during the final showing, and five minutes after the
last customer had departed an enormous roll of white
plastic was gently carried in through the panic doors and
laid across the stalls. The odd-looking structure itself took
only a couple of hours to erect, but we were all there until
breakfast time because the aperture plates in the projectors
had to be filed down little by little until the image fitted into
the screen with no overspill. At eight am we breathlessly
tried out various bits of film on the huge white monster, and
were overwhelmed by the sight of the six stars of *On the
Town* marching gaily towards us, though the difference
may simply have been one of contrast because the old
screen had been so dirty.

   We advertised our new toy widely and somewhat dis-
honestly (first outside London – screen of the future –
amazing new depth – 3-D without glasses). The week
before Christmas, however, is scarcely the best time to start
a new fashion, and we only did well by having the gall to
inaugurate our Synchro-Screen with a double-X exploitation programme of astounding ineptitude. *The Devil's
Weed*, a scruffy little American melodrama of drug addiction, was combined with *Forbidden Rapture*, a piece of
Swedish impenetrability with subtitles. (The distributor
had offered us, in place of either, or even in addition to
both, an item called *Chained for Life*, about girl Siamese

twins, real ones, who fall in love with the same man; but even George's faint sense of good taste rebelled at this.) If, however, the two thousand patrons who spent part of their Sunday with us went home holding their noses at the entertainment, they were full of praise for the Synchro-Screen, and word of mouth undoubtedly bucked up the Christmas trade. The screen must have paid for itself even before the undergraduates came back in January, and it transpired that they quite liked it too; but waiting in the wings to claim their share of the spotlight were 3-D proper; the so-called wide screen; and CinemaScope.*

3-D with glasses was nothing new at all. One of the first attractions to be released in the process in 1953 was nothing more than a re-issue of a Pete Smith novelty short made in 1935, and once again red-and-green-lensed throwaway specs were provided to go with it. It was called *Metroscopix*, and during its brief running time so many hard and spiky objects were hurled at the camera as to make the audience dizzy from ducking them. The reason for the 3-D effect, at its best in the polaroid process which allows full colour, is that our two eyes see things from slightly different angles, which is why we can see around a ball and register that it is spherical rather than flat. If you photograph a scene through two synchronized cameras corresponding in position to one's two eyes; print one result on polaroid film which is horizontally graded and the other on polaroid film which is vertically graded; project the two films on top of each other; and view the result through spectacles with one horizontally-graded and one vertically-graded polaroid lens; then the brain will separate out the two images, giving an effect of three dimensions

*For obscure reasons Fox gave up this famous trademark after a few years and replaced it with Panavision; but the method is virtually identical, and in referring here to the original form I keep to the original name.

which is most notable when something advances rapidly towards, or retreats rapidly from, the camera.

The first film to use polaroid 3-D effects was an independent quickie undistinguished by production values, acting or story line. It was called *Bwana Devil*, and its publicity alleged that it was shot in Natural Vision and would provide the spectator with 'a lion in your lap, a lover in your arms'. It took a fortune, mainly for the producer, whose extra costs were no more than using two rolls of film in adjacent cameras. It was the exhibitor who had to install mechanically or electrically synchronized projectors and bear the risks involved in buying or renting the heavy polaroid spectacles. But when the producer whistles, the exhibitor always jumps. 3-D came – and went – like a fever. One day nobody had heard of it; the next there were twenty films in production and every traveller was urging us to convert and be ready. In Britain nobody paid much heed until the major studios got into the game, and the first evidence of that was the memorable trade show of Warners' *House of Wax*. A hasty revamp of *Mystery of the Wax Museum*, it simplified the story but was a poor production. However, it did have an 'X' certificate and contained scenes which were twice as frightening in three dimensions as they would have been in two. Knives were brandished in our faces, a head was guillotined into our laps, and there was a man with a ping-pong bat who seemed to bounce his elasticated ball almost to the back wall of the theatre. The censor let it all pass except for a brief scene in which the chorus girls waggled their lace-frilled bottoms into the front rows. The West End trade presentation, for which numbered tickets were hard to come by, had the additional advantage of stereophonic sound; when the monster hurled a chair over the hero's head, we heard it crash behind us. George had his chequebook at the ready before he left his seat.

Alas, Warners expressed themselves regretfully unable to take our money, as they had a general commitment to the ABC circuit which, although not yet ready to install 3-D equipment, had put *House of Wax* on hold just in case. This was an extremely annoying state of affairs to would-be pioneers such as ourselves, for if *Bwana Devil* was the best level we could attain, 3-D would last no longer than a fairground sideshow. Luckily, an overnight decision on the part of Hollywood mogul Harry Cohn brought our old friends Columbia into 3-D with a whole range of barely tolerable (but promotable) westerns and crime thrillers, all apparently made in a matter of days, and looking it. Dudley Pritchard brought his boss down to see us, knowing that Columbia did not have a prayer with ABC; and over dinner at a country inn we allowed ourselves to be wooed and won. Out of what was available, at fifty per cent per show, the choice of the first attraction in the new process was easy. Though essentially no more than a moderate black-and-white support, *Man in the Dark* had the advantage of a reliable star in Edmond O'Brien, and a suitably gimmicky plot about a convict who lost his memory after submitting to a brain operation to remove his criminal tendencies. What was more, it ran for only 67 minutes, so that a centre break was the only one required. (Both projectors being in simultaneous use, intervals were required for reloading after each reel. In the old days that would have meant every ten minutes, but George splashed out on giant spool cases which took 35 minutes each.) Most important, *Man in the Dark* assaulted its audience in every way known to science and showmen. You were shot at, stamped on, kissed, blackjacked, knifed, operated on with scalpel and scissors; a hatchet came whizzing at you, as did a car out of control; a spider crawled at you across its web; a body fell from your grasp out of a top floor window; and you were finally taken for a ride on a roller coaster. What more could a sophisticated audience require?

Once again, technicians and workmen assaulted the Rex's aged machinery. In order to achieve the necessary brilliance a metallic screen surface was needed, so the Synchro-Screen was painted over, thus losing whatever effect it had. But again we were the very first in East Anglia; drawing strangers from miles around, *Man in the Dark* ran for two weeks to full and appreciative houses, coasted along quite happily for a third, and was later revived to general satisfaction. During the first week of its run ABC, clearly piqued at having lost the race, announced in the *Daily News* that they had booked *House of Wax* ('3-D as it *should* be seen') to play at the Victoria in less than a month. More than a little piqued myself, I inserted in our advertisement for *Man in the Dark* a new line: '"Better than *House of Wax*", say our delighted patrons!' Two days later we received a letter from ABC's solicitors, threatening legal action unless this line were removed and an apology rendered. It concluded: 'It is not apparent how your patrons can have been able to judge between *Man in the Dark* and *House of Wax*, since the latter has not yet played in Cambridge.'

I replied cheerily, pointing out that there was a regular train service between Cambridge and London, and that some of our patrons even owned cars. I also enclosed a paper signed by six of my friends who were prepared to perjure themselves by agreeing with what our advertisement said; and we heard no more. *House of Wax* duly played at the Victoria, where to our surprise it did only fair business and was taken off after two weeks. This may have seemed like a small triumph, but it showed that the novelty of 3-D was wearing off and that, as always, the quality of the film itself was what mattered. For the rest of the summer therefore we played the hell out of every 3-D film while there was still a weekend audience ready to respond. The most successful was a piece of independent hokum called *Gorilla at Large*, about murders in a circus, where the murderer turned out to be Anne Bancroft in a gorilla skin! There seemed to be nothing, however, that we could play in term time except the MacLaren shorts: MGM asked far too high a premium for *Kiss Me Kate*, and then at the last moment cancelled the 3-D version and released the film 'flat'. So that was virtually the end, apart from a pre-Christmas revival of *House of Wax*. The trade rather hastily realized that 3-D was not the answer to its prayers, and many exhibitors were unable to afford the equipment. The few interesting films which started out in 3-D, such as Hitchcock's *Dial M For Murder*, were finished and released in the more conventional way.

It was fun while it lasted. Perhaps what really killed 3-D in public esteem was not the low content standard but the fact that audiences, in addition to buying a ticket, had to hand over another sixpence for the hire of glasses which were heavy and inconvenient to wear, especially if one already sported spectacles; most people found it necessary to hold them in place during the exhibition. We lost out too. The glasses cost us one-and-six a pair to buy; but collection and sterilization were so difficult, and losses so considerable, that we were soon out of pocket. A simpler solution came in a reversion to the old type of throwaway cardboard frames with polaroid lenses; these could be sold outright for sixpence and kept by the purchaser until they fell apart. The snag was that they came in boxes of a thousand each, and these were not returnable once opened, which could lead to great unhappiness if one had to open a box for the last half-dozen patrons of one's very last 3-D performance. Besides, the profit margin of one halfpenny per pair scarcely covered the cost of distribution and staff borrowings. Nor did the process improve our public relations image. Every other patron seemed to be resentful ('This is an outrage! I've already bought my ticket!') or apologetic ('Can I bring the sixpence on Monday?') or perplexed ('How do they work?'). One schoolgirl who did not have sixpence to spare offered me three penny stamps and an apple in lieu. There was even an American whose complaint was that the things were ridiculously cheap; to such lack of commercial acumen he attributed Britain's collapsing economic structure. And I shall always remember the little old lady who came in one afternoon on a pensioner's ticket and made her way over to the little table from which the glasses were sold.

'Are you selling toffee?' she asked. 'I want some toffee to suck in the pictures.'

I was filling in for the circus lady, and gladly donned my other hat in order to sell her a packet of Maltesers. Meanwhile I tried to explain to her about such things as 3-D and glasses, but the facts did not seem to crystallize. 'Oh, no,' she said finally with an air of distaste. 'I only wanted the toffee. I won't bother with them other things.'

'But you won't see anything without them,' I persisted. 'It'll hurt your eyes. Here, don't tell anybody, have a pair on me.'

She became indignant. 'You leave my eyes alone. I've never worn glasses for seventy-two years and I'm not going to start now.' She shook her head so firmly that I feared it would fall off, and marched into the auditorium. I had to give up; but nearly three hours later I happened to catch her coming out.

'How did you get on?' I asked.

She paused thoughtfully. 'Oh, not so bad. But I think

you want something doing to your machines. It were all a bit fuzzy, like.'

The trade would never have permitted so quick a death for 3-D had there not been on the horizon a potentially more fruitful and lasting gimmick. In Hollywood in 1952 there had been advanced the theory that the way to fight the inroads of television on world audiences was to develop a screen which was not only bigger but of a shape different from the one which had served the industry for more than fifty years. These changes were intended to show up the paltriness of the home set. And so from that day forth the old four-by-three, which had been good enough for *Gone with the Wind* and *Citizen Kane* and *The Grapes of Wrath*, was officially labelled 'postage stamp' and condemned to instant extinction. The simplest way of 'improving' on it was to use all the same equipment bar the screen, the lens and the aperture plate. The latter was replaced by one with less height, preventing the top and bottom of the old picture area from being projected. The remaining middle strip was then put through a magnifying lens and captured on a larger, wider screen of the same dimensions as the aperture plate. The audience was thus getting less picture content than before, but that less was bigger; one major drawback to it was that greater magnification led to poorer definition. The elementary process was known as 'wide screen' except by MGM, who called it Metroscope. (They would.) But what it was called hardly mattered; a process so economical could not fail to be enthusiastically adopted by every exhibitor in the country in the hope that it would improve his declining business. From now on, films made before 1952, made for the old ratio, could be shown only in this mutilated form, missing the heads of actors and the feet of dancers and totally ruining the work of any director with a sense of visual composition. Even the few cinema managers who realized the desecration they were wreaking on fine films found themselves unable to do anything about it, for the new electrically-controlled screen masking was variable only in width, not in height; and few projectionists would have bothered to change it for older films anyway. The new films were of course photographed so that all the essential action occurred in the middle strip of the frame which was to be projected, and this meant that cinemas like the Rex, which stuck to the old screen shape as long as they could, found that very little was happening in the top and bottom third of their picture, and that the actors in the middle seemed very small and remote. And since television sets were committed to the old four-by-three ratio, post-1952 films came to seem disappointing in that medium, while the older classics retained their freshness and vigour.

Still another monster loomed. CinemaScope, under some other name, was a thirty-year-old French invention which until now had been dismissed as impracticable and unnecessary. Its screen ratio is very wide indeed, roughly five units long to two units high, so that while effective for the display of panoramas, snakes and funerals it is usually the kiss of death to anything more intimate. The scene is photographed through an anamorphic (wide-angle) lens which squeezes the image sideways into the usual 35mm film frame. (Look at a strip of CinemaScope film and you will find everybody looking emaciated.) The projector is then fitted with a complementary lens which 'unsqueezes' the projected picture on to the *extra* wide screen in a shape which certainly cannot be confused with what is available on television. The Twentieth Century-Fox studios, which now patented the process and imposed it upon the industry, claimed it as their own invention, which it was not, and said that it gave 3-D effects without glasses, which it did not.

But in sheer desperation because of falling receipts they committed themselves to a long schedule of CinemaScope movies, which encouraged other studios to follow suit for fear of being left out in the cold. Cinemas throughout the world were then obliged to convert to the new process (which could co-exist with the 'wide-screen' films) because if they did not they would find themselves short of product. The industry was in fact doubly harmed, because at the same time there was introduced a new cheap colour process called De Luxe (or Warnercolor for films from the Warner studio). This had a blue base, and when over-magnified (which it always was) presented the front half of the audience with a random arrangement of bobbing blue dots trying to compose themselves into a picture. Only a few people with an eye for quality wondered in what sense these developments could be called progress, but as P. T. Barnum said, there's a sucker born every minute, and the public was easily fooled into thinking that it was getting something miraculous at no extra cost.

In order to show CinemaScope films it was necessary to be granted a licence by Fox, and George and I, bemused by the way the business was changing, thought we had better go along to see a demonstration at the Odeon in Tottenham Court Road. There, in the company of such visiting luminaries as Gene Kelly and Jose Ferrer, we watched, amid sheep-like applause, an enormous grainy picture of Westminster Bridge with the Thames flowing downhill from the left and uphill towards the right. (It took a couple of years to get the distortions out of the lenses, and these were compounded by the deep curvature of the screen, which was necessary if all parts of the picture were to be equally in focus.) After similarly unprepossessing shots of New York on the up-and-down Hudson, we were shown the 'Diamonds Are a Girl's Best Friend' number from

Gentlemen Prefer Blondes, first in the old screen shape and then in CinemaScope. (I much preferred the former.) Then Mr Spyros Skouras, presiding genius of Fox, came on in person and proved entirely unable to pronounce the name of his new process. Some spokesperson for the exhibitors next stood up and thanked Mr Skouras for saving the industry, and we all went home. George and I were not in the least impressed, but in the weeks that followed we began to hear whispers that ABC was resisting Fox's demand for full stereophonic sound to be expensively installed in every cinema licensed for CinemaScope, which might just let us in if George's chequebook was still open. We were not entirely surprised when the London branch manager of Fox rang us one day to offer tickets for the West End première of *The Robe*, the first film in CinemaScope.

'What's the point?' asked George blandly. 'We won't get the film, will we?'

There was a pause. 'I wouldn't be too sure about that,' came the answer we expected. 'Stay up in town after the première, and come to see me the next morning.'

Although slightly underwhelmed by *The Robe*, we could see the attraction of acquiring for the Rex a permanent flow of first-run product which would stand us in good stead for the six months of the year when few undergraduates were around, and we walked into the Soho Square offices in barely suppressed anticipation. It transpired that Fox, unable to get the guarantees it required from Rank or ABC, was proposing to form its own independent circuit of CinemaScope halls, many of them virtual fleapits astonished by this turn of good fortune. Continuity of product would be guaranteed for three years, and in return for higher-than-usual rentals there would be a grant towards conversion costs. There seemed to be no hidden

snags – we even negotiated a sliding scale – and we asked
Western Electric to make an immediate survey, bearing in
mind that we would need a screen high as well as wide so
that we could come down to four-by-three for the older
films which were our real bread and butter. The specialists
reported that the Rex was ideally suited for this purpose;
we rang Fox delightedly and asked for the contract to be
put in the post. Two weeks later, on the day before the
necessary conversion was to begin, the vital paper had still
not arrived despite three more phone calls, and George
began to make such remarks as: 'There's a nasty smell of
Fox about.' Then the engineers came in and asked where
the screen materials were: Fox, they said, always supplied
direct to the theatre. We rang Fox again, more in anger
than in sorrow. Ah yes, they said, the Miracle Mirror
materials; unfortunately delivery had slowed up and they
were not yet able to allocate a sufficient quantity to us. No,
no other white plastic would do; it had to have their own
trademarked Miracle Mirror finish. No, it could not be
spray-painted in situ. We would have to wait for the
Miracle Mirror, that was in the agreement. 'What agreement?' yelled George, dancing up and down. 'We never
got the bloody agreement!' Then he hurled the phone at me
and added: 'Tell him if he ever finds the bloody agreement
he knows what he can do with it, and I hope it's in a stiff
cover.'

We scarcely needed to be told what had happened. ABC
had seen the light, and Fox had found excuses to abandon
its much-heralded independent circuit. We kept Fox films
out of the Rex for a year, and only gave in when another
row between the renter and ABC gave us at least a share of
the first runs. Alas, none of them made a penny profit, for
by then it was not the shape of the screen that mattered but
the stars and the story; and I was sad to see the monster

screen go up in the Rex, which was by now among the last
of the East Anglian cinemas to install it. But at least we
were able to keep a good height, so that old films could be
shown in their proper ratio in the middle of it.

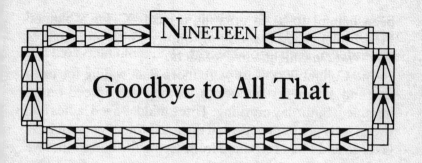

NINETEEN

Goodbye to All That

How the Rex in 1954 came to hit the front pages of several national newspapers takes a little explaining. The producer Stanley Kramer was making for Columbia a series of critically-acclaimed but modestly budgeted programme pictures. None of them took much at the box office, but the Rex had been pleased to get them first run, for they included *Death of a Salesman, The Four Poster, The Juggler, The Sniper*, and *The Five Thousand Fingers of Dr T*, all of which kept our reputation high if not our spirits. One of the later items in the package was an unlikely-sounding story about motor-cycle hooligans who take over and terrorize a small Californian town until the police arrive to round them up. Originally called *The Cyclists' Raid*, it was changed to *The Wild One* in order to cash in on its rising star, the moody Marlon Brando, then causing great interest as Hollywood's 'new type of man'. The trade next learned with considerable surprise that the British Board of Film Censors had firmly banned *The Wild One* on the grounds that it did not clearly show retribution descending on the gang, and therefore might encourage imitation in remote British villages. The press had a couple of field days with the news, and it occurred to me that, since a local watch committee can always overturn the censor's decision if it so wishes, and since Cambridge had recently been helpful to us in granting a local 'X' for a banned French film called *Stain on the Snow*, a plea on behalf of *The Wild One* might work wonders.

The Columbia powers were more than willing for us to try, and at our first request a viewing was agreed on an imminent Saturday morning. Three middle-aged ladies and two elderly gentlemen turned up, and I told them that both George and I had refrained from seeing the film so that we could not influence their judgement; however, I did pass among them with copies of a press handout lauding to the skies the previous work of Stanley Kramer. I mentioned a few other worthy cases in which BBFC decisions had been reversed by local authorities, including *Snow White and the Seven Dwarfs*, from which children had originally been restricted. I added that the Rex had no wish to encourage violence, but felt that in Cambridge *The Wild One* would be regarded solely as art. I then let them get on with it, parking myself in a distant corner by a radiator.

The Wild One was a nicely photographed picture, with a startling pre-credits shot of an empty road which slowly becomes packed with roaring motor bikes, but dramatically it seemed a dull and undeveloped little melodrama without much idea of what it wanted to say. I took an instinctive dislike to the new star, and winced at some of the senseless town-wrecking near the end. Harry Habbin, our accounts clerk, peeked at most of it through the little porthole above his desk, and I could hear him tut-tutting; George came in, sat by me for a while, and went to sleep. At the end, the ladies and gentlemen filed out with rather frosty good mornings, and their spokesman said I would be hearing from them. That, I felt, was that. But on the following Tuesday their letter arrived to advise us that *The Wild One* might be played at the Rex with an 'X' certificate.

We hastened to confirm a contract by telegram that very day; Columbia was even quicker to demand a fortnight's run and fifty per cent of the takings. I issued the story to the local press, not thinking of any wider consequences, but the *Daily News* rang Fleet Street and suddenly the proverbial balloon went up. The *Daily Express* rang George at midnight for a quote, and told him what we had suspected but not wanted to know, that every other local authority approached had turned the film down flat. Next morning we were their second lead on the front page and filled an entire column under the heading

ONE CITY
WILL SHOW
WILD ONE
BRANDO

The story, very kindly, even informed enthusiasts of the cost of a day return ticket from the metropolis to our university backwater. Suddenly we were besieged by enquiries. One man rang from Glamorgan and another from Manchester, and several film societies and motor-cycle clubs rang to enquire about party rates. Connery Chappell sent a *Picturegoer* team to invent a double-page feature including a few lines by me: for fifteen guineas I did not mind being billed as 'the daring young cinema manager who shows films that no one else will'.

All this activity gave George one of his very worst ideas. First, he said, we must step up the prices, and second, we must run a very short programme to get all the crowds in. Vainly did I plead that *The Wild One* was not a film with universal appeal, that word of mouth was unlikely to be enthusiastic, that it was essential to keep faith with one's regular audience. He was adamant. *The Wild One* is over in 79 minutes, but all he would allow in the way of support was four UPA cartoons which, popular as Mr Magoo and his cohorts then were, added up with trailers and intervals to a programme of barely two hours, not enough for a twelve-hundred-seat cinema: it would have taken almost that time to fill all the seats even had there been a constant queue, which there was not. A great many people did come, but as they never found the slightest difficulty in getting in, they all used the cheaper seats, and complained of the constant irritating movement from other people's comings and goings. George quickly realized his error, and for the second week we put in *The Four Poster* as support. But it was too late; over the run we played to very average business. Our normal audiences gave *The Wild One* a wide berth, the gap being partially filled by teddy boys and a sprinkling of London sophisticates and actors, the latter category led by Beatrice Lillie and Jon Pertwee. On the whole the rest of England did not seem to miss *The Wild One*; and I never found out what kind of reception it had in Maesteg, the only Welsh community licensed to show it.*

The Rex's most freakish attraction was undoubtedly *Genevieve*, but that was a story with a happier ending. Between 1954 and 1956, in fact, it played the Rex on no fewer than fourteen separate bookings; and we only got it in the first place by waiting until ABC thought its appeal had been exhausted. It premièred in London in the summer of 1953, when the unusual heat must have wilted the critics' percipience, for it received the mildest of praise and went straight out on release to do the mildest of business, since it contained no star names, did not bear the Ealing seal of

---

*Fifteen years after these excitements, in 1969, the censor reconsidered his decision and *The Wild One* was generally released with an 'X' certificate. It played on the Odeon circuit as a second feature and most of those who saw it thought it dull.

approval, and had a heroine who turned out to be not a woman but a vintage car. It was the public who discovered *Genevieve* to be a sunny, sexy comedy about two engaging couples having a race along the roads and lanes of southern England; but only towards the end of August did the national press begin to run stories about how a quartet of new stars was being created – John Gregson, Dinah Sheridan, Kay Kendall, Kenneth More – because all over the country *Genevieve* was doing better on its second runs than on its first. George and I nodded significantly to each other, but we were still helpless, because in Cambridge ABC had the automatic option to take as many repeat runs as they liked. In September they brought it back for a week at the Central, where it broke the house record; so there was still no hope for us, since they would certainly play it again at the Tivoli and Playhouse. They did, but we could not believe it when we heard that they had been short-sighted enough to place the third run in early January, before the university term began. *Genevieve*, the massive countrywide hit of the autumn, and a movie ideally suited to our young, bright, audiences, had never had a Cambridge playdate in term time.

As casually as we could, we worked the subject into our next conversations with Rank: 'Might give *Genevieve* another run sometime, if ABC have finished with it.'

'What have they had? Four weeks? Oh yes, you can have that, no problem.'

'Last week of term, then. Let's say a double bill with *The Lavender Hill Mob*.'

And so it was. If ABC ever realized their mistake, they never vented their fury on us. Just to confirm things, we guaranteed subsequent bookings at the Kinema; but first we watched with interest undergraduate reaction to our foyer posters at the Rex, and the excitement gave us an

CINEMA REX BALLROOM

MAGRATH *Best Value in Show Business!* AVENUE
PHONE 59659   PHONE 54355

Mon.-Wed. Open 1.30.
By popular request we are again pleased to present Anna Magnani and Burt Lancaster in Tennessee William's

THE ROSE TATTOO

(A) in VistaVision.
The film that won for Magnani the Oscar award for "the best actress of the year." Also starring Marisa Pavan and Ben Cooper.
1.45, 5.15, 8.45.

also

Bob Hope, Tony Martin, Rosemary Clooney, Arlene Dahl in

HERE COME THE GIRLS

(Tech.) 3.45, 7.15. (A)

Thurs.-Sat. Open 1.40.
Danny Kaye, Mai Zetterling in
KNOCK ON WOOD (U)
Also   Helen
Hayes,   Van
Heflin. MY SON
JOHN (U).

DANCING

To-night   7.30 p.m. to 1 a.m.
CASTLE AND DISTRICT DARTS LEAGUE
Competitions followed by dancing.

Wednesday   8 p.m. to 11.30 p.m.
Admission 2/6.
Ladies 1/6 before 8.30 p.m.

Thurs., June 7th. 8 p.m. to 2 a.m.
JAZZ CLUB END OF TERM BALL
Humphrey Lyttelton and his Band
Full Buffet.
Proctorial Permission.
Tickets 10/- from Millers, Rex, King and Harpers, Volunteer.

Sat. Children's skating 2.15 & 4.30 p.m.

KINEMA
PHONE MILL ROAD 56961

Mon.-Wed. Open 2.00 Adults only.
Cambridge Premiere of Jean Gabin in
THE TRUTH ABOUT OUR MARRIAGE (X)
2.15, 5.35, 8.55.
Also Fernandel in CASIMIR (A) 3.45, 7.05.

The George Webb Empire The design may have been clumsy, but it made maximum use of the space. This is June 1956: even after my departure George maintained his connection with the University Jazz Club, much to the distress of residents in Magrath Avenue.

early cue to extend our booking to six days. When the time came, we had no difficulty in breaking the house record (not counting *A Queen is Crowned*). The Saturday was particularly remarkable. A flu epidemic had robbed us of half our staff, and George had promised that both he and

Mrs Webb would be available as required. When we opened at two o'clock, however, there were few people about, so he decided that everybody had gone to the football match and that he, having over-indulged at lunch, would nip off home for forty winks. This left one usherette in the circle and me in the stalls; and at 2.35 pm, just as *Genevieve* was about to go on, the crowds arrived in their hundreds, noisy and expecting a good time. I have a vivid recollection of making several efforts to get to the phone and dial George's number, and of being swept back by the inflowing tide. When I did manage it, all I was able to say was: 'Come quick!' He did, bringing additional reinforcements in the shape of two of his sons, both quite adequately trained as usherettes. By the time order was restored, there was a patient queue down Magrath Avenue, and it did not shorten until nine o'clock that evening. *Genevieve*, again combined with an Ealing comedy, was back at the Rex six weeks later, and played every term for the rest of my stay.

During my second and third years at the Rex, we seemed during term quite unable to make a mistake. Put another way, each slight disappointment was followed by half-a-dozen copper-bottomed successes, which is not a bad average for any cinema. I believe our most successful seven-day programme (again excepting *A Queen is Crowned*) was a combination of Chaplin's *Modern Times* with a re-run of Tati's *Monsieur Hulot's Holiday*; but the place was constantly on the boil. Ealing comedies, Marx Brothers, Bob Hope, Alastair Sim, MGM musicals, Frank Capra, Alfred Hitchcock, Orson Welles, Noël Coward, Ernst Lubitsch, Marcel Carné, Ingmar Bergman, Cary Grant, Tracy and Hepburn, Laurel and Hardy were among our staples, each name capable of drawing a reliable crowd. We even started a Roy Rogers Club on Saturday mornings.

This concession was operated by a fly-by-night company which, in return for a weekly fee, supplied a box of badges and a trailer in which the movie cowboy knelt down on the canyon floor in order to pray with his horse Trigger. ('Well, Lord, I reckon I ain't much use down here all by myself . . .') I did not mind being Uncle Leslie once a week, leading the community singing and handing out balloons, but I was diffident about attending the magistrates' court for the purpose of sanctifying this activity with a special licence. I was even less amused when it turned out that I had chanced on one of those local beaks who like to be funny at the applicant's expense. 'Are you Mr Roy Rogers?' he asked me over his glasses, with one eye on the *Daily News* reporter. I stayed long enough to see him get his come-uppance at the hands of an irresistibly low defendant accused of ringing up twelve Cambridge matrons and making the same obscene remark: 'I've got twelve inches of hard cop here, do you want any?'

Despite the boredom of the long afternoons when nobody came in, I doubt whether I could have devised for myself at that time a more entertaining lifestyle than the one I was enjoying. I was a square peg in a square hole; but I knew that it was a kind of fantasy life which had lasted as long as it had because it was the natural culmination of my long love affair with the cinema. Even so, it ought not to have lasted longer than the two years I originally allowed for it. By now, I should be justifying my education, pleasing my mother, and earning some proper money in case, for example, I felt like getting married – an event about which, having read Somerset Maugham on the subject, I had decided to postpone thought until reaching the age of thirty. There was, after all, not much else now that I could do for George. We had even given ourselves competition by inviting undergraduates to patronize the Kinema, and were in double jeopardy if in so doing we offended the regulars of that hall; but we forgot to worry when *The Battleship Potemkin* and *The Birth of a Nation* (in a sound version) played to such packed houses that we wished we had shown them at the Rex. Furthermore, by offering dazzlingly low rates we even tempted the CU Film Society's Sunday morning shows away from the Central to the Rex, although George, predictably, said that he could not possibly afford to pay the staff extra for attending on these occasions. To him the Film Society members were especially welcome in the winter, as they were hardy chaps who would not mind the initial low temperature, while their hundreds of young bodies would heat up the cinema nicely for the afternoon.

One way or another, therefore, my days were filled with excitement and my nights with conversation. I enjoyed as much university society as I wanted; I had free passes to every show in town; my friends all stayed for a drink after visiting the Rex to see a film. Still, after eighteen months I began to look out, rather furtively at first, for other jobs.

I tried the film studios and television, the latter taking me memorably to Langham Place for a BBC interview with General Sir Guy Williams, who wanted to know what I thought of affairs in Guatemala, but never seemed to watch television himself. In the advertising field I filled in endless questionnaires for J. Walter Thompson. In journalism I could have chosen jobs among half a dozen journals vaguely linked with artistic endeavour, but two of them folded while I was considering their offers, and the working conditions of the others seemed like a retrograde step even from the squalor of the manager's office at the Rex. What did appeal to me was the possibility of a Commonwealth Fund Fellowship to study the art of the motion picture at the University of Southern California in Los Angeles, right on Hollywood's doorstep. I was interviewed by several senior trusties of the film industry, including Michael Balcon, Kenneth MacGowan, and Arthur Elton, and was eventually told (in the spring of 1954) that I had just missed being selected and was advised to try again next year. This was sufficient inducement to spend another twelve months at the Rex, but when the time came round again I did not get the fellowship, this time because I had been able to obtain no firm guarantee of work in the British film industry on my return.

In my anger and disappointment I was spurred to action. During the intervening months I had obtained vague offers of employment both from Granada Television (where I was interviewed by Sidney Bernstein himself, who was looking for a personal assistant, and tripped over his office doormat on the way in); and from the Rank Organisation, who were signing up executive trainees for a three-year course. I would have preferred Granada's pleasing informality, and besides, it offered the chance of an entirely new field; but they dilly-dallied about a starting date, and kept asking me to stay in touch and stand by. Meanwhile Rank had a contract ready, and would not wait, so I took the plunge and signed on with them. George's dismay when I informed him of my plans was offset to some extent by his belief that he had now learned enough about films to do my job as well as his own, thus saving the whole pitiful amount of my salary, which after an acrimonious scene had been brought up to £8 10s a week, but no share of profits. On the one hand I had a suspicion that both he and Cambridge might miss me just a little; on the other, I had had my fill of both, and felt the need, like Chaplin's little tramp, to walk away from the camera into a new sunset.

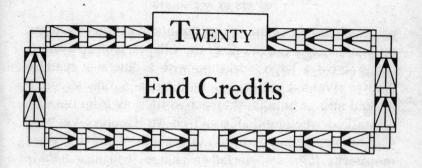

TWENTY

End Credits

It was nearly thirty years later. On my way to spend a weekend in Norfolk, I had the opportunity, while passing through Cambridge, to find out what had happened to the Rex. I knew that sometime in the sixties George Webb had sold it and had gone back into road haulage; but he and I had not met or spoken for many years. No antagonism, just lack of mutual interests.

I enquired at the newspaper office, where I had gone for old photographs, but the adenoidal girl behind the counter said casually; 'The Rex? Where on earth was that?' While browsing through the city centre bookshops I asked several other people, the majority of whom thought that the Rex had gone over to bingo. Clearly I had to be sure; and so in my gold-coloured Rover I turned right at the Magdalene lights, swept past the cottage of long-departed Mrs Lavis, climbed the solemn grey hill of Hertford Street and so regained the unrelieved dismalness of Magrath Avenue, where in all the intervening years only one thing had changed. The Rex buildings were no longer there. Not a wall of them remained, just a few low spurs of the brick foundations. Cars were parked amid the debris, making the whole space seem far too small to have housed both ballroom and cinema and the two thousand people who sometimes crowded into them on a Saturday night.

I found I could not manage even a wry smile. I sighed

painfully and drove on, taking a random country route on my way to Ely. And in one of the villages, a biggish one, I came across a large workshop with a blue sign reading George Webb Enterprises. Parking in a side street, I walked into an antique shop across the way from the sign and asked whether that could be Mr George Webb of Cambridge, the big chap with the bald head and the Hitler moustache. 'Oh,' said the lady in charge, 'you mean *old* Mr Webb. Yes, I see him about sometimes, but of course his sons take care of the business.'

I drove on, through King's Lynn, which I had not visited since one day when George had taken me out there to help him decide whether to buy up a little independent cinema called the Pilot, which was going cheap. It proved to be in the middle of dockland and seemed to us to have far too few houses near it to be worth the risk in the strained atmosphere of the cinema industry in the fifties. I now turned a corner, and there was the Pilot, looking spruce and well managed, and displaying a queue of children for a revival of *E.T.* Now I could smile; but I was smiling at a kind of mirage, for when I drove back that way a few days later the Pilot had closing notices up, with a message from the owner thanking the citizens of King's Lynn for forty years of loyal support.

It was not until the next time I visited Cambridge that I discovered from the files of the public library that George had in fact died a few months before my previous visit. I was shown an obituary from the *Cambridge News*, which bore the heading 'Cambridge Loses a Flamboyant Personality', and gave his age as sixty three. He had had heart trouble for years, it seemed, but persisted in ignoring the advice of his doctors. The notice told of his garage and his family farm, but concentrated on his tenure of the Rex and the Kinema, which were said to have made him 'a household word'. I was surprised to find myself mentioned – 'then a young Cambridge graduate but now an international film and television impresario' – as an influence in making George's cinemas 'come alive'. University students, it seemed, once felt that Cambridge life was incomplete without weekly visits to the Rex; and it was felt that the ghosts of many thousands of undergraduate cyclists must still haunt the Magrath Avenue area, their black gowns flapping in the evening breeze. George's son Bob commented on typical Webb innovations which seemed to have happened after my time: exhibitions of all-in wrestling in the ballroom, cups of tea in the cinema. In the latter case, it was said, George used to turn down the heating so that customers would be sure to want the tea. That figured. Conversely he turned up the heat ten minutes before the ice-cream interval. George was a tryer, there was no doubt of that.

Some months later, rather masochistically perhaps, I made a rare trip back to Bolton. Here, after my sisters moved south, and my aunts died one by one, two cousins are all that remain of my once extensive family. My father had lived to see his eighty-seventh birthday, but my mother died at seventy-one in 1956, soon after I took her on a final Isle of Man holiday during which we saw Charles Laughton in *Hobson's Choice* at the Onchan Picture House. For our very last Bolton film together, though at the time we did not know it was that, we braved the insufficiently heated Capitol on a bitter February afternoon to see *The Blackboard Jungle*, and reckoned nothing of it, since authority was shown with its back to the wall, and nobody wore pearls or dinner jackets or set his face against the stars.

Without my mother now, Bolton in the 1980s seemed a joyless and inhospitable place. Perhaps that was partly because there were no illuminated cinema canopies to brighten the streets. The *Evening News* told me, and personal observation confirmed, that the twenty-eight cinemas of my boyhood had been reduced to one. The Lido it once was, the most cheapjack of the thirties newcomers.

Now it was Studios One, Two and Three, but between them on a cold Sunday evening they seemed to be attracting very few customers, even by showing three films prohibited to persons under the age of eighteen: *Sudden Impact*, *Scarface*, *The Honorary Consul*. I strolled down the slope of Bradshawgate, and was dismayed to find a petrol station and an open car park occupying the space where the Queen's used to be. That wide corner seemed wider than ever. There was too much sky. No longer could I even imagine the metallic whirring of those ancient projectors, nor catch a whiff of that heady scent which fifty years earlier had made me a film fan.

Moving a few blocks west, I discovered that my magnificent Odeon, though reprieved from demolition, had suffered a sad name change, to Top Rank Bingo. The only word for its new appearance was melancholy, especially since nobody had bothered to clean off the ingrained dirt which formed on the white-tiled façade a ghostly image of the original name. I passed on to the Regal, which had become a skating rink again and was called the Navada. The Rialto had at some fairly recent date become the Apollo, but was now firmly shuttered. The Capitol had been modernized into a sports centre. As for the Grand and Theatre Royal, it was impossible to be sure exactly where they had once stood, for most of the south side of Churchgate had been turned into a concrete supermarket block. I continued my tour by car. Bolton seemed suddenly to have shrunk, not only because the brightly coloured posters of the cinema outposts, once renewed every week, were no longer visible even as torn remnants; but because Victoria Square had become a vast pedestrian precinct, and many of the remembered shops had retreated to the stale warmth and muzak of an Arndale Centre. The town was a cleaner but duller place, with front doors from Taiwan, and graceless modern windows replacing all the old sashes and casements. The ancient Man and Scythe pub, in the shadow of the Churchgate cross, seemed even more out of place than it had in my boyhood, with its gilded inscription on blackened oak beams:

> A.D. 1251   Rebuilt 1636
> In this ancient hostelry
> James Stanley
> 7th Earl of Derby
> passed the last few hours of his life
> prior to his execution
> Wed 15 Oct 1651

Then, to my amazement, I saw that across the road Ye Olde Pastie Shoppe flourished still, with its bow windows intact and a sign I had forgotten: ESTABLISHED 1667. Next day when I passed at lunchtime there was a moving queue, and the smell which wafted on the breeze was so appealing that I could not resist joining the throng. Inside, I thought I recognized the sixtyish lady behind the counter as the young daughter of the family who had sometimes served me while my mother queued at the Capitol. I said: 'I had one of your pasties in 1933 and it was so good that I've come back for another.' This made me *persona grata*: I was not only introduced to a member of staff who had joined as a lad in 1933 but urged to try with my pastie a carton of black peas with vinegar, a delicacy which I had not experienced since the old Bolton days of the New Year Fair, when my visits to the black pea tent used to alternate with sessions on the Waltzer, the Caterpillar and the Moon Rocket.

The pastie was marvellous. I took it with the peas in a paper bag, and consumed both in the cold air, standing at the back end of Silverwell Street car park where it overlooks the graves in the parish churchyard. After that, Bolton seemed quite a welcoming town again. Next time I pass by I must try its fish and chips. They are still reckoned to be the best in the North of England.

Index

Principal references are given.
Films and stars merely listed are not included.